GOVERNANCE
AND
PERFORMANCE:
NEW PERSPECTIVES

Edited by

CAROLYN J. HEINRICH
LAURENCE E. LYNN, JR.

Georgetown University Press
Washington, D.C.

Georgetown University Press, Washington, D.C.
© 2000 by Georgetown University Press. All rights reserved.
Printed in the United States of America

10 9 8 7 6 5 4 3 2 1   2000

This volume is printed on acid-free offset book paper.

Library of Congress Cataloging-in-Publication Data

Governance and performance : new perspectives / edited by Carolyn J. Heinrich,
Laurence E. Lynn, Jr.
        p. cm.
    Papers presented at a workshop held at the University of Arizona in May
1999.
    Includes index.
    ISBN 0-87840-798-7 (cloth : acid-free paper)—ISBN 0-87840-799-5
(paper : acid-free paper)
    1. Public administration—Congresses. I. Heinrich, Carolyn J. II. Lynn,
Laurence E., 1937–

JA35.5 .G68 2000
351.73—dc21
                                                        00-026364

Contents

Biographies

Howard S. Bloom is chief social scientist for the Manpower Demonstration Research Corporation (MDRC). Prior to that, he was a professor of public administration in the Robert F. Wagner School of Public Service at New York University for twelve years and at Harvard University for eight years. Bloom has been a principal investigator for numerous large-scale multisite program evaluations, mainly in the field of employment policy, and primarily based on the use of randomized experiments. He has written several books and numerous articles on these and related topics.

Anthony S. Bryk is the director of the Center for School Improvement, Marshall Field IV Professor of Urban Education, of Sociology, and of the Social Sciences at the University of Chicago, and senior director of the Consortium on Chicago School Research. Bryk has developed new statistical methods in education that have contributed to studies of school effects. Among his current interests are the social organization of schools and school restructuring to improve student learning.

Amy Kneedler Donahue is assistant professor of political science and public and urban affairs at the University of Connecticut. She serves as an analyst for the Government Performance Project at the Alan K. Campbell Public Affairs Institute at Syracuse University. The Government Performance Project is an initiative funded by the Pew Charitable Trusts to assess the effectiveness of government management systems. Her research interests focus on analysis of productive efficiency in the provision of local public services, particularly the influence of managerial decision processes on public production technologies, organizational outputs, policy outcomes, and cost efficiency.

John W. Ellwood is currently professor of public policy and associate dean of the Goldman School of Public Policy of the University of California, Berkeley. Trained as a political scientist, he spent six years as a staff member on Capitol Hill. Prior to coming to Berkeley, Ellwood taught at Princeton University's Woodrow Wilson School, the Hubert H. Humphrey Institute of Public Affairs at the University of Minnesota, and Dartmouth College's Amos Tuck School of Business Administration.

Jo Ann G. Ewalt is assistant professor of political science at Northern Kentucky University, where she teaches courses on research methods and public policy analysis at the undergraduate level and in the master's program in public administration. Her research interests include policy implementation and program evaluation.

Thomas H. Hammond is professor of political science at Michigan State University. His primary research interests are in the development of formal theories of political institutions, public administration, and public management. His most recent publication is "Political Institutions, Public Management, and Policy Choice" in the *Journal of Public Administration Research and Theory.*

Carolyn J. Heinrich is assistant professor of public policy analysis at the University of North Carolina, Chapel Hill. She is also a research affiliate of the Northwestern University-University of Chicago Joint Center for Poverty Research. Her most recent publications appear in the *Journal of Policy Analysis and Management* and the *Journal of Public Administration Research and Theory.*

Carolyn J. Hill is a doctoral student at the Harris Graduate School of Public Policy Studies at the University of Chicago. Her dissertation examines implementation and governance in welfare-to-work programs and implications for program effectiveness.

Patricia W. Ingraham is distinguished professor of public administration and political science at the Maxwell School of Citizenship and Public Affairs and director of the Alan K. Campbell Public Affairs Institute at Syracuse University. Ingraham served as a staff member of the National Commission on the Public Service. She is a fellow of the National Academy of Public Administration, an international fellow of the Canadian Centre for Management Development, and past president of the National Association of Schools of Public Affairs and Administration (1995–96). She is the author or editor of a number of books and articles related to public management and reform.

Brian A. Jacob is a doctoral student in public policy at the University of Chicago and a research analyst at the Consortium on Chicago School Research. His dissertation examines the impact of Chicago's high-stakes testing and retention policy on student achievement.

Edward T. Jennings, Jr., is professor of public administration and political science in the Martin School of Public Policy and Administration at the University of Kentucky. He is past president of the American Society for Public Administration. His research has explored topics in comparative state policy analysis, intergovernmental policy and management, welfare policy, employment and training programs, literacy, land-use mediation, and community development. He is co-author or co-editor of four books and monographs, the most recent of which is *Welfare System Reform: Coordinating Federal, State, and Local Public Assistance Programs.*

Jack H. Knott is the director of the Institute of Government and Public Affairs (IGPA) and professor of political science at the University of Illinois. Prior to coming to the University of Illinois he served as the chair of the political science department and as the director of the Institute of Public Policy and Social Research (IPPSR) at Michigan State University.

Laurence E. Lynn, Jr., is the Sydney Stein, Jr., Professor of Public Management at the School of Social Service Administration and at the Harris Graduate School of Public Policy Studies at the University of Chicago. He is the author of numerous books and articles on public management, the most recent of which is *Public Management as Art, Science, and Profession.* He has held senior policy planning positions in the U.S. government and has taught at Stanford University's Graduate School of Business and at Harvard University's Kennedy School of Government.

Kenneth J. Meier is Charles Puryear Professor of Liberal Arts and coordinator of the Program in American Politics at Texas A&M University. He is a former editor of the *American Journal of Political Science.* A student of bureaucracy and politics, his most recent books are *Substantively Weighted Analytical Techniques: A New Approach to Analysis for Programs and Policy* (with Jeff Gill) and *The Politics of Fertility Control Policy* (with Deborah McFarlane). He is currently working on a series of studies involving organizational structure, management, and performance.

H. Brinton Milward is the McClelland Professor of Public Management and director of the School of Public Administration and Policy at the University of Arizona. He has focused much of his recent work on understanding how to manage networks of organizations efficiently that jointly produce public services such as mental health. He is also studying the impact of privatization on public service provision. Among his recent publications is a book co-edited with Donald Kettl, *The State of Public Management.* Milward is a past president of the National Association of Schools of Public Affairs and Administration and has served on the Policy Council of the Association for Public Policy Analysis and Management.

Laurence J. O'Toole, Jr., is professor in the Department of Political Science and senior research associate in the Fanning Institute for Leadership and Community Development at the University of Georgia. His research focuses primarily on policy implementation, especially in networked settings. Among his recent books are *Institutions, Policy and Outputs for Acidification; Participation and the Quality of Environmental Decision Making* (co-editor); *American Intergovernmental Relations* (editor, 3d edition); and *Advancing Public Management* (co-editor with Jeffrey Brudney and Hal G. Rainey).

Keith G. Provan is a professor in the College of Business and Public Administration at the University of Arizona. He holds joint appointments with the School of Public Administration and Policy and the Department of Management and Policy. His research interests have focused on the study of interorganizational and network relationships, including network structure, evolution, governance, and effectiveness. Provan has previously taught at the University of Kentucky, Vanderbilt University, and Rochester Institute of Technology.

James Riccio specializes in the study of work-related programs and policies for welfare recipients and other disadvantaged groups. He is currently research director for MDRC's Jobs-Plus demonstration, an employment initiative for public housing residents in seven cities. Riccio previously directed MDRC's long-term evaluation of California's GAIN program, the nation's largest welfare-to-work program of its type. He has also studied welfare reform in Britain as a recipient of an Atlantic Fellowship in Public Policy, and he serves as an adviser on several current British evaluations.

Melissa Roderick is an associate professor at the School of Social Service Administration at the University of Chicago and co-director of the Consortium on Chicago School Research. Roderick is the lead principal investigator of the consortium's integrated program of research evaluating the effects of Chicago's efforts to end social promotion. She is an expert in urban minority adolescent development and urban high schools and has conducted research on school dropout, truancy, and the effects of grade retention.

Jodi R. Sandfort is assistant professor of public administration and senior research associate, Center for Policy Research, at the Maxwell School of Citizenship and Public Affairs at Syracuse University. She has recently published academic work in the *Social Service Review, Journal of Poverty, Children and Youth Services Review,* and *Contemporary Sociology.*

Preface

This volume is a product of a research project that originated with the question: Is it possible to derive a body of knowledge on public sector governance and management that is useful both to practitioners and to scholars by using the more rigorous theories, models, and methods of the social sciences? Public management research had for some time been based on the investigation of so-called "best practices" through observational research and case studies. While the very best of this experiential research exhibited considerable verisimilitude and insight, resonating with the world as public managers know it, a growing number of critics had begun to question a lack of rigor that undermined the validity and generalizability of its conclusions. It appeared to be too easy for investigators to discover just what they wanted to discover in the field through a biased selection of cases and evidence. But governance and public management are exceedingly complex, frustrating the reductionist propensities of social science. Were formal theories, models, and methods adequate to the challenge?

Paul C. Light, then director of the public policy program at the Pew Charitable Trusts, was willing to invest significant resources in seeking some answers. The resulting grant to the University of Chicago and to its subcontractor, the Manpower Demonstration Research Corporation (MDRC), funded the research and other activities that are the basis for this book. We are deeply indebted to him for his foresight in structuring the grant and for his willingness to take a chance by committing foundation resources to a field of research—governance and public management—that seldom proves attractive to a philanthropic community more interested in bold innovation than in the less glamorous project of understanding how governing institutions can function more effectively. We have continued to receive encouragement and support from Rebecca Rimel, president of the Pew Charitable Trusts, and from Michael Delli Carpini, Light's successor at Pew.

The papers collected in this volume were first presented at a workshop on "Models, Methods, and Data for the Empirical Study of Governance and Public Management" held at the School of Public Administration and Policy, University of Arizona, in May 1999. The success of this workshop was due in large measure to the encouragement and support of H. Brinton Milward, the school's director, who embraced the idea of the workshop almost immediately and arranged for our use of the first rate facilities of his school. Brint is an important friend and partner in this project.

The idea of the workshop was also welcomed and supported by the authors themselves. Their willingness to prepare high quality manuscripts, to meet deadlines for submissions, revisions, and editorial changes, and to accomplish all that is necessary for the production of an edited volume has been nothing short of remarkable. We are grateful to our authors for their enthusiasm and their intellectual and personal contributions to the success of this project.

The idea that the workshop papers might constitute an important contribution to the literature on public management and governance had the early and encouraging support of John Samples of Georgetown University Press. With publication projects of this sort, it seldom goes as well as it has with John and the Press staff, who have also agreed to publish in due course a companion volume. We deeply appreciate the commitment of Georgetown University Press to this research project.

In addition, several of our colleagues at the University of Chicago have been indispensable to this project. Annie Zhang is a gifted and experienced programmer and data analyst, and her expertise has facilitated our work at every stage. Carolyn J. Hill is completing her doctoral studies at the Irving B. Harris Graduate School of Public Policy Studies. She is a co-author of two of the chapters in this volume, but more than that, she is an exceptionally conscientious and hardworking partner in all our efforts. Keith Madderom, associate dean for administration at the School of Social Service Administration, University of Chicago, and Sue Fournier, his associate, have assisted with the administration of the Pew grant with uncommon skill, freeing us to concentrate on the substantive challenges of the research. To all of these friends, we are grateful.

Finally, we believe that the questions with which this project began have been answered. Rigorous, interdisciplinary empirical research on governance and public management is not only possible, it is essential if we are to understand some of the more complex problems of public administration: promoting the effectiveness of public policies and programs that are implemented through dispersed networks of public and private organizations. In his concluding essay, John Ellwood provides historical context and appropriate cautionary observations for this project, but optimism is warranted.

Carolyn J. Heinrich
Laurence E. Lynn, Jr.
The University of Chicago

CHAPTER 1

Studying Governance and Public Management: Why? How?*

Laurence E. Lynn, Jr., Carolyn J. Heinrich, and Carolyn J. Hill

$\mathbf{H}$ow can public-sector regimes, agencies, programs, and activities be organized and managed to achieve public purposes? This general question is the concern of officials in all branches and at all levels of the public sector: legislators, elected and appointed executives, and judges at federal, state, and local levels of government. Underlying it is an even broader question: How can government continually improve performance so as to earn the respect of citizens who pay for and whose lives are affected by its programs and regulatory activities? The fact that this question is of fundamental importance in politics, policy implementation, public administration, and public management motivates the systematic study of governance, that is, research whose objective is determining how, why, and with what consequences public-sector activity is structured and managed.

The term "governance" is widespread in both public and private sectors, in characterizing both global and local arrangements, and in reference to both formal and informal norms and understandings. Because the term has strong intuitive appeal, precise definitions are seldom thought to be necessary by those who use it. As a result, when authors identify "governance" as important to achieving policy or organizational objectives, it may be unclear whether the reference is to organizational structures, administrative processes, managerial judgment, systems of incentives and rules, administrative philosophies, or combinations of these elements.[1]

Despite ambiguity of definitions, governance generally refers to the means for achieving direction, control, and coordination of wholly or partially autonomous individuals or organizations on behalf of interests to which they jointly contribute. Thus we speak of the governance of global financial markets and of local public schools, of the European Union and of federally administered social programs, of international humanitarian aid distribution, and of networks of public service providers.

In this chapter, we introduce a particular way of defining and thinking about governance that served as general background for the individual contributions included in this volume.[2] Funded by a grant from the Pew Charitable Trusts, around thirty individuals from fifteen academic and research institutions convened at the School of Public Administration and Policy, University of Arizona, in May 1999 for the presentation and discussion of ten papers addressing the general theme of "Models, Methods, and Data for the Empirical Study of Governance and Public Management." In recent decades case-based, best practices research has been the most popular approach to the study of government and managerial effectiveness, at least in public administration and public policy studies. The goal of the Arizona workshop was to explore how rigorous, theory-based research that draws on the most recent advances in social science theories and statistical methods might expand our empirical understanding of governance and government performance in useful ways. Although the focus of this volume is on U.S. domestic policy and program implementation, many of the approaches easily generalize to wider domains of interest.

This opening chapter places the contributions to this volume in the context of the workshop theme. The concluding chapter, by John W. Ellwood, professor of public policy at the Goldman School of Public Policy, University of California, Berkeley, and a workshop participant, assesses these contributions, and the workshop project as a whole, in light of earlier empirical approaches to the study governance dating back to the Carnegie school.

What Is Governance?

In its broadest sense, the study of governance concerns the relationship between governance and government performance. In the empirical analysis of public policies and their implementation, the term "governance" may be defined as *regimes of laws, administrative rules, judicial rulings, and practices that constrain, prescribe, and enable government activity,* where such activity is broadly defined as the production and delivery of publicly supported goods and services.[3] Two separate intellectual traditions have contributed to the etymology of the term "governance" in public administration (Milward 1999; O'Toole 1999). First, the study of institutions has emphasized the multilayered, structural context of rule-governed understandings. Public choice scholars are among the primary contributors to the institutional roots of governance research. Second, the study of networks has emphasized "the role of multiple social actors in networks of negotiation, implementation, and delivery. . . . 'Governance' requires social partners and the knowledge of how to concert action among them . . . " (O'Toole 1999).

Questions that can be usefully explored within a governance context include: (1) How much formal control should be retained by authoritative decision makers and how much delegated to subordinates and officers, and how do the answers vary across political and professional settings? (2) How can particular ideas, or the objectives of particular, powerful stakeholders, or goals such as "efficiency" or "high reliability" be incorporated into an existing governance regime in such a way as to promote its success? (3) How can a governance regime be designed to ensure priority in resource allocation and attention to particular goals and objectives? (4) How can diverse governance regimes (e.g., across states, across municipalities within a state, or across local offices) be induced to converge on the achievement of particular policy objectives? (5) To the extent that government performance depends on competence and reliability at the street levels of government (e.g., in public school classrooms, local welfare offices, or clinical treatment facilities), how can governance be organized to ensure greater competence or attention to particular priorities?

The scope of governance study may encompass both "strictly" positive research as well as analysis of the empirical content or implications of normative propositions. Knowledge about governance acquired through both approaches can prove useful in analyzing and designing governance systems (e.g., to implement public education, health care, or public assistance reforms). The study of governance is complicated, however, by its broad scope and defining elements—the nature of its configuration, the political interests and activities that shape it and exercise influence, and the formal and informal rules and authority that characterize the execution of public policies.

Governance implies an arrangement of distinct but interrelated elements—statutes, including policy mandates; organizational, financial, and programmatic structures; resource levels; administrative rules and guidelines; and institutionalized rules and norms— that constrains and enables the tasks, priorities, and values that are incorporated into regulatory, service production, and service delivery processes. The fact that governance implies configurations rather than the mere summing up of independent elements constitutes a formidable challenge to administrative reform, to managerial practice, and to systematic research on government performance (Ostrom 1986).

A given governance regime distributes resources and responsibility for functions and operations within and between offices and organizations in the public and private sectors (see, e.g., Heinrich and Lynn, in this volume).[4] Through these distributions, governance links the objectives of various and diverse stakeholders (e.g., citizens expressing themselves as voters, respondents to polls, and consumers; organized interest groups; and elected and appointed officials) with the activities that take place at the operational levels of government. Stakeholders are likely to disagree, often sharply, over these distributions, fueling political competition for the control of public administration that affects government operations at every level (Moe 1989). Because a governance regime must balance competing interests and objectives, its creation necessarily entails choosing among the particular interests and objectives to be given priority. Governance is, therefore, inherently political, involving bargaining and compromise, winners and losers, ambiguity and uncertainty, and constituting a second formidable challenge to the study of governance.

Elected executives, legislators, stakeholders, and other policymakers often act as if their exercise of authority over executive agencies affords significant control over what government does and achieves. But governance comprises both formal authority (statutes, administrative guidelines, judicial decrees) and the informal exercise of judgment by the numerous actors and entities involved in implementing public policies and programs. Therefore, the links between expressions of legislative intent and actual government operations may be loose and unreliable, and outcomes may not conform to expectations, especially if conflicts over the means and ends of governance are intense. Effective influence over government activity may begin with formal authority, but it is not wholly determined by it. Discrepancies between authorized and actual activities constitute a third challenge to the study and practice of governance.

A Logic of Governance

Any particular governance arrangement—within a policy domain (e.g., environmental protection), with respect to a type of government activity (e.g., regulation), within a particular jurisdiction (e.g., a state or a city), or within a particular organization (e.g., a department of human services) or organizational field (e.g., child-serving agencies)—may be interpreted as reflecting what we shall term "the logic of governance." The logic of governance, set forth in greater detail below, is not intended to be a comprehensive theory of bureaucracy, government performance, or public management. Rather, it is a schematic or heuristic framework that identifies how the values and interests of citizens, legislative enactments and oversight, executive and organizational structures and roles, and judicial review are linked through a dynamic, interactive, and continuous sociopolitical process. This process induces the performance of public programs and agencies and mediates the consequences of particular strategies for change or reform of government activities.

This logic of governance is derived substantially from the literature and concepts of political economy. We do not mean to argue that political economy provides a complete or, in particular contexts, even an adequate causal account of the social processes that affect government outcomes. We do argue, however, that the positive theory of political economy provides an exceptionally useful framework for organizing and integrating the potential contributions to the study of governance from many different disciplines and fields. Such integration is a primary goal of our approach.

The logic of governance can be characterized as follows:[5]

- Legislators legislate. Legislating means creating coalitions to support and enact specific bills. Coalitions involve, in the first instance, both houses of a legislature and the elected executive, but may include (implicitly) the courts and (explicitly) bureaucrats, who often control the resources of information and technical competence.

- Why do legislators legislate and enacting coalitions form? Reelection is certainly a motive, but on any given issue, legislators' positions may have little or no bearing on their reelection prospects—most have safe seats and adequate war chests to finance campaigns. So a legislative coalition reflects mixed motives based on present and future interests in issues. Useful concepts to describe what legislators do include "deck stacking," that is, crafting legislative mandates so that they favor particular actors and interests, and making "a durable deal," that is, anticipating and forestalling future threats to a legislative mandate by making its undoing difficult.

- "Deck stacking" is about governance, about creating structures and processes that distribute authority and responsibility in ways that benefit favored groups. This is accomplished by specifying administrative decision rules, defining decision criteria, adjusting evidentiary burdens, enfranchising or empowering particular actors, and subsidizing particular interests. The objective of governance arrangements may or may not be about efficiency or about performance in any objective sense, even when these terms are found in statutory language. Governance may be about creating symbolic activity, distributing resources to favored interests, or even preventing efficient administration of controversial policies.

- Unelected public managers, especially those whose civil service status protects them from political reprisals, are potential threats to the durability of any deal. In general, enacting coalitions do not wish to allow bureaucrats authority to decide what to do subject to little direction or constraint. Therefore, they create governance arrangements specifically to narrow or prescribe the range of executive-administrative discretion and thus ensure compliance with the coalition's multifarious intentions.

- The control of bureaucrats can take two distinct forms: *ex ante* controls, designed to preclude noncompliant decisions and actions, and *ex post* controls, designed to detect and punish noncompliance after the fact. The former give rise to principal-agent problems, that is, controls over bureaucratic activity that are ineffective because formal accountability is problematic. The latter, the legislative version of managing by exception, allows for more flexible *ex post* monitoring based on the "fire alarms" set off by interested parties but that may come into play too late to be effective.

- In summary, governance, as a product of legislative action, comprises structures and processes guiding administrative activity that create constraints and controls (both *ex ante* and *ex post*) and that confer or allow autonomy and discretion on the part of administrative actors, all toward fulfilling the purposes of the enacting coalition.

The story so far concerns enactment of legislation that establishes structural and procedural foundations of administration and that constrains and enables the tasks, priorities, and values that are incorporated into regulatory, service production, and service delivery processes of the public sector. The story continues into the implementation of legislative mandates.

- Administrative discretion, which is implicated both in achieving and in thwarting the objectives of the legislative deal, is exercised by actors at various levels of government and within departmental hierarchies, from executives at the federal level to front-line employees in local offices. Within hierarchies, higher-level managers may use (or be directed by legislation to use) their discretion to create additional constraints and controls on lower-level managers and workers. The drift away from legislative intent may originate at lower levels in the system, where actors may be relatively immune to the values of the deal makers.[6]
- As a corollary to the above, there is less need for managerial judgment when legislative directives (or other formal guidelines) are practically definitive. The need for management arises under three conditions: (1) when an enacting coalition has explicitly delegated the "figuring out" of appropriate action to executive agencies; (2) when there is ambiguity in the mandate, providing unintended opportunity for managers to figure things out to fulfill their own purposes; and (3) when fulfilling legislative or administrative objectives requires judgment in interpreting and enforcing rules and standards in

particular cases. In fact, there is virtually always a need for management with respect to public-sector activity, and, therefore, managerial behavior is almost always a factor in government performance.

- Governance regimes, even those with substantial ex ante controls, create or allow for substantial discretion at the street or front-line levels of public organizations, where the primary work of service delivery and regulation is performed. Thus front-line workers and their supervisors, viewed as actors in their own right, may have substantial influence on government outcomes by virtue of their interpretations of rules and standards and their judgments in individual cases. Indeed, it is their performance, for example, in the awarding of contracts or in performing or supervising casework in ways that lead to scandal or harm, perhaps detected through *ex post* control mechanisms, that triggers legislative review and reform of the governance arrangements that permitted adverse outcomes.

Within a governance framework, two distinct or paradigmatic approaches to public management may be identified:

- Public managers may be viewed as optimizing outcomes within a given governance regime or arrangement. Many approaches to public-sector leadership, entrepreneurship, political management, best practices, and innovation explicitly or implicitly take the structures of formal and informal authority as given and, therefore, as circumscribing a manager's maneuvering room.[7] This essentially short-run view of public management emphasizes the quotidian, repetitive aspects of managerial roles and features the psychology, tactics, and political communications aspects of management.
- Alternatively, public managers may be viewed as proactive participants in coalition politics, as representatives of elected executives, as representatives of agency constituencies, or as goal-seeking actors in their own right. This view, less well developed in the literature, is implicit in the notion of "iron triangles" and issue networks.[8] In the literature on social control, it is implicit in the notion of bureaucracy. It is also explicit in some spatial models of coalition politics (see Knott and Hammond, in this volume). This longer-run view broad-

ens the subject of public management to the wider domain of governance and the administrative control of bureaucracy and the content of management to include the design of governance arrangements.

This logic of governance, as we have emphasized, is not the only one that might be used to interpret the dynamics of policy and program implementation. For example, the hypothesis of "deck stacking" is sharply contested by critical legal theorists and by legal idealists, who have altogether different explanations for why legislation takes the form that it does (Mashaw 1990). Moreover, it is hard to falsify "deck stacking," that is, to investigate the extent to which and how bureaucrats thwart the purposes of enacting coalitions and the nature of the a priori purposes that are served by government activities. Thus the empirical usefulness of the approach may be questioned. As an alternative, network analysis might be used to construct interpretations of policymaking that emphasize the centrality of continuing social and political relationships and communication among stakeholders and other actors internal and external to executive agencies (see Milward and Provan, in this volume). Systems models might be constructed to help organize thinking around the notion of a production or transformation process linking inputs to outputs via organizations, managers, and technologies (Scott 1992; O'Toole and Meier, in this volume).

We believe that the logic of governance is an insightful heuristic because it requires investigators to recognize the formally hierarchical, essentially political, and loosely coupled nature of policy enactment and program implementation structures and processes. The investigator is encouraged to take into account the endogenous nature of factors often assumed to be exogenous, such as local implementation structures or service and resource provider behavior (Moe 1985). Further, the investigator's attention is drawn to influences on operations and outcomes originating at various levels of administration, such as formal mandates in legislation, administrative guidelines, or the discretionary strategies chosen by managers. Thus the investigator recognizes the importance of both formal and informal authority and the relationships between them.

Governance research using this logic enlarges the intellectual scope of what has been called "implementation analysis." Within a governance framework, investigators can explore the determinants of policy and program impacts without becoming distracted by the alleged dichotomy between exogenous (or top-down) and street-level (or bottom-up) explanations of outcomes or performance. For example, Elmore (1979, p. 605) argues that "applying forward and backward mapping to the same problem gives much different results. . . . The crucial difference of perspectives stems from whether one chooses to rely primarily on formal devices of command and control that centralize authority or on informal devices of delegation and discretion that disperse authority."

Empirical governance research conceptualized through a logic of governance can conceivably accommodate both top-down and bottom-up perspectives without having as its central focus the primacy of one or the other. In effect, the governance researcher employs theory-based insights (from both exogenous and street-level perspectives) to analyze a governance regime and its consequences (see Jennings and Ewalt, and Sandfort, both in this volume) in a kind of ex post backward mapping. In general, the logic of governance encourages investigators to contextualize their models and data analyses in drawing general conclusions from necessarily incomplete data and information.

Limits to Governance

Governance research may explore the empirical content of policy changes and, especially, the limits that formal changes may encounter. Attempts to relocate decision-making authority, for example, often do little to alter actual decision-making processes. Bimber's (1994) study of several efforts to decentralize public school governance illustrates this point. He found that, despite an expressed desire for decentralization and the subsequent implementation of site-based management, "years after decentralization was introduced, governance structures . . . either remained centrally controlled or represented a hybrid of centralized and decentralized arrangements" (p. vii). Bimber attributes this finding to the difficulty of separating decisions about various aspects of school operations that are in fact highly interrelated. It is difficult, for example, to give one group meaningful authority over personnel without also giving that group a measure of fiscal autonomy. It is similarly ineffective to give "schools discretion over use of maintenance funds while reserving authority to veto repair decisions and requiring use of overworked district maintenance workers" (p. 3).

The limited effectiveness that reforms of formal structures and processes may have suggests the need for other theory-based approaches to evaluating the determinants of government performance. Nevertheless, governance is still one tool that can facilitate public-sector improvement. Appropriate governance is essential to implementing agreed-on goals and to facilitating and institutionalizing new norms of practice and performance—both key elements in meaningful reform. Governance, moreover, is an end in itself, a translation of competing interests and values into operational guidance for policies and programs and into political property rights that preserve the stability of a legislative deal.

Altering incentives through formal structures will improve performance only if the changes are made in a way designed to affect how informal authority influences the behavior of subordinate managers and primary workers. To improve program performance or to change core organizational practices, it may be necessary to make changes in governance within a comprehensive framework designed to change core values and commitments. As Bimber (1994) and others have shown, simply redistributing formal authority may have little effect on desired outcomes, despite claims to the contrary by many administrative reformers. Hence, every reform agenda must consider the need for associated governance changes, where formal processes and structures of governance must be viewed as necessary but not sufficient for public-sector improvement.

The Study of Governance

The study of governance must confront the three intellectual challenges identified earlier: (1) constructing and assessing the influence of configurations of variables rather than of individual variables or simple correlations, (2) taking into account the political nature of these configurations, and (3) recognizing the importance of informal authority, an endogenous factor, as mediating between formal authority and outcomes. Moreover, a conceptual framework for such research—whether the logic of governance sketched in the preceding section or some other framework—is essential to developing rigorous research designs and data analysis strategies. Such a framework helps investigators identify potentially significant interrelationships and select theories appropriate to formulating and testing explanations or propositions concerning why, how, and with what consequences governance affects government performance.

Within a framework of governance, which emphasizes formal and informal structures that predispose action, the study of public management is concerned with action itself, with the discretionary actions of actors in managerial roles subject to formal authority.[9] The research problem is to explain government results, outcomes, impacts, or performance in ways that allow for the separate identification of both governance arrangements and of public management. That is, the problem is separating how the deck is stacked from the particular impact of how managers figure things out and exercise discretion within a governance arrangement.[10]

The research problem is complicated by the fact, noted earlier, that effectiveness or efficient performance may or may not be the goal of a legislative coalition; there is frequently no well-organized political constituency for performance or results per se.[11] Moreover, organizations created by and accountable to legislative coalitions seldom resemble the kinds of organizations that organization theorists would create; rational actors in legislatures do not necessarily create rational organizations to execute their mandates (a proposition implied by Arrow's impossibility theorem). Potential members of winning coalitions often negotiate to the point of obsession over the details of administration in order to *preclude* effective administration of a program that might alienate constituencies or damage particular interests.

Models and Methods

Can the methods of positive social science contribute to sorting out the consequences of deck stacking and managerial choices and to producing reliable and significant knowledge about governance? Is such a research program worth the considerable effort required to do it well, given the requirements for expensive and extensive data and the complexity of the tools needed to ensure statistical reliability? The answer is not obvious.

If they are to produce knowledge for practice, the models and methods of social science require the researcher to make simplifying assumptions that reduce a problem to an essential and manageable causal logic (see, e.g., Ingraham and Donahue, in this volume). In modeling phenomena as complex as governance, the sacrifice of verisimilitude may assume away too many essentials for the results to be of much practical interest. It is inherently difficult to derive predictions and create empirical models that permit positive tests of nontrivial, theory-grounded hypotheses concerning structures, processes, and action. The price of rigor may be quite high. Moreover, synthesizing the findings from many models does not necessarily overcome the individual shortcomings of any one model. The configurational nature of governance remains an issue.

Formal empirical research, furthermore, is hardly the only approach to obtaining useful knowledge about governance; materials ranging from biography and journalistic accounts to oral histories and case studies often provide important insights into the internal logic and results of government. A knowledge of best practices derived from field research and richly textured case studies may be, and is in the minds of many, more appropriate for investigating the subtle complexities of governance.

These arguments do not, however, constitute a prima facie argument against studying governance using positive methods. Qualitative, narrative, and hermeneutic methods have the advantage of accommodating subtlety, nuance, and complexity. The chief advantages of positive methods are their transparency to those who were uninvolved; the fact that conjectures and hypotheses must survive formal, a priori tests of their validity; and the possibility of generalizing findings beyond the specific contexts of the research. Thus qualitative research may be most useful in identifying the many factors that may matter to government performance or the constituent elements of a governance regime, that is, the contents of administrative "black boxes." Research that systematically employs models and statistical methods may be most useful in identifying which factors, elements, or configurations are most influential, or influential at all, and the magnitude of importance of these factors relative both to other variables in the model and to omitted variables. In general, research that employs theory, empirical methods, and systematically obtained data and observations is likely to be the primary source of fundamental and durable knowledge that transcends particular times, places, and contexts.

The Logic of Governance Applied

To construct an organizing framework for empirical research, it is useful to recognize that the logic of governance involves a hierarchy of relationships:

- between citizen preferences and interests expressed politically and legislative choice;
- between legislative preferences and the formal structures and processes of public agencies;
- between formal authority and the structure and management of organizations, programs, and administrative activities;
- between organization, management, and administration and the core technologies and primary work of public agencies;
- between primary work and outputs or results, that is, the availability, quality, and cost of publicly sponsored goods and services;
- between outputs or results and stakeholder assessments; and
- between stakeholder assessments and reactions and, back to the top of the list, political preferences and interests.

Empirical research may reveal, or field observation may suggest, that governance in particular contexts may be broken down into subanalyses of loosely coupled or decoupled administrative units. Too often, however, the possibility that broader patterns of interrelationships decisively affect outcomes is not adequately incorporated into explanation or interpretation. It is possible, for example, that work performance or client outcomes may be attributable to client characteristics, to worker and treatment characteristics, or to patterns of interaction between clients, treatments, and workers. The significance of local or hierarchical organizational and management variables, or of systemwide incentives, should not, however, be ruled out. It may be the case that the pattern and magnitude of client, worker, and treatment effects is influenced by the characteristics of governance regimes, an important consideration in assembling evidence of value to public managers.

To further illustrate: The logic of governance outlined in the previous section can be expressed as a basic "reduced form" model:

$$O = f(E, C, T, S, M)$$

where O = outputs/outcomes (individual-level and/or organizational outputs or outcomes); E = environmental factors; C = client characteristics; T = treatments (primary work or core processes or technology); S = structures; and M = managerial roles and actions.

Table 1.1 lists some examples of variables used in governance research for each of these reduced-form model components. The reduced form is a framework, not a theory. In specific policy contexts, the "true" model may be one in which the marginal effect of many elements is zero. The purpose of theory-based research within this framework is to identify the most parsimonious model for specific contexts.

In its reduced form, this model estimates the relative associations of the various independent variables to the dependent variable. A complex causal structure, however, almost certainly underlies these relationships in the true model: interdependencies undoubtedly exist among (and within) E, C, T, S, O, and M. Theories relevant to governance may be adduced to assist in specifying and testing these underlying causal structures or processes. Governance researchers may begin with a relatively parsimonious "political economy view" of the public sector, captured in the logic of governance, and gradually introduce elements of considerable conceptual complexity, including those variables suggested by bureaucratic theory and by sociological and social psychological perspectives on organizational and interorganizational behavior. These more complex theoretical frameworks assist in modeling the heterogeneity of governance contexts. In particular, they may include a constellation of relevant variables and causal models, and enable the researcher to isolate the relative effects of constructs that are of theoretical or practical interest.

Postulating and establishing causal relationships (or strong statistical associations) at the individual level are generally more tractable problems than postulating the effects of governance arrangements on these associations, or on outcomes related to organizational characteristics. For example, analyzing the associations between student background characteristics and student outcomes measured by test scores is relatively straightforward compared with determining whether the average student does better with particular kinds of instruction or in particular schools, or determining whether instituting high-stakes testing or merit pay for teachers affects student achievement (see, e.g., Roderick, Jacob, and Bryk, in this volume).

TABLE 1.1

Reduced-Form Logic of Governance

Reduced-form model component	Examples of variables
O = Outputs/outcomes (individual-level and/or organizational-level)	Precisely defined, empirically measured variables Broadly defined, not necessarily client-oriented variables
E = Environmental Factors	Political structures Level of external authority/monitoring Performance of the economy Market structure/degree of competition Funding constraints/dependencies Characteristics of eligible or target population Legal institutions/practice Technological dynamism
C = Client Characteristics	Client attributes/characteristics/behavior
T = Treatments (primary work/core processes/technology)	Organizational mission/objectives Determination of target populations, recruitment or eligibility criteria Program treatment/technology (including scope/intensity of services)
S = Structures	Organization type Level of integration/coordination Centralization of control Functional differentiation Administrative rules/incentives Budgetary allocations Contractual arrangements Institutional culture/values
M = Managerial roles and actions	Leadership practices—characteristics, attitudes, behavior (including, e.g., innovation and goal-setting, worker motivation, recognition and support, problem-solving, and delegation of authority or work tasks) Staff-management relations, communication and decision-making tools and arrangements Professionalism/career concerns Monitoring/control/accountability mechanisms (including performance standards, incentives, and sanctions)

Given the undoubted importance of configurational, political, formal and informal aspects of governance, and its complex causal structure, how does an investigator evaluate the contributions of public management skill to government outcomes? That actors (whether managers or front-line staff) have discretion may be intentional or unintentional. One may desire to isolate the discretionary contributions to government outcomes controlling for contextual factors, which requires fairly rich data sets (see Riccio, Bloom, and Hill in this volume). Research that tests the empirical relevance of various, often competing, perspectives on the public management contribution will constitute important intellectual capital for public management practice.

Research on Governance

A logic of governance can accommodate a wide range of theories, models, and methods, but not the relatively atheoretical eclecticism that is popular with many governance and public management researchers. To assess the contributions—as well as the challenges—of theory-based governance research, we have reviewed a "literature of governance." To identify such a literature, we restricted the domain to the logic of governance outlined earlier and to characteristics of individual contributions. Within this context, we assessed monographs, articles, and working papers that met at least one of the following five criteria:

- framed questions or propositions to advance theoretical and empirical modeling;
- developed theory-based models or frameworks with multiple components for empirically testing hypotheses;
- defined and operationalized specific concepts or variables;
- provided guidance for data collection and determining appropriate methods for empirical research; or
- presented convincing and appropriately framed findings.

We compiled a sample of more than 500 studies by applying these criteria, which is illustrative rather than exhaustive of literature exploring governance from the viewpoints of various disciplines, subdisciplines, professional fields, and subfields of study.[12] Other researchers will undoubtedly include other contributions in their versions of a literature addressing this or another logic of governance. A goal of our effort is to assess the models and methods that have been used in governance research, and to identify common pitfalls as well as promising approaches to the study of governance.

Knowing "what we know" and "how we know it" concerning governance and public management is enhanced by routinely and characteristically drawing on research from theoretical and empirical sources in a wide variety of disciplines and professional fields. Such habits of search and synthesis promote empirical research that is adequately conceptualized and carefully specified and tip the odds in favor of research designs that account for a logic of governance. The papers included in this volume exemplify research that attempts to meet this challenge.

The Papers

Following is a synopsis of each of the ten papers included in this volume (chapters 2–11). Each paper is part of a larger research project of the authors. Assembled in this volume, these particular papers illustrate a range of theoretical and methodological possibilities of empirical governance research conceived as an intellectual enterprise that transcends the boundaries of disciplines, subdisciplines, and professional fields. Our hope is that this broad awareness will stimulate further high quality research on governance.

Chapter 2: *Evaluating Chicago's Efforts to End Social Promotion, by Melissa Roderick, Brian Jacob, and Anthony Bryk.*

In an ambitious, multilevel research project, Roderick, Jacob, and Bryk study the relationships between the structure and management of public schools and educational technologies, and between educational practices and student performance. They draw on the wealth of data generated by the Consortium on Chicago School Research, which, in collaboration with the Chicago Public Schools (CPS), is developing data sets and methods to evaluate the CPS systemwide administrative reform to end "social promotion" (or automatic grade advancement) and increase students' achievement. In earlier research, Roderick and Camburn (1997) used hierarchical generalized linear models to test hypotheses about students' likelihood of failing courses and of subsequent recovery from failing a grade. They found a number of important relationships among individual- and school-level variables that suggested that "governance and instructional environments . . . matter" (p. 32).

Roderick, Jacob, and Bryk build on their own earlier work and use three-level hierarchical linear models to analyze changes in students' grades and test scores over time (the first level); students' characteristics and their promotion, retention, and summer school participation within schools and across years (the second level); and the effectiveness of schools' responses to these policies as a function of school demographics and characteristics, policy implementation and teachers' classroom strategies, and the school environment and "prior school development" (the third level). This study also includes an extensive qualitative component with intensive case studies of each school's approach to policy implementation and a longitudinal investigation of students' experiences under the promotional policy.

Roderick, Jacob, and Bryk present preliminary findings that suggest significant policy implementation effects (e.g., of extra instructional time and other resources invested during the school year before testing) on student achievement gains. In continuing research, the authors will disentangle the student achievement effects into possible component effects of: (1) testing or instrumentation, that is, improvements in test-taking skills; (2) motivational or behavioral changes on the part of students in a high-stakes testing environment; (3) changes in instruction made by teachers; and (4) program effects of a special after-school program. We expect this work will set a new precedent for empirical modeling in educational research that aims to get inside the classroom as well as the school unit in investigating the link between administrative policies, educational approaches, and student achievement.

Chapter 3: *Governance and Performance: The Influence of Program Structure and Management on Job Training Partnership Act (JTPA) Program Outcomes, by Carolyn J. Heinrich and Laurence E. Lynn, Jr.*

Heinrich and Lynn also employ a multilevel approach to the study of governance and management in federally funded job-training programs. They develop an empirical model of the formal structures of control and accountability in state and local Job Training Partnership Act (JTPA) programs and investigate the effects of these governance structures and management practices on participant (or client) outcomes. They use hierarchical, time-varying data from the National JTPA Study (including information about individual participants and local program structures and operations) to identify the separate contributions of administrative structures, management strategies, and client characteristics to program outcomes. Their research was intended not only to explain further JTPA program outcomes within a governance context, but also to indicate the types of insights that can be gained in the study of governance and public management through theory-based, empirical research using multilevel, multisite data sets.

In their descriptive analyses, they found strong associations among the choices of organizational and administrative structures in JTPA service delivery areas and the types of administrative policies and incentives that are adopted at both state and local levels to motivate performance. For example, they showed that when private-sector representatives assumed more formal authority in program administrative entities, they appeared to emphasize measured performance and to adopt administrative practices (e.g., more performance-based contracting and contracts with for-profit organizations) that also demanded accountability for results. To evaluate relationships such as these empirically and further explain the role of governance and management factors in producing JTPA client earnings and employment outcomes, Heinrich and Lynn estimated hierarchical linear models that included all six components of the model of governance described in the introductory portion of this chapter.

From their hierarchical linear model they were able to explain nearly all of the cross-site variation in client earnings and employment outcomes. In general, they found that organizational structure is an important influence on program outcomes, as is management to the extent that managers choose the structural arrangements governing program operations. In addition, the effects of management strategies on client outcomes were larger for more straightforward, easily monitored incentive policies that contributed to a coherent focus on program goals among management and staff. These results not only generate useful insights for further public administration research, but they demonstrate the potential for using multilevel, multisite data sets in the study of governance and public management.

Chapter 4: *Driving Caseloads Down: Welfare Policy Choices and Administrative Action in the States, by Edward T. Jennings, Jr., and Jo Ann G. Ewalt.*

In their study of state-level welfare policy choices and administrative actions, Jennings and Ewalt evaluate two arguments about how to reduce welfare caseloads. The first asserts that a top-down reorientation of the system toward the goal of client self-sufficiency will bring about desired behavioral changes in welfare recipients. The second contends that behavioral change among welfare recipients requires administrative and cultural reform given that it is the actions of administrators that shape "street-level" activity. In evaluating these two arguments, they use information from a survey of state government administrators, along with administrative and census data, to explore the translation of federal law into state action and state action to local action, focusing on the restrictiveness of state policy choices. In particular, they examine the fit or congruence between state policy choices and administrative goals, between administrative goals and organizational processes, and between administrative actions and policy outcomes (i.e., caseload reductions).

Jennings and Ewalt estimate a multivariate model of caseload reductions for forty-four states, including predictors or controls for state goals and strategies, implementation activities related to emphases on client work and changing office culture, a measure of the restrictiveness of state policies, and environmental factors. Their model findings suggest that the link between state policy restrictiveness and administrative policy goals is weak because state program administrators have not developed policy goals consistent with the indicated level of policy restrictiveness. They also examine specific patterns of administrative activity and find a strong link between policy restrictiveness, administrative actions, and caseload declines. Thus states are developing programmatic approaches consistent with the overarching policy objective of reducing welfare caseloads. Although they find evidence to support both arguments about how to reduce caseloads, Jennings and Ewalt conclude that administrative reforms have the most influence on program outcomes.

Chapter 5: *Examining the Effect of Welfare-to-Work Structures and Services on a Desired Policy Outcome, by Jodi R. Sandfort.*

While Jennings and Ewalt explore how variations in state policies, implementation strategies, and goals are related to changes in welfare program outcomes, Sandfort focuses on the structure and management of welfare programs within a single state. She studied the decentralized service delivery structures of welfare-to-work programs in eighty-two Michigan counties to address the question: Does county-level variation in service delivery structures and technology have a measurable impact on the proportion of a county's welfare caseload that combines welfare and work, and ultimately, moves into the workforce? Sandfort specifically investigates the effectiveness of the "Work First" (immediate labor force attachment) welfare-to-work model introduced in 1994, and the "Project Zero" pilot initiative (case management with additional supportive services) being tested within some of the counties.

Sandfort's development of empirical models for assessing the influence of county-level program structures, primary work technologies, and management of welfare-to-work program outcomes is informed by her prior qualitative research, including telephone interviews with managers of public welfare offices and local welfare-to-work programs. In her current research she uses census and county-level administrative data to develop empirical measures for environmental, client, structural (service provider), and treatment and technology factors, in addition to outcome measures (the proportion of a county's caseload that is working). Management variables are not explicitly incorporated into her models but are implied, as she suggests, in county choices for service technology and service delivery structures.

Sandfort finds a statistically significant positive effect of participation in the Project Zero pilot on county-level outcomes, and a negative relationship between the number of Work First providers and the proportion of welfare recipients who were working. She applies the findings of her qualitative research to aid in the interpretation of these results because, as she acknowledges, there was substantial variation in the Work First service provider technologies and the Project Zero interventions that she was unable to explore empirically with available data. She encourages future researchers to develop new empirical models that can disentangle the effects of program management and complex, inter- and intraorganizational relationships in local service delivery structures on program outcomes.

Chapter 6: *Management, Organizational Characteristics, and Performance: The Case of Welfare-to-Work Programs, by James Riccio, Howard Bloom, and Carolyn J. Hill.*

Riccio, Bloom, and Hill investigate how management practices, organizational characteristics, and service technology influence the implementation of welfare-to-work programs in seventy-two local offices within twenty-two counties and eight states. They use administrative records and survey data collected by the Manpower Demonstration Research Corporation (MDRC) during experimental evaluations of these programs to formulate hypotheses and empirical models for testing. Having found statistically significant differences in the impact on earnings, labor force participation, and welfare receipt across the seventy-two local offices, they constructed measures of local office management and staff policies and practices (e.g., enforcement of the participation mandate for program participants) and explore their relationships to program impacts.

The information obtained from MDRC surveys of welfare-to-work program managers and staff encompasses a wide range of perceptions, beliefs, characteristics, and service delivery practices that not only define the nature of the welfare-to-work intervention, its organizational context and culture, and management processes, but may also influence the effective operation of these programs. Riccio, Bloom, and Hill use this information to construct measures that will allow them to estimate the separate effects of these organizational factors on program impacts (controlling for client characteristics and environmental factors), and that also capture the degree of variation or agreement among staff in perceptions, beliefs, and practices within the local offices. Their ongoing research will assess whether variation in these aspects of management within and across welfare-to-work program offices helps to explain the observed variation in office impacts on earnings, labor force participation, and welfare receipt.

The authors will use the multilevel, multisite experimental data to construct eight measures of welfare-to-work program impacts that will serve as the dependent variables in their models of organizational performance. They will also explore three alternative approaches to estimating: (1) aggregate-level regression models, (2) individual-level regression models with interactions, and (3) hierarchical or multilevel models. They anticipate that their research will not only generate substantive findings in the area of welfare-to-work (i.e., increasing knowledge about what drives performance), but that it will also help to provide methodological guidance for future research in other human services settings (i.e., improving the measurement of performance).

Chapter 7: Congressional Committees and Policy Change: Explaining Legislative Outcomes in Banking, Trucking, Airline, and Telecommunications Deregulation, by Jack H. Knott and Thomas H. Hammond.

Knott and Hammond's is the only work included in this volume that focuses on the enactment of legislation that establishes the structural and procedural foundations of administrative and policy implementation activities. They construct a formal (spatial) model of legislative policymaking to examine the varying effect of congressional committees on policy outcomes and to identify conditions under which legislative committees are likely to be effective in fostering or blocking policy change. They apply their theoretical model to four case studies of deregulation in the banking, trucking, airline and telecommunications industries.

Knott and Hammond aim to identify conditions under which the policy status quo is in equilibrium and conditions under which it can be changed. These include exogenous changes such as court rulings, exploitation of legislative loopholes or regulatory "cheating," unilateral presidential actions, independent administrative actions by regulatory agencies, and congressional committees with overlapping jurisdictions. In the context of deregulation, they employ a simplified model that focuses on actors with policy preferences on a continuum ranging from strongly pro-competition to strongly anticompetition. For each case, they model exogenous changes in the policy status quo, the legislative responses, and the legislative outcomes to form some generalizations about the conditions under which committees effectively block or promote policy change.

They find that (1) the degree of influence of congressional committees depends on relationships between actors' policy preferences and the location along a continuum of the status quo policy, while changes in status quo location affect the relative power of actors; (2) the president is one actor whose support is essential for a committee to change the status quo; (3) legislative procedures directly affect the conditions under which legislative committees are powerful; and (4) the coalition necessary to change the status quo is considerably larger than the one required to protect it. In general, their modeling efforts generate conceptual insights about relationships and influence in an area of complex legislative, policy, and political interactions, while also assessing their empirical implications for legislative outcomes.

Chapter 8: How Networks Are Governed, by H. Brinton Milward and Keith G. Provan.

Milward and Provan's theoretical contributions to the study of governance describe networks as governing mechanisms or regimes, consisting of grants, contracts, and agreements to produce public services jointly and manage decentralized programs at the community level. Drawing on earlier research by Milward (1994), they characterize networks as the "mainstay of the hollow state," where the hollow state implies "joint production and several degrees of separation between the source and use of government funds," that is, a number of layers between the source and use of public funds. Although their work in this volume is primarily theoretical, their substantial empirical research on networks of nonprofit organizations that jointly produce mental health services in communities across the United States underlies many of their conceptual insights.

Milward and Provan emphasize that governance in multitiered networks involves much more than a simple chain of principal-agent relationships. They make a helpful distinction between network governance structures based on contractual (more formal, principal-agent) ties, and interorganizational networks held together by historical patterns of collaboration, interdependence, informal or personal relationships, and trust. They also argue that networks must cultivate both of these types of ties or relationships to be effective. It is well-defined principal-agent relationships combined with strong, trust-based ties that facilitate network governance and guide all actors or parties to actions that encourage achievement of their long-term mutual objectives.

One additional contribution of Milward and Provan's work that is important for governance research is their development of the concept of stability in network governance. Both their theoretical and empirical investigations of networks suggest that systems in flux—primarily with respect to client base, funding, and leadership—are less effective in coordinating administrative and service delivery processes. A key finding of their empirical research that explored the links between network governance and the mental health outcomes of clients was that human service systems that are stable are more likely to perform well than systems in transition.

Chapter 9: Networks, Hierarchies, and Public Management: Modeling the Nonlinearities, by Laurence J. O'Toole, Jr., and Kenneth J. Meier.

Like Milward and Provan, O'Toole and Meier recognize networks as increasingly prominent and prevalent public management structures, and they investigate the ways that network managers and other network actors shape the outcomes of public policy. One of a number of contributions this work makes is to define precisely, through a formal model as well as narrative, three core concepts frequently employed in the study of network management: hierarchy, network, and management. For example, hierarchy is described as a stabilizing or buffering arrangement, that is, a stable set of relations with formal, tightly connected, superior-subordinate authority linkages. A network is defined as two or more units in which all major components are not incorporated within a single, hierarchical array of formal relationships.

Focusing on networks in formation or in flux, O'Toole and Meier develop a formal model of overall network management that allows one to specify the functions and nonlinear, interactive relationships within both hierarchies and network forms of governance. Their model defines network management along a continuum from designated hierarchy (or complete stability) to total structural fluidity and instability (networks), with the objective of generating precise model predictions that might be empirically tested. In addition, they identify three forms of management or management tasks: (1) stabilizing internal system operations, (2) exploiting shocks in the environment, and (3) buffering the organization from environmental shocks.

Although they do not test their formal model empirically, O'Toole and Meier derive a number of interesting propositions for future empirical research. For example, they posit that a major difference between networks and hierarchies lies in how they are affected by external shocks from the environment. Networks are alleged to have fewer buffering capabilities, but because they are inherently less stable, the shocks that penetrate them are also predicted to have less impact on outcomes. In the context of their autoregressive approach to capturing the dynamics of repeated interactions among network participants, they also predict that as hierarchy increases, the role of management becomes less important. In many ways, as they acknowledge, their work initiates a new research agenda, and one that they hope also motivates more empirical testing in this important area of governance research.

Chapter 10: Dissecting the Black Box Revisited: Characterizing Government Management Capacity, by Patricia W. Ingraham and Amy Kneedler Donahue.

Ingraham and Donahue's research is more directly focused on the primary work and administrative activities of public managers than any other chapter in this volume. In their work, which is part of a larger, ongoing empirical research project, they develop a conceptual framework and analytical approach to facilitate, in their words, "a comprehensive and valid evaluation of government management." With the objectives of improving public management practices, communicating the results of government management systems to the public, and supporting research, they address three prominent public management questions: How well do public entities perform? How does management influence performance? How can management be assessed?

Their conceptual model identifies four "management subsystems" of government management capacity: financial, human resources, capital, and information technology. For public managers to be effective, they argue, these subsystems not only must perform well independently but must also be well coordinated and mutually supporting. A major goal of their research is to examine how leadership and other managerial attributes and resources strengthen the capacity of these subsystems and contribute to organizational effectiveness. In their model, relationships among management subsystems and their implications for effective public management practices vary along two dimensions: integration (achieved through leadership, the use of information, and resource allocations), and the presence of a formalized system of managing for results.

A substantial product of their research to date is specifying a system of indicators for criteria-based assessment that allows one to characterize government performance along the two dimensions of integration and managing for results. The evaluation criteria apply to both the level of government management capacity and the contributions of its capacity, allowing one to consider not only the strengths and weaknesses of a government's management systems but also the degree to which they affect government's overall ability to manage.

Ingraham and Donahue encourage debate about these evaluation criteria for government management. Their model of management subsystems and evaluation criteria might also provide guidance to public management scholars who are initiating empirical research in an area that has been lacking in more rigorous, well-defined conceptualizations and measures of leadership and management components. Although their focus is on empirical research, Ingraham and Donahue have not yet reached that stage in their larger project. We expect that it will be in empirical work—where concepts are operationalized and precise measures of management factors are imperative—that the merits and import of their models and criteria will be further appraised.

Chapter 11: *Prospects for the Study of the Governance of Public Organizations and Policies, by John W. Ellwood.*

In the concluding chapter of this volume, John Ellwood appraises the current state of research aimed at building a theory-based empirical literature on the governance of public policies. While he is encouraged by the new theories and better data that researchers in this volume are using to evaluate governance mechanisms, he remains skeptical about our ability to model governance given its inherently political nature.

Ellwood argues that public organizations or governance regimes are less accountable than private sector organizations because they lack a "balance sheet" or "single-issue accountability" that provides clear incentives to management, while at the same time, exercising the coercive or monopoly power of the state. He argues further that contemporary public choice theory rarely focuses on objectives related to increasing governmental performance or social welfare. Rather, according to Ellwood, models are concerned with legislative, bureaucratic, and interest group behaviors that "create situations in which individuals and groups profit at the expense of the society as a whole." The processes by which these "situations" are created, that is, in which public policy is developed and implemented, are also fundamentally unstable, characterized by multiple and frequently conflicting goals that are left partially or wholly unresolved by policy makers.

The absence of a stable equilibrium from which outcomes can be analytically derived complicates research efforts to evaluate the effectiveness of governance regimes and policies. For example, Ellwood asks, "Who should determine what the goals of a given policy should be?" Who, and at what level of a governance regime, should determine which policy alternative will achieve particular policy goals? How do scholars engaged in empirical research begin to define appropriate measures of governmental effectiveness when the objective of a given policy and the choices made about policy implementation may be unclear? As Ellwood argues, "to the extent that this remains the case, the researcher must impose the dependent variable for her or his study of the governance of public policies." He notes further that the public policies addressed in this volume, those that aim to produce government outputs that change individual and group behaviors, are among the most difficult to study.

In the past, Ellwood says, scholars have commonly faced a trade-off between policy relevance and scientific rigor in the study of public governance. With better data and improved statistical techniques, he observes, the authors in this volume are able to escape this trade-off and return to a line of research abandoned by Herbert Simon and his colleagues in the late 1930s: developing and testing models that "assess the effects of a wide variety of independent variables on policy outcomes." He reserves judgment, however, on the ultimate contributions of this approach to governance research. Can the results of governance models be replicated using data from other jurisdictions or for other policies in the same jurisdiction? he asks. We can only come to know this by continuing to pursue theory-based empirical research on the governance of public policies and institutions.

References

Altshuler, Alan, William Morrill, Harold Wolman, and Faith Mitchell, editors. 1999. *Governance and opportunity in metropolitan America.* Washington, D.C.: National Academy Press.

Bimber, Bruce. 1994. *The decentralization mirage: Comparing decision-making arrangements in four high schools.* Santa Monica, Calif.: Rand Corporation.

Elmore, Richard. 1979. Backward mapping: Implementation research and policy decisions. *Political Science Quarterly,* 94(4): 601–16.

Fiorina, Morris. 1982. Legislative choice of regulatory forms. *Public Choice,* 39(1): 33–66.

Horn, Murray J., and Kenneth Shepsle. 1989. Commentary on "Administrative arrangements and the political control of agencies": Administrative process and organizational form as legislative response to agency costs. *Virginia Law Review,* 75: 499–508.

Kingdon, John. 1984. *Agendas, alternatives, and public policies.* Boston: Little, Brown.

Mashaw, Jerry. 1990. Explaining administrative process: Normative, positive, and critical stories of legal development. *Journal of Law, Economics, and Organization,* 6 (Special Issue): 267–98.

McCubbins, Mathew, Roger Noll, and Barry Weingast. 1987. Administrative procedures as instruments of political control. *Journal of Law, Economics, and Organization,* 3(2): 243–77.

―――. 1989. Structure and process, politics and policy: Administrative arrangements and the political control of agencies. *Virginia Law Review,* 75: 431–83.

McCubbins, Mathew, and Thomas Schwartz. 1984. Congressional oversight overlooked: Police patrols vs. fire alarms. *American Journal of Political Science,* 28: 165–79.

Milward, H. Brinton. 1994. Nonprofit contracting and the hollow state. *Public Administration Review,* 54: 73–77.

―――. January 1999. Personal communication to Laurence E. Lynn, Jr .

Moe, Terry M. 1985. Control and feedback in economic regulation: The case of the NLRB. *American Political Science Review*, 79(4): 1094–116.

———. 1989. The politics of bureaucratic structure. In *Can the government govern?* Edited by J. Chubb and P. Peterson. Washington, D.C.: Brookings Institution, pp. 267–329.

———. 1990. The politics of structural choice: Toward a theory of public bureaucracy. In *Organization theory: From Chester Barnard to the present and beyond,* edited by O. Williamson. Oxford: Oxford University Press, pp. 116–53.

Niskanen, William. 1975. Bureaucrats and politicians. *Journal of Law and Economics*, 18: 617–43.

Noll, Roger, and Barry Weingast. 1991. Rational actor theory, social norms, and policy implementation: Applications to administrative processes and bureaucratic culture. In *The economic approach to politics: A critical reassessment of the theory of rational action,* edited by K. R. Monroe. New York: HarperCollins, pp. 327–58.

Ostrom, Elinor. 1986. An agenda for the study of institutions. *Public Choice,* 48(1): 3–25.

O'Toole, Laurence, Jr. February 1990. Personal communication to Laurence E. Lynn, Jr.

Roderick, Melissa, and Eric Camburn. 1997. Risk and Recovery: Course Failures in the Early Years of High School. The University of Chicago, School of Social Service Administration, unpublished paper, January 1997.

Scott, W. Richard. 1992. *Organizations: Rational, natural, and open systems,* 3d ed. Englewood Cliffs, N.J.: Prentice-Hall.

Shepsle, Kenneth, and Barry Weingast. 1981. Structure-induced equilibrium and legislative choice. *Public Choice,* 37(3): 503–19.

Simon, Herbert. 1964. On the concept of organizational goal. *Administrative Science Quarterly,* 9: 1–11.

Weingast, Barry, and M. Moran. 1983. Bureaucratic discretion or congressional control? Regulatory policy-making by the Federal Trade Commission. *Journal of Political Economy,* 91: 765–800.

Endnotes

*The research for this chapter was funded by a grant from The Pew Charitable Trusts.

1. For example, appropriate governance is widely regarded as essential to public education reform, yet there are few precise definitions of the term in the literature. A recent report by the

National Research Council, *Governance and Opportunity in Metropolitan America,* implied that governance is "the structure of political institutions," including, for example, the home rule powers of municipalities (Altshuler et al. 1999, p. 8).

2. Each workshop participant was provided a copy of a much longer study, "The Empirical Study of Governance: Theories, Models, and Methods," by Laurence E. Lynn, Jr., Carolyn J. Heinrich, and Carolyn J. Hill of the University of Chicago. A book based on that manuscript is forthcoming from Georgetown University Press.

3. Investigators may, of course, choose a policy (e.g., child protection), a specific program (e.g., the Job Training Partnership Act), or an organization (e.g., the Illinois Department of Children and Family Services) as the focus of governance research; and either individual outcomes or average outcomes by office or type of activity (e.g., performance contracts) as the unit of analysis.

4. We use the terms "configuration," "regime," "arrangement," and "system," interchangeably, even though each term has a somewhat different connotation. They have in common the idea of many interacting elements whose collective effect is nonadditive, and that is our meaning.

5. This section is based on the work of Fiorina (1982); Horn and Shepsle (1989); McCubbins, Noll, and Weingast (1987, 1989); McCubbins and Schwartz (1984); Moe (1989, 1990); Noll and Weingast (1991); Shepsle and Weingast (1981); Weingast and Moran (1983); and related work.

6. In the same vein, a drift away from executive, as opposed to legislative, intent may originate at lower levels, where workers are allied with members of legislative coalitions and their constituencies.

7. Assuming a structure of constraints, opportunities, and information distribution as given or exogenous is also incorporated in formal reasoning. See, for example, Simon (1964) and Niskanen (1975).

8. An exception is Kingdon (1984).

9. A managerial role is one that incorporates formal authority over subordinate actors, multiple tasks, both programmed and unprogrammed activity, and an opportunity to exercise judgment in selecting actions.

10. The manager's influence on deck stacking is a separate matter, relatively easily depicted in spatial matters but difficult to study empirically.

11. The Job Training Partnership Act (JTPA) is an example where measured performance was a legislated goal (Heinrich and Lynn,

this volume). The picture is far murkier in the case of, for example, public education and public assistance, where there tend to be multiple, often conflicting goals incorporated in formal mandates.

12. Our analysis of this literature, and its link to the logic of governance we outline in this chapter, will be included in our forthcoming book to be published by Georgetown University Press.

CHAPTER 2

Evaluating Chicago's Efforts to End Social Promotion

Melissa Roderick, Brian A. Jacob, and Anthony S. Bryk

In the first chapter of this volume, Lynn, Heinrich, and Hill argue that architects of large-scale administrative reform seldom consider how what that reform ultimately becomes depends upon the decisions that administration makes at various levels and by the nature of the context in which it is implemented. They call for studies that pay attention to the hierarchical system of government organizations and that collect data from multiple sites and different environments in order to understand how environment shapes reaction to policies and how different levels of decision making within organizations ultimately shape policy implementation.

The study of schools provides an ideal setting for such research. How a systemwide administrative reform influences school practice and, ultimately, student performance depends on the decisions made by principals at the school level and by teachers at the classroom level. How policies shape school performance also depends on the ecological environment in which they operate—the resources available within the school and community and the nature of the clients they serve. There is a long history in education research of studying how schools buffer themselves from administrative reform and how they adapt reforms to address the complexities, realities, and multiple objectives of teaching (Elmore 1996; Meyer and Rowan 1978; Meyer, Scott, and Deal 1981; Meyer et al. 1978; Scott and Meyer 1981; Tyack and Cuban 1995; Weick 1976).

Most prior research in this area, however, has been qualitative. As Lynn and his colleagues note, the quantitative study of governance introduces new challenges for researchers and requires data sets and methods that can analyze variance in outcomes as well as in implementation.

This chapter describes a new study of Chicago Public Schools' efforts to end social promotion. We begin with a description of the Chicago initiative and the main questions it raises for research. We then describe the data sets and methods used to examine the effects of this policy on student achievement and instruction. A main focus of our work is to understand variation in policy implementation in the more than 400 elementary schools in Chicago and to examine the factors that shape the responses and their effects. After presenting our methodological approach to estimating policy effects and across-school variance, we illustrate how this model can be used to examine one of the central questions raised by this initiative: To what extent have Chicago's efforts influenced achievement in the year prior to testing?

This chapter provides an example of one approach to studying the impact of a systemwide policy that addresses two aspects of research highlighted by Lynn, Heinrich, and Hill as critical for cutting-edge research on governance: (1) the collection of data from multiple sites and multiple environments, and (2) the construction of data sets that pay attention to components of the framework proposed by these authors for how governance decisions influence outputs—data on outcomes, environmental factors, client characteristics, treatment, structural arrangements, and managerial roles and actions. This evaluation also provides an example of the kinds of data sets and statistical methods that can be used in addressing these questions.

Chicago's Effort to End Social Promotion

In 1996 the Chicago Public Schools (CPS) began an ambitious initiative aimed at ending social promotion (or automatic passing from one grade to the next) and raising student achievement. Chicago's efforts were heralded by President Clinton in his 1999 State of the Union address and have spurred a wave of similar reform in school systems around the country. The centerpiece of this initiative is promotion standards for the third, sixth, and eighth grades. Students in these grades must now achieve a minimum score on standardized tests in reading and mathematics in order to be promoted to the next grade. Students who do not are required to participate in a special summer school program, Summer Bridge, and retake the test at the end of the summer. Those who again fail are retained in their grade for the next year; if they are age fifteen, they are instead sent to new alternative schools called "transition centers." In the first two years of the new policy, over one-third of third, sixth, and eighth graders failed to meet the promotion standards. More than 22,000 students attended Summer Bridge, and at the end of the summer, one-third of the attendees met the standard and were promoted. In both 1997 and 1998, CPS retained almost one in five eligible third graders and approximately 10 percent of sixth- and eighth-grade students. In 1998 almost 1,600 students, mostly third graders, were retained for a second time.

The CPS policy was enacted to address two concerns. The first was that students were having difficulty in later grades, and particularly in high school, because they were allowed to progress through elementary school without attaining even minimum levels of basic skills. The second was a concern raised by teachers that they could not pursue higher standards or be accountable for poor student performance because students did not have the skills to move on to more advanced material.

The CPS promotion initiative aims to address these problems through a combination of efforts during the school year before promotion, over the summer, and in the retention year. In the year before promotion, the policy seeks to use the threat of retention as an incentive for students to work harder and for parents to monitor their children's performance more closely. The policy aims to focus teachers' attention on those who are not mastering the material and sends a strong message that they must cover material that will raise students' skills. Students who are at risk are given extended instructional time during the school year through Lighthouse, an afterschool program begun in 1997 and expanded in 1998. Lighthouse provides schools with funds to extend the school day and for a centrally developed curriculum focused on reading and mathematics.

The second major component of the policy, Summer Bridge, provides additional, more focused instruction time and a second chance to pass the standard during the summer. The much heralded Summer Bridge program provides smaller classes and a centrally developed curriculum over six weeks. Summer Bridge participants are then retested in August, and if they meet the standard, they are promoted to the next grade.

The policy also directs even more resources in the retained year to keep students on task and get them back on track. Schools that have been hard hit by retention have been provided extra teachers and reduced classroom sizes for retained students. Retained students are required to participate in the Lighthouse after-school program. CPS has begun experimenting with a range of additional strategies to accelerate further the progress of these students, including mid-year opportunities for retained students to pass the standard and rejoin their classmates. In summary, the CPS effort combines high-stakes testing with multiple chances to pass the standard and progressively targeted interventions, all aimed at improving the achievement of students with the lowest skills.

The Debate over Ending Social Promotion

Proponents of such initiatives, including many central city superintendents and education policymakers, argue that it will benefit all students. They argue that setting standards and providing extra resources to schools offer children with low skills needed intervention to redress prior problems, laying the basis for long-run school success. Although low-achieving students should benefit the most, proponents argue that all students benefit from more focused instruction and from classrooms in which all students are working harder and are on task. Proponents also argue that by reducing diversity in classroom achievement the policy addresses educators' concerns that social promotion hampers the ability to teach grade-appropriate material. Thus all students should benefit because their teachers in later grades will be able to pursue higher skills and more grade-appropriate content.

Critics worry about the potential negative effects on instruction and on students who are retained. They contend that the policy leads to too great a focus on test preparation and basic skills drills and to teachers limiting content coverage, slowing down rather than increasing the pace of instruction. A National Academy of Sciences panel on the appropriate use of testing cautioned against the sole use of test scores in making promotion decisions and took the stand that high-stakes testing should occur only after instructional changes have been made and not, as the Chicago policy intends, as a method to motivate teachers to change instruction (Heubert and Hauser 1999).

Critics also argue that the practice of retaining students has not proved successful in increasing achievement, even with extra resources for remediation. Studies find that grade retention is associated with, at best, moderate and, at worst, no positive effects on long-run achievement and school performance (Alexander, Entwistle, and Dauber 1994; Gottfredson, Fink, and Graham 1994; Holmes and Matthews 1984; Holmes 1989; Jackson 1975; Shepard, Smith, and Marion 1996). Clearly, students perceive retention as a failure and often as a punishment. A stigma is attached, and if it were not, the threat of nonpromotion would not work as a motivating factor (Byrnes 1989). Although the long-term effects of retention on self-esteem and learning attitudes are unclear (Alexander, Entwistle, and Dauber 1994; Gottfredson, Fink, and Graham 1994; Holmes and Matthews 1984; Holmes 1989), a consistent finding is that students who are retained are more likely to drop out of school, regardless of the grade in which retention occurs (Hess and Lauber 1985; Barro and Kolstad 1987; Grissom and Shepard 1989; Roderick 1994). Thus critics argue that retention and the placement of students in transition centers may benefit those who are promoted while creating sacrificial lambs of the most vulnerable Chicago students.

Prior studies of the use of such testing have generally confirmed negative effects on retained students. In the early 1980s, New York City embarked on a similar effort, giving students who had been socially promoted before the policy was enacted extra summer resources and reduced class sizes the following year. In an evaluation of the New York initiative, Ernest House found that students who had been retained had similar test scores in later grades to a matched group of low-performing students who had been promoted before the policy began (New York City Board of Education 1988; House 1998). House concludes that retention and extra resources did not benefit the students who were retained. He found, moreover, that retained students dropped out at significantly higher rates (40% versus 25%) than the matched group of previously promoted, low-achieving students.

House's study focused on the impact of retention. We know of no study that has looked at the effect on students in the year prior to testing. Indeed, there is very little research to support or negate the central theory that underlies Chicago's promotion initiative—that setting standards for students will lead to higher achievement and more focused instruction, that raising students' skills before promotion will improve their long-run learning trajectory, and that changing the distribution of achievement in post-testing grades will promote greater instructional pacing and more opportunity to learn. Presumably much of the effect of the promotional policy should take place in the year before students take the test, when motivational, instructional, and programmatic supports such as Summer Bridge are in place. Yet we know little about whether the introduction of high stakes tests with linked support efforts such as Summer Bridge and Lighthouse leads to greater learning gains for students who are promoted and whether those gains are sustained over time. Nor do we know whether reducing the spread of achievement in the year after a student is promoted will actually lead teachers to cover more in the way of either content or skills.

Past research clearly supports the CPS policy in one area: greater instructional time has positive effects, particularly when it occurs during the summer (Fusaro 1997; Levin and Tsang 1987; Smith 1998). Previous research finds that many impoverished students lose skills during the summer and that this "summer learning loss" may be an important reason for poor children often falling behind their more advantaged counterparts (Entwistle, Alexander, and Olson 1997; Heyns 1987). In addition, a mechanism by which ending social promotion purportedly shapes achievement is through motivation affect. When students meet a challenge, work hard, and succeed, research suggests they would have acquired improved coping strategies, more positive learning attitudes, and more resilient behaviors. Thus how passing or failing shapes students' sense of their competence and efficacy may be particularly critical to the long-term impact of this policy.

Research Questions and Overview of the Study

This study has three main goals. The first is to test the degree of evidence for the hypothesized negative and positive effects of the social promotion policy by examining short- and long-term effects on student achievement and educational outcomes, on instruction, and on parental involvement. The second goal is to examine how the various components of the policy influence its net effects and the effects on different groups of students. The components of the policy include both the design of the policy across time—during the year before retention, during the summer, and in the retention year—and its components at each time point. At each time point, the policy proposes to shape these outcomes through a combination of changes in student and parent behavior, changes in instruction, and through program efforts such as Lighthouse. Central to disentangling effects at each time point is understanding whether variation across schools in both program design and instructional effects are correlated with student performance under the policy. The third goal of this study is to examine variation in policy implementation at the school and classroom levels and relate it to student outcomes.

Defining Critical Outcomes

The bottom line of this policy is clearly achievement. Equally important, however, is understanding whether achievement benefits come with a tradeoff, in the form of negative student attitudes toward school and school progress, and whether the benefits and costs of the policy are distributed differently across students. The evidence here is unclear. Opponents suggest that average to above-average students may benefit from the policy but that the lowest-achieving students, particularly those who are retained, may suffer in the form of lowered self-esteem and higher rates of school dropout while gaining little in terms of achievement. An equally plausible scenario is that this policy redirects resources to the highest-risk students and may benefit these students at the cost for average to above-average students of reduced opportunity to learn and lower long-run achievement.

To judge these claims, our evaluation of the Chicago policy focuses on short- and long-term effects on students in four areas: achievement gains; educational attainment (e.g., rates of school dropout); self-concepts and school engagement; and learning attitudes (e.g., help-seeking or avoidance behavior, attributional and learning strategies, and work effort). A unique aspect of this study is our focus on the effect of promotion standards both prior to and after retention or promotion and on evaluating the effect of the policy on each of these outcomes for students both at risk and not at risk under the policy.

Effects on Instruction.   One of the main questions surrounding the social promotion policy is its effect on instruction. Critics argue that the policy forces teachers to emphasize test preparation and basic skills to the exclusion of other subject matter and skills. A recent Consortium on Chicago School Research study found that the curriculum in Chicago schools is already plagued by high levels of repetition (Smith, Smith, and Bryk 1998). Critics contend that this policy will exacerbate the problem and, in particular, will lead teachers to eschew content such as science or social studies for a sole focus on mathematics and reading. On the other hand, the social promotion policy may redirect instructional resources to students who need the most help. It may also allow students in later grades to pursue more grade-appropriate skills and content because students with low skills had either caught up before promotion or been retained. This debate, then, leads us to focus on instructional effects in three areas: choice of instructional methods—test preparation versus instructional techniques such as reading books or undertaking projects that are associated with a greater depth of knowledge; content and subject matter coverage; and pacing, or opportunity to learn at grade-appropriate levels. We consider these instructional effects in the year before and in the year after promotion testing.

Parents. An often overlooked set of outcomes in the debate over ending social promotion is the effect that such policies may have on parental involvement in their child's education. CPS policy provides significant incentive both for parents to be more involved in monitoring and assisting in their children's school work and for teachers to work more closely with parents. Research has consistently found that the level of parent involvement is critical for school success. These incentives may work to the extent that parents are aware of the policy and of their children's skills in relation to the policy. It may, however, be that parents of those students most affected would be the least likely to know about the policy or comprehend their child's risk. An important component of this study is our attention to how the policy may shape parental involvement and parent-teacher communication.

Studying the Components of the Initiative

As described previously, Chicago's approach is not a single policy. Rather, it is an integrated set of initiatives during the school year before testing, over the summer, and during the retention year all focusing attention on the students performing most poorly. It is also evolving. As CPS policy has evolved, the administration both has directed extra resources to retained and at-risk students and has continued to raise the standard. In both 1998 and 1999, the standard was raised for eighth graders. In the year 2000, CPS plans to raise the standard again for all three grades. A main focus of this research, then, is to disentangle the web of effects associated with the various components of the initiative on various groups of students. What happens in the year before testing, when students presumably are working harder and receiving more focused and extra instruction? What is the effect of summer school? What happens to students in the year after promotion or retention? And how do changes in the policy over time shape its effect?

Documenting Variation in Implementation and Impact across Schools

Our initial work on this evaluation compared the performance of the third-, sixth-, and eighth-grade students in 1997 and 1998 who faced the promotion standard with that of a 1995 cohort of students—those who were promoted even if they did not meet the standard (Roderick et al. 1999). We found that many more students in 1997 and 1998 were meeting minimum test score cutoffs, in part because of an increase in the proportion of students who met the test score required for promotion during the school year, and in part because of the effect of the Summer Bridge program. Improvement in passing rates during the school year was concentrated among sixth and eighth graders. Among third graders there was little increase between 1995, 1997, and 1998 in the proportion who met the minimum test score cutoff for promotion by the end of the school year.

Schools also differed widely in passing rates. By a rough cut, we would expect that a student would be at risk of not passing if, in order to meet the minimum standard, the student needed to achieve above-average learning gains in a grade. Using students test scores in June of the year prior to testing, we considered students at high risk of failing the standard if they needed to increase their reading or mathematics scores on the Iowa Test of Basic Skills by 1.5 grade equivalents or greater in a year in order to meet the promotion test cutoff. We considered students at moderate risk of nonpromotion if they needed to make up 0.5 to 1.5 grade equivalents in a year.

Figures 2.1, 2.2, and 2.3 present the across-school distribution in the percentage of moderate- to high-risk students who were able to pass the standard in reading by June in the third, sixth, and eighth grades in 1997.[1] As illustrated in these figures, there was wide variation in passing across schools. For example, in 49 schools, less than 20 percent of at-risk third graders raised their test scores to the minimum required for promotion. In other schools, the majority of at-risk third graders were able to meet the test cutoff and were promoted. There is variation in school performance across all three grades, although this variation was greatest in the third grade. Figures 2.1–2.3 also illustrate that passing rates were the lowest in third grade and highest in eighth grade, an effect we will consider further in this chapter.

Why are some schools doing a better job than others in raising their students' test scores to the promotion test cutoff? To address this question, we must first consider variation in the implementation of the policy programmatically and in its impact on instruction and school processes. A first source of variation across schools that

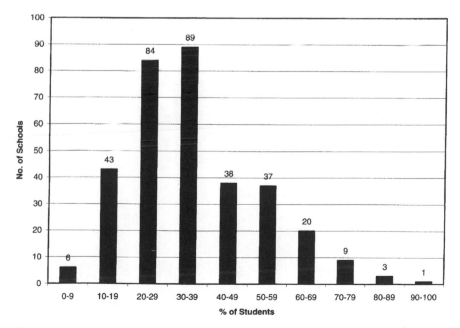

FIGURE 2.1   *Percent of at-risk third graders meeting the standard in reading in 1997*

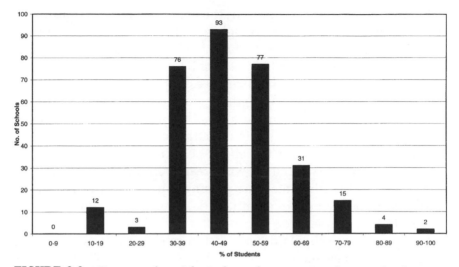

FIGURE 2.2   *Percent of at-risk sixth graders meeting the standard in reading in 1997*

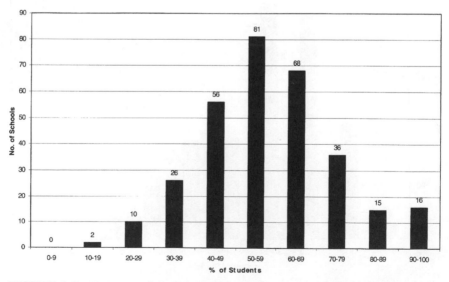

FIGURE 2.3   *Percent of at-risk eighth graders meeting the standard in reading in 1997*

might affect student performance is in the decisions schools make about how to use new resources and design the retention program. We call this variation in "program design." Schools have been given great flexibility in determining which students receive extra resources and how to link after-school programs to the school day. Some schools are reserving Lighthouse slots for retained students, while others are requiring all at-risk students to participate. Some are reserving Lighthouse only for the earlier grades, while others are requiring all third-, sixth-, and eighth-grade students to participate. Schools are also differing in their implementation of the Bridge program and their management of the retention experience.

A second, and equally important, source of variation in implementation is in the instructional effect—how principals and teachers understand the task they face, the nature and level of their response, and the strategies they use to approach the task. When a teacher faces a group of students who did not meet a promotion criterion, but did participate in a summer program and once again failed, what should that teacher do? When teachers know that a high percentage of their students may be at risk of not passing, what strategies do they employ to assist them? The CPS policy is an accountability measure. It provides strong incentives, sanctions, and resources to reach a goal, but it does not prescribe the strategies and methods that teachers and principals should use to reach that goal. Nor is there any consensus among the education community about what is an optimal solution. Summer Bridge does have a prescribed curriculum and, clearly, any outcome incentive that uses a test for evaluation provides a strong signal to prepare children for the test. Beyond these elements, however, teachers and principals have been largely left alone in deciding how to manage their task. Presumably, different teachers and different principals will approach this task differently.

This policy provides an opportunity to investigate what instructional strategies may be more effective both in the year before promotion (getting students "up to speed") and in the year after for those who are retained. Critical areas of investigation are: (1) the degree to which the promotion policy influences teachers' decisions regarding goals for student learning and choice of content coverage, instructional techniques, and instructional materials; (2) time spent on test preparation; (3) the degree to which teachers attempt to tailor instruction to address differing student risk; (4) how teachers who have classes with retained students approach the instructional task; and (5) how the policy affects teachers' relationships with one another, with parents, and with their students.

Modeling Across-School Variation in Implementation and Effects

Simply documenting variation in implementation does not allow one to understand the processes that shape the level and nature of teacher response. An equally important question, and one that is germane to the study of governance, is: How can we understand why different teachers and different schools respond differently to the policy? One colleague, for example, told the story of a new eighth-grade teacher who had two students who were retained and needed to retake the test in January. Concerned about the effect on their self-esteem, this teacher decided that her entire class should prepare for the test during the month of December. Another teacher recounts how her principal walked into her classroom every day and critiqued her if she was not drilling her students on basic skills or if she was using material that did not offer multiple-choice answers to prepare students for the test. Another principal applauds the policy because it has allowed her to push teachers to diagnose students early in the year and develop individual progress plans, an approach that is consistent with her vision for student learning and the broader instructional mission of the school. Are these examples of how the incentives embedded in the policy shape instruction, or are these examples of how the reaction of educators reveals their underlying capacity to respond to the new challenges the policy poses?

To address this question, one must devise a theoretical framework for how the characteristics of teachers, schools, and the environment shape the implementation response. We hypothesize that the way schools and teachers implement this policy is shaped by four factors:

1. the capacity of teachers, including their teaching experience, their own instructional orientation, their sense of efficacy toward their students, and their prior training;
2. the capacity of the community in the school to manage change and pursue instructional improvement, including the degree of professional community, instructional orientation

of the school environment, resources within the school for instructional support, extent of principal leadership, and prior trends in achievement within the school;

3. the environment of the school, including student body and community characteristics; and

4. the nature of the task teachers face, which we define as the skills gap and concentration level. These relationships are described in figure 2.4.

The fourth characteristic—the task teachers face—may be one of the most important factors influencing variation in both implementation and school outcomes. Quite simply, a teacher for whom most students in the classroom are performing substantially below grade level faces a different task in raising an individual student's test scores than does a teacher for whom one or two students are at risk. Similarly, a student with third-grade reading skills in eighth grade has a very different task than a student who needs to raise his or her test score a year and four months in a school year. Thus schools vary

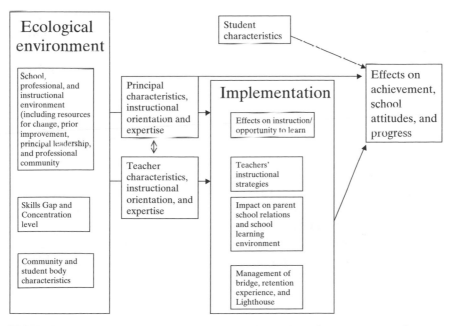

FIGURE 2.4   *A model for how school and teacher characteristics shape variation in implementation and outcomes*

widely in what we term the "concentration of risk" and the "skills gap" that they are being asked to close. The concentration of risk could be a positive or a negative under this policy. On the one hand, high levels of concentration may constrain the ability of teachers to spend individual time with students, leading to poorer outcomes for students. On the other hand, high levels of concentration may allow teachers and schools to implement more broad-based changes in programming and instruction and may provide the potential for peer effects that would produce greater benefits for individual students.

Finally, in the third area—the environment of the school—it is important to realize that this policy does not operate in isolation. It is part of a larger school reform effort in which the mayor has assumed governance of CPS and initiated major efforts in capital improvement and in the extent of monitoring and assessment of individual school performance. The policy comes after a decade of school reform efforts in which local schools were given more autonomy in managing their own governance and curricula, funds, and in hiring principals. Under this previous reform, some schools improved rapidly while others stagnated or deteriorated. The policy also comes at a time when test scores systemwide have been improving. Thus, in some schools, this policy is being implemented in an environment of general improvement and where previous reforms may have laid the foundation for positive responses in reaction to this challenge, while in other stagnating or deteriorating schools this policy may add yet additional pressure to schools already debilitated and resource poor.

Data Sources

Evaluating CPS's promotion efforts calls for attention to multiple outcomes and impacts, including the evaluation of the multiple components of the policy and documentation and analysis of variation in impact and implementation across schools and classrooms. It requires longitudinal data to assess changes in behavior, achievement, and school performance; data that allow us to document variation in effects and in the implementation across schools, teachers, and students; and data that allow us to link these outcomes to the characteristics of schools, teachers, and students. For most independent researchers, assembling such a data set would be daunting and, indeed, even seem implausible because of the need for pre-policy longitudinal data.

Over the past nine years, the Consortium on Chicago School Research has worked to develop data sets and methods that provide the capacity to address these multilevel sets of questions. The purpose of the consortium is to undertake research to assist in implementing school reform, assess its progress over time, and more generally to support school improvement in Chicago. There are few, if any, comparable organizations able to study a single school system with equal depth and technical capability. Among the factors that contribute to this capacity are a comprehensive data archive and ongoing surveys. In this section, we describe how the data sets assembled by the consortium provide a base with which to examine the impact, process, and implementation components of this study.

Quantitative Data Sources

At the core of the consortium's data archive are the official school records provided by the Chicago Public Schools with linked survey data. The CPS data archive contains extensive school records on successive cohorts of CPS students. It includes scores on the Iowa Test of Basic Skills, including summer test scores; demographic and administrative history data; and high school transcript files for all students enrolled in CPS from 1986 to the present.

Administrative data provide extensive information on student characteristics including race and ethnicity, grade retention, school moves, attendance status, and special education and bilingual education participation. These extensive school records provide a base from which to study achievement growth and high school performance of various cohorts of students both prior to and after the new promotion initiative.

Critical to the work of the consortium is the ongoing "Charting Reform" survey project. This project surveys students, teachers, and principals every two to three years. In 1994, 1997, and 1999, the consortium surveyed all CPS sixth-, eighth-, and tenth-grade students and all principals and teachers, or approximately 13,000 teachers and 55,000 students in each survey year. In 1999, surveys included a supplement pertaining to the promotion initiative. In the summer of 1999, the consortium surveyed all sixth- and eighth-grade students and teachers in the Summer Bridge program. The next scheduled round of survey administration is in 2001. Each student's survey can be linked to his or her individual school records. Teacher data are linked to grade, department, and school. Thus in 2001 the consortium will have three waves of survey data for eighth graders who faced the promotion gate in 1999 (sixth, eighth, and ninth or tenth grades) and two waves of survey data from sixth graders (sixth and seventh or eighth grades.)

Survey data are central to this evaluation in four respects. First, survey data from teachers and students allow us to obtain key dependent variables necessary to examine the effect of the policy on instruction and on student outcomes in addition to those available on official school transcripts. In each survey, teachers are asked to report time spent on test preparation, content coverage in reading and mathematics, instructional strategies, and choice of instructional media. Content coverage scales have been analyzed to provide measures of curriculum pacing across grades and across time (Smith, Smith, and Bryk 1998). Each measure is placed on a common scale designed to analyze change over time. In addition, information on teachers' communication with parents and levels of parent-teacher trust allows us to chart the effect of the policy on parent-teacher relations. Student surveys provide key longitudinal measures of engagement in school, perception of support from teachers, challenge in coursework, levels of peer support for academic work, parental monitoring, and self-reports of homework and attendance.

Second, data from teacher and student surveys will allow us to obtain measures for each of the school and teacher characteristics identified in figure 2.4. The Charting Reform surveys were designed to provide key measures of school environment and instructional orientation of schools in 1994, 1997, and 1999. School environment includes the focus on student learning, the degree of principal leadership, a focus on innovation in the classroom, and collegiality among teachers. Third, the supplement to the 1999 teacher, principal, and student surveys allows us to develop measures of policy implementation at the school and classroom levels. The 1999 teacher and principal supplements assessed teachers' views of the effect of the policy on students, on the broader environment of the school, and on their own behavior. We asked teachers their view of retention and how the policy fits with their own instructional goals. Survey items asked teachers to report on the strategies they used to raise student test scores. The student supplement asked students to report on their own behavior, awareness of their risk, attitudes toward the policy and testing, and their involvement in programs such as Lighthouse. Additional information from principal surveys and a supplemental phone survey provide data on the implementation of Lighthouse in each school and the management of the retention program.

Finally, teacher surveys provide additional background information, including each teacher's educational qualifications, experience and tenure, and demographic characteristics. Measures from teacher surveys are used to characterize teachers' sense of efficacy with their students, their professional development, and their own instructional objectives. Principal surveys collect additional information on the level of external resources in the school, such as links with external partners and other major initiatives at the school level.

Qualitative Data

Although this chapter focuses on the design of the quantitative component of the evaluation, the evaluation has a parallel qualitative component. The qualitative study provides a more intensive investigation of the experiences of individual teachers, students, and schools. The qualitative component is studying the implementation of the initiative in five schools and is looking at the experiences of 100 sixth- and eighth-grade students with the policy. Since spring 1999, we have been following these students, their families, and their teachers through the process of the promotion testing initiative. Students will be followed through the end of the retention or promotion year, June 2000. This qualitative component will provide both case studies of teachers and schools and data on the experiences of individual students. Because this chapter focuses on the quantitative aspect of the study, we do not discuss in detail the components of the qualitative aspect of the evaluation.

Modeling the Effects of the Policy on Achievement: A Three-Level HLM

The previous section described how the use of longitudinal survey data and official school transcripts allow us to address the central research questions posed in this study. Critical to this process is developing methodological approaches that allow us to obtain robust estimates of policy effects and that allow us to model across-school variation. Perhaps the most important methodological question is how to measure effects on achievement. In this section, we describe our general model and illustrate how that model can be used to estimate effects on achievement in the year prior to testing.

The General Model

Our general approach is to use a before-after estimation strategy in which we compare the learning gains of students in the year prior to and after promotion retention with those of students in grades prior to policy implementation, correcting for the fact that student test scores have been rising throughout the decade. This model obtains an estimate of the difference in the observed achievement growth for each student who faced the promotion testing standard over and above what we would expect given their growth trajectory in prior grades and learning gains of like students in the year before the promotion testing policy. Growth curve analysis provides two significant advantages. First, it allows us to estimate gains in the years before and after the promotion policy based on a student's trend over several years, rather than on only one point prior. Second, growth curve analysis allows us to examine the effect of the policy in shaping a student's achievement trajectory in the years after promotion or retention. Of particular interest is the question of whether positive effects dissipate over time (for example, gains are followed by lower than expected gains the subsequent year).

We use a three-level hierarchical model to estimate patterns in achievement growth across students and across time in schools using scores on the Iowa Test of Basic Skills (ITBS) from 1992 to 1998. Hierarchical linear modeling (HLM) is one of a class of models designed to examine school-level differences in student-level outcomes (Bryk and Raudenbush 1992). The HLM framework has several distinct advantages. First, it yields consistent standard errors that take into account the correlation of errors within schools. Second, it provides estimated Bayes residuals that take into account the relative information provided by each observation. Third, it provides a convenient framework in which to examine and model variation across students and schools. This model is estimated separately for third-, sixth-, and eighth-grade students. For explication purposes, we present the three-level model for sixth grade.

Level 1: Measurement. Level 1 is a measurement model where all variables are centered so that grade has a value of zero in the grade prior to the promotion testing year (fifth grade).[2] In a model for the sixth grade, Y_{ijk} is that achievement at grade i for student j in school k. This model is estimated using both ITBS Grade Equivalent metrics, used by the school system, and equated Rasch scale scores, corrected for form effects.

$$Y_{ijk} = \pi_{0jk} + \pi_{1jk}\text{Grade} + \pi_{2jk}\text{SixthGrade} + \pi_{3jk}\text{PostGatoCrade} + \pi_{4jk}\text{Repeat} + e_{ijk}$$

where π_{0jk} measures the latent or predicted fifth grade score; π_{1jk} measures the annual student growth rate or learning trend; π_{2jk} measures the sixth grade "value-added"; and π_{3jk} measures the value-added in the post-gate years.[3]

"Sixth grade" is a dummy variable that equals ono if the grade is sixth grade and zero otherwise. As described above, since π_{0jk} is the predicted fifth-grade scores and π_{1jk} is the student's growth trend, the coefficient on sixth grade is interpreted as the extent to which the student's observed sixth-grade test score deviates from the value one would have predicted based on prior achievement. We refer to this coefficient as the "sixth-grade value-added."

Level 2: Student Model. Level 2 models the π coefficients as a function of student characteristics.[4]

$$\pi_{0jk} = \beta_{00k} + \beta_{01k}(1997) + \beta_{02k}(1998) + r_{0jk}$$

$$\pi_{1jk} = \beta_{10k} + \beta_{11k}(1997) + \beta_{12k}(1998) + r_{1jk}$$

$$\pi_{2jk} = \beta_{20k} + \beta_{21k}(1997) + \beta_{22k}(1998) + r_{2jk}$$

$$\pi_{3jk} = \beta_{30k} + \beta_{31k}(1997)*\text{Path} + \beta_{32k}(1998)*\text{Path} + r_{3jk}$$

$$\pi_{4jk} = \beta_{40k} \text{ (assumed fixed for simplicity of this illustration)}$$

In this equation, 1997 and 1998 are dummy variables that indicate whether the student was part of the 1997 or 1998 sixth-grade cohort.[5] All other year cohorts (i.e., 1992–96) are captured in the intercept. The year dummies accomplish three objectives in this model. First, by modeling π_{0jk} and π_{1jk} across schools, we control for systemwide and individual school trends in achievement. Second, the coefficients β_{21k} and β_{22k} indicate the extent to which the value-added terms of students in these years deviate from the value-added terms of students in the pre-policy cohorts. Hence we refer to β_{21k} and β_{22k} as the "gate-year policy effect" for sixth graders in 1997 and 1998.[6] Third, the vector β_{31k} allows us to capture the achievement effect in the year(s) after the promotion testing grade. Here, path is a series of dummy variables, each of which indicates the "path" a student followed in the policy—for example, whether students were promoted, retained, or participated in Summer Bridge. The coefficient on the path variable, then, measures the achievement gain or loss (above the predicted score) made by students in this path in the next academic year.

Once we have estimates of the pre- and post-testing effects on achievement, we can extend these models to examine how achievement effects vary by student characteristics—for example, by race, ethnicity, and gender and by student risk under the policy. We can incorporate a measure of risk, which we estimate from a separate HLM that brings together all prior math and reading data for the student. Risk can then be defined as the distance between the promotion standard and a student's latent score in the pre-gate grade.

At Level 3, we allow our estimates of the effect of students in school k to vary across schools and by school characteristics. We are primarily interested in the coefficients β_{21k} and β_{22k}. For example, if we consider the policy effect during the first year of the policy (1997), then β_{21k} is the mean sixth-grade value-added in school k in 1997. The estimated Bayes residual for this coefficient provides a measure of the relative effectiveness of school k in responding to the policy. We can then model β_{21k} and β_{22k} as a function of school demographics and as a function of survey measures of the implementation of the policy and as a function of the school environment and prior school development.

Estimating Policy Year Effects on Achievement

A central premise of CPS's effort to end social promotion is that by setting standards and providing extra instructional time to students during the school year, students will learn more in the year before the test and will be brought up to the test score cutoff. Yet as we noted earlier, few studies of high-stakes testing have looked at whether such policies actually lead to greater learning gains in the year before testing. A starting place for our analysis, then, is to examine the nature of these policy year effects.

Tables 2.1 and 2.2 present preliminary estimates of the achievement effect associated with the policy in the year before testing ("policy year") for third, sixth, and eighth graders. By "policy year effects" we refer to achievement gains during the school year before testing, which does not include the effect of the Summer Bridge program. Table 2.1 estimates the effect in reading. Table 2.2 presents results for mathematics. These results were estimated using a 20 percent random sample of students. The CPS initiative began in 1996 for eighth graders and was expanded to third and sixth graders in 1997.

These models were estimated using ITBS scores in grade equivalent metrics.[7] The promotion criteria were based on students' ITBS scores reported in grade equivalents according to national norms. Because testing occurred in early May, a student at the national norm would receive a score of that grade plus eight months. Thus a sixth grader is at the national norm if his or her ITBS score is a 5.8. The promotion criterion for third graders was set a 2.8, one year below grade level. Students in the sixth and eighth grades faced more lenient standards. Sixth graders must have reached a 5.3 in reading and mathematics, a year and one-half below grade level, to be promoted. In 1997 eighth graders were required to achieve a minimum test score of 7.0, 1.8 years below grade level, to be promoted.

The coefficient on the intercept provides a measure of the latent test score in the grade prior to testing. Consider the results for sixth-grade reading. Prior to the implementation of the policy, we would predict that the average fifth-grade reading test score was a 4.8, approximately one year below grade level. The average increase in ITBS test scores in reading in grades prior to sixth grade was 0.88. Thus prior to the policy, CPS students learned roughly nine-tenths of what one would expect a student at the national norm to learn in a year. The sixth-grade value-added for these students in the years prior to the policy was moderate (.06 g.e.), although statistically significant. Thus on average, in the years prior to the policy, the sixth-grade increase in ITBS test scores was 0.94 grade equivalents. In the years prior to the policy, the third, sixth, and eighth grades

TABLE 2.1
Gate Year Policy Effects in Reading

Student Fixed Effects	Third Grade		Sixth Grade		Eighth Grade	
	Coefficient	t-ratio	Coefficient	t-ratio	Coefficient	t-ratio
Score in Pregate Grade						
Prepolicy	2.23	103.2	4.80	159.5	6.67	182.1
1996					0.80	3.4
1997	0.01	0.9	0.12	5.9	−0.02	−0.7
1998	0.07	4.7	0.09	4.8	0.19	7.6
Average Learning Rate						
Prepolicy	0.68	81.3	0.88	193.3	0.97	186.2
1996					−0.03	−5.6
1997	−0.07	5.6	0.02	4.4	−0.08	−17.1
1998	−0.05	3.4	−0.02	−4.1	−0.03	−5.9
Gate Year Value-Added						
Prepolicy	0.09	11.3	0.06	9.4	−0.09	−9.4
1996					0.15	6.8
1997	−0.01	−0.3	0.02	1.0	0.36	16.0
1998	0.16	7.0	0.27	14.2	0.30	13.2

TABLE 2.1 (*continued*)
Gate Year Policy Effects in Reading

	Variance Components					
Student Random Effects	**Variance**	**p-value**	**Variance**	**p-value**	**Variance**	**p-value**
Score in Pregate Grade	0.629	0.000	1.072	0.000	1.640	0.000
Average Learning Rate	0.163	0.000	0.027	0.000	0.025	0.000
Gate Year Value-Added	0.484	0.000	0.235	0.000	0.433	0.000
Level 1	0.169	0.000	0.358	0.000	0.442	0.000
School Random Effects						
Pregate Mean Score	0.194	0.000	0.387	0.000	0.545	0.000
Average Learning Rate	0.020	0.000	0.007	0.000	0.007	0.000
1996 Policy Effect					0.008	0.000
1997 Policy Effect	0.038	0.000	0.031	0.000	0.050	0.000
1998 Policy Effect	0.019	0.000	0.042	0.000	0.073	0.000

Note: Based on a 20 percent random sample of student test score data. The third grade model differs slightly from the model described in the text.

TABLE 2.2
Gate Year Policy Effects in Math

Student Fixed Effects	Third Grade		Sixth Grade		Eighth Grade	
	Coefficient	t-ratio	Coefficient	t-ratio	Coefficient	t-ratio
Score in Pregate Grade						
Prepolicy	2.65	156.8	5.01	187.2	6.85	206.9
1996	0.02	1.4	0.03	1.9	−0.11	−6.0
1997	0.09	5.1	0.06	3.3	−0.07	−3.5
1998					0.06	3.1
Average Learning Rate						
Prepolicy	0.92	111.0	0.83	163.6	0.90	197.0
1996	0.03	1.7	0.01	3.0	−0.05	−14.1
1997	0.02	1.1	0.01	2.0	−0.04	−14.1
1998					−0.02	−5.0
Gate Year Value-Added						
Prepolicy	−0.22	−16.0	0.24	30.8	−0.07	−7.9
1996	−0.07	−2.9	0.17	12.1	0.21	14.3
1997	0.16	5.9	0.18	11.9	0.49	30.9
1998					0.32	20.7

TABLE 2.2 (*continued*)
Gate Year Policy Effects in Math

	Variance Components					
Student Random Effects	Variance	p-value	Variance	p-value	Variance	p-value
Score in Pregate Grade	0.397	0.000	0.936	0.000	1.321	0.000
Average Learning Rate	0.163	0.000	0.026	0.000	0.020	0.000
Gate Year Value-Added	0.274	0.000	0.029	0.000	0.108	0.000
Level 1	0.169	0.000	0.175	0.000	0.201	0.000
School Random Effects						
Pregate Mean Score	0.108	0.000	0.304	0.000	0.444	0.000
Average Learning Rate	0.020	0.000	0.009	0.000	0.007	0.000
1996 Policy Effect					0.025	0.000
1997 Policy Effect	0.046	0.000	0.032	0.000	0.043	0.000
1998 Policy Effect	0.034	0.000	0.044	0.000	0.040	0.000

Note: Based on a 20 percent random sample of student test score data. The third grade model differs slightly from the model described in the text.

were testing grades for a statewide assessment program, the Illinois Goals Assessment Program. This might have created a small testing effect, which is indicated in a modest sixth-grade value-added in prepolicy years.

The 1997 cohort entered sixth grade slightly better prepared than previous cohorts, as indicated by the 0.12 coefficient on the 1997 dummy variable for the score in the pregate grade. Nevertheless, they showed virtually identical learning gains to prior cohorts in the grades prior to sixth grade. The value-added term for the 1997 cohort is not significant in reading, suggesting that in the first year of implementation, there was no aggregate policy effect in reading achievement. This was not true in mathematics, where we find a 0.17 grade equivalent coefficient on the gate-year effect for sixth graders in 1997. There is a substantial effect in reading in 1998. The coefficient of 0.27 indicates that students in this cohort learned over one-quarter of a year more during sixth grade than their comparable peers prior to the policy. Based on the prior learning rate of 0.88, this represents, on average, a 31 percent increase in achievement in sixth grade in 1998.

Several points are apparent from this brief examination of results. First, there is considerable evidence of policy-year effects on gate-year achievement. In 1998, for example, effects ranged in size from 0.16 for third-grade reading to 0.32 for eighth-grade mathematics. Considering differing learning rates across grades, these effects are equivalent to a 20 to 30 percent increase in achievement in that grade.

Second, there appears to be a substantial implementation effect of the policy. In both the third and sixth grades, there is little to no policy effect in reading and a moderate policy effect in mathematics among sixth graders during the first year of implementation. In 1998, however, significant policy effects appear across all three grades. Similarly, effects are small but significant in the first year of implementation in the eighth grade (1996) and are substantially larger in both 1997 and 1998. This implementation effect might not be surprising. First, incentive effects for students to work harder should be higher in the second year, after students in these grades have been in a classroom with others who were retained under the policy. Second, we might expect that it would take schools and teachers time to make significant changes in instruction. Third, many more schools received extra resources in 1998 in the form of the Lighthouse after-school program, suggesting that program effects should be larger in 1998.

This discussion of how we should interpret implementation effects underscores the importance of disentangling achievement effects. The central question is: How do we interpret the nature of these relatively large achievement effects? First, there may be a testing or instrumentation effect of the policy, meaning that students may simply be taking the test more seriously or may be improving their test-taking skills. Second, the promotion standard may have motivated students and led them to study harder and learn more during the school year. Both of these effects would suggest that learning gains during the school year are caused by students changing their behavior owing to the high-stakes testing environment. A third explanation is that because of the promotion standard, teachers may have changed their instruction to focus more on improving students' basic skills or may have spent more time working with these students to raise their performance—what we would call an "instructional effect." Fourth there may be a positive effect of students participating in the Lighthouse after-school program—what we call a "program effect."

These alternative explanations also come into play when looking at a second trend among the results. The policy seems to have had the largest effect on eighth graders, even after accounting for differences in learning rates across the grades. In some ways, this finding is surprising. The rhetoric of early intervention surmises that sixth and eighth grade would be too late to intervene to remediate poor skills. Opponents of the policy might see this trend as evidence that most of the policy effect is because of incentive effects on students. Clearly, the CPS initiative relies heavily on incentive effects for students and on producing gains that are accrued in short, intensive periods. In this respect, this finding might not be surprising. Eighth graders face the greatest costs of not meeting the standard. If they do not pass, they cannot graduate from elementary school. Eighth graders may also have the greatest capacity to shape their school performance via their own motivation and effort. Third graders will be less sensitive to the threat of retention, are less likely able to shape their own learning by effort, and may be less likely with intensive spurts of attention to overcome barriers.

On the other hand, the same incentives might also occur for teachers. Eighth-grade teachers may be responding to the policy by focusing significant attention on those students at risk and might be making appropriate changes in instruction to address these students' problems. Eighth-grade teachers might have more room in their instructional program to shift instructional objectives and time and might be more likely to see retention as a bad thing for adolescents, who are faced with the prospect of not going to high school. Third-grade teachers, who are already focusing on basic skills, may be less likely to make significant changes to their instruction as a result of this initiative and might also be more inclined to believe that retention is a positive thing for children. As discussed previously, in disentangling these various interpretations we will examine how variation across grades, schools, classrooms in programming approaches, and teachers' and students' attitudes toward the policy are associated with these effects.

Estimating Across-School Variation in Achievement Effects

A significant advantage of the HLM framework is that by allowing the coefficients at level 2 to vary randomly across schools, for example, we can obtain estimates of across-school variation in the effects of the policy on achievement. The variance components associated with each of the estimated coefficients are presented in the lower half of tables 2.1 and 2.2. Not surprisingly, there is significant variation in the pregate mean test scores and growth rates across schools. This implies that elementary schools across the city vary widely in the achievement and average yearly increase in the test scores of their students. More important, we find significant variation in the policy effect in all grades, subjects, and years. Consider, for example, sixth-grade reading in 1998, for which there was an average policy effect of 0.27 grade equivalents. The variance component associated with this effect is 0.042. This suggests that the estimated achievement value added ranged in the middle 95 percent of schools from −0.13 to 0.67 [0.27 ± 1.96* sqrt (.042)]. Thus in the most successful schools, the sixth-grade value added in 1998 was as high as two-thirds of a year increase in achievement. In the least successful schools, by contrast, achievement gains in the sixth grade in 1998 were 0.13 grade equivalents lower than expected.

This significant across-school variation in the magnitude of the policy effects suggests two further steps in the analysis. The first is to begin to examine how these effects vary across student characteristics. One might expect, for example, that the effect of this policy may differ between students at high, moderate, and low levels of risk given that these students face different incentive effects and different tasks. The second step is to model this variation across schools by first accounting for differences in the kinds of students school serve and, second, by considering the components of the model outlined by Lynn, Heinrich, and Hill. How do the magnitude of these policy effects vary by the characteristics of the schools, including the characteristics of the student body, the proportion of students at risk in the school, and the skills gap? How does variation in the treatment—what we have called "program effects"—shape students' performance? And to what extent can the policy-year effects be linked to characteristics of either teachers' and principals' reactions to the policy—what we call "instructional effects"—or to measures of the underlying quality of the school environment, such as teacher characteristics and instructional program?

Conclusion

The debate over ending social promotion is one of the most important policy questions in education today. Many school systems are pursuing polices such as Chicago's while simultaneously struggling with the potential negative effects of grade retention on students. Helping school systems design effective approaches for raising achievement requires that one understand how systemwide policies and programs shape student performance and teacher behavior, and what school and instructional characteristics improve the capacity of students and teachers to respond successfully to high-stakes testing approaches. The goal of this study is to bring a rigorous and multifaceted approach to the central questions and conundrums raised by such initiatives—for example, effects on instruction and students and the distribution of benefits and costs of the policy across various populations.

Our initial analysis of pre-testing-year effects highlighted an area most often neglected in the debate and research over ending social promotion. We find evidence that the initiative, as implemented in Chicago, was associated with positive achievement effects in the year before promotion testing in at least the second year of implementation. Our results raise many more questions than they answer and highlight areas that we will address in further research. How much of these achievement gains are a result of students working harder, teachers changing their behavior, or schools providing extra and targeted instructional time for students? We also do not know whether these achievement gains can be sustained over time or whether trade-offs may include negative effects on instruction or on students who do not make the test score cutoff and are retained. These questions can be answered by extending our model to examine post-testing-year effects for promoted and retained students and by examining the effects on outcomes in addition to achievement.

The goal of this chapter was to provide a case example of what Lynn and his colleagues called for in developing data sets, methods, and research that enhance the study of governance. Often, in evaluation research, variation in implementation is viewed as "noise" that results in a weakening of policy effects and that needs to be controlled in order to find the true effect of programs when implemented as originally conceived. Such an approach lends itself to randomized experiments that seek to control the implementation and environmental conditions as much as possible. This is clearly not an option when studying the effect of a systemwide policy such as Chicago's initiative. More recently, evaluators have begun to look at variation in implementation as a way of studying various treatments, such as looking at differences across states in the design of welfare-to-work programs. This approach allows for estimating dosage effects—for example, how variation in the level and intensity of treatments are associated with differential effects.

In this evaluation, we have taken a different approach to studying variation in implementation and effects. First, we hope to use across-school differences in implementation and in reaction to the policy as a means of gaining insight into why we are observing or not observing effects. Second, this approach affords the opportunity to move beyond an evaluation of the specific policy to investigating the factors that shape how teachers and principals translate policies within their schools and classrooms. This is the study of governance. We hope this chapter illustrates the potential for this approach to move the debate beyond competing treatments—for example, ending social promotion versus pursuing standard-raising initiatives in other ways—to a more informed understanding of the mechanisms by which the many external policies aimed at schools may actually shape the behavior and performance of the individuals charged with meeting the objectives of those initiatives.

References

Alexander, Karl, Doris Entwistle, and Susan Dauber. 1994. *On the success of failure: A reassessment of the effects of retention in the primary grades.* Melbourne: Cambridge University Press.

Barro, Stephen, and Andrew Kolstad. 1987. *Who drops out of high school? Findings from High School and Beyond* (Publication No. CS 87-397c). Washington, D.C.: U.S. Department of Education, National Center for Education Statistics.

Bryk, Anthony, and S. Raudenbush. 1992. *Ilierarchical linear models: Applications and data analysis methods.* London: Sage.

Byrnes, Deborah. 1989. Attitudes of students, parents, and educators toward repeating a grade. In *Flunking grades: Research and policies on retention,* edited by Lorrie Shepard and Mary Lee Smith. London: Falmer Press.

Elmoro, Richard. 1996. Getting to scale with good educational practice. *Harvard Education Review,* 66 (1): 1–26.

Entwistle, Doris, Karl Alexander, and Linda Olson. 1997. *Children, schools, and inequality.* Boulder, Colo.: Westview Press.

Fusaro, Joseph. 1997. The effect of full-day kindergarten on student achievement: A meta-analysis. *Child Study Journal,* 27 (4): 269–77.

Gottfredson, Denise, Carolyn Molden Fink, and Nanette Graham. 1994. Grade retention and problem behavior. *American Educational Research Journal,* 31 (4): 761–84.

Grissom, J. B., and L. A. Shepard. 1989. Repeating and dropping out of school. In *Flunking grades: Research and policies on retention,* edited by Lorrie A. Shepard and Mary Lee Smith. London: Falmer Press.

Hess, G. Alfred, and Diane Lauber. 1985. *Dropouts from the Chicago Public Schools.* Chicago: Chicago Panel on Public Schools Policy and Finance.

Heubert, J. P., and R. M. Hauser, eds. 1999. High Stakes: Testing for tracking, promotion, and graduation. Washington, D.C.: National Academy Press.

Heyns, Barbara. 1987. Schooling and cognitive development: Is there a season for learning? *Child Development,* 58: 1151–60.

Holmes, Thomas C. 1989. The fourth R: Retention. *Journal of Research and Development in Education,* 17 (1): 1–6.

Holmes, Thomas, and Kenneth Matthews. 1984. The effects of nonpromotion on elementary and junior high school pupils: A meta-analysis. *Review of Educational Research,* 54 (2): 225–36.

House, Ernest. 1998. The predictable failure of Chicago's student retention program. Unpublished manuscript, University of Colorado
School of Education, Boulder, Colo.

Jackson, Gregg. 1975. The research evidence of the effects of grade retention. *Review of Educational Research,* 45: 613–35.

Levin, Henry, and Mun Tsang. 1987. The economics of student time.
Economics of Education Review, 6 (4): 357–64.

Meyer, John, and Brian Rowan. 1978. The structure of educational organizations. In *Environments and organizations,* edited by Marshall W.
Meyer. San Francisco: Jossey-Bass.

Meyer, John, Richard Scott, and Terrence Deal. 1981. Institutional and
technical sources of organizational structure: Explaining the structure of educational organizations. In *Organization and the human
services,* edited by Herman D. Stein. Philadelphia: Temple University Press.

Meyer, John, Richard Scott, Sally Cole, and JoAnn Intili. 1978. Instructional dissensus and institutional consensus in schools. In *Environments and organizations,* edited by Marshall W. Meyer. San
Francisco: Jossey-Bass.

New York City Board of Education, Office of Educational Assessment.
1988. *A follow-up study of the 1982–1983 promotion gates students.*
New York: New York City Board of Education.

Roderick, Melissa. 1994. Grade retention and school dropout. *American Educational Research Journal,* 31 (4): 729–61.

Roderick, Melissa, Anthony Bryk, Brian Jacob, John Easton, and Elaine
Allensworth. 1999. *Ending social promotion in Chicago: Results
from the first two years.* Chicago: Consortium on Chicago School Research.

Scott, W. Richard and John W. Meyer. 1981. The organization of societal
sectors: Propositions and early evidence. In *The new institu-
tionalism in organizational analysis,* edited by Walter W. Powell and
Paul J. DiMaggio. Chicago: University of Chicago Press, pp. 108–42.

Shepard, Lorrie, Mary Lee Smith, and Scott Marion. 1996. Failed evidence on grade retention. *Psychology in the Schools,* 33: 251–61.

Smith, BetsAnn. 1998. *It's about time: Opportunities to learn in Chicago's elementary schools.* Chicago: Consortium on Chicago School
Research.

Smith, Julia, BetsAnn Smith, and Anthony Bryk. 1998. *Setting the
pace: Opportunity to learn in Chicago's elementary schools.* Chicago: Consortium on Chicago School Research.

Tyack, David, and Larry Cuban. 1995. *Tinkering toward utopia.* Cambridge, Mass.: Harvard University Press.

Weick, Karl. 1976. Educational organizations as loosely coupled systems. *Administrative Science Quarterly* 21: 1–19.

Endnotes

1. These figures provide data on passing rates for students who were not exempted under the policy, such as bilingual or special education students, and for whom test scores were available. Schools with fewer than ten students at risk were excluded from the analysis.

2. The model presented estimated a linear growth curve at level 1. We have experimented with alternative nonlinear models such as quadratic curves but found they made little difference.

3. Repeat is a dummy variable that equals one when a pregate grade is repeated. This control is for any prior retention experience.

4. For the purpose of this example, school k is the school in which a student experiences the sixth grade. Bryk is currently working on an extension to HLM with Raudenbush and Congdon to represent the fact formally that students may be nested in different schools over time. This new program will be available for use in this work.

5. In sixth grade, we estimate a policy year effect for 1997 and 1998 and treat 1996 as a prepolicy year. The eighth grade model differs in this respect. Because the program began in 1996 for eighth graders, 1996 is a postpolicy year.

6. On average, we would expect that the gate year value added would be zero before the policy. However, because third, sixth, and eighth grades have historically been testing years for a statewide test, the Illinois Goals Assessment Program, we might expect a previous testing effect at these grades. In earlier versions of this work, we experimented with various specifications for the year effects, including estimating a value added for each testing year using a vector of dummy variables. This specification best fit the data.

7. For ease of interpretation, we present the result when ITBS scores are left in Grade Equivalent metrics, the metric CPS uses when making promotion decisions. We are re-estimating these models using Rasch scale scores, which allow us to correct for form effects.

Governance and Performance: The Influence of Program Structure and Management on Job Training Partnership Act (JTPA) Program Outcomes

*Carolyn J. Heinrich and Laurence E. Lynn, Jr.**

The Job Training Partnership Act (JTPA), enacted in 1982 as a major initiative of the Reagan administration, created what became a $5 billion federally funded employment and training program for disadvantaged workers.[1] Under JTPA states are directed to provide services to "those who can benefit from, and are most in need of, such opportunities" and are required to measure results by "the increased employment and earnings of participants and the reduction in welfare dependency.[2]

Three important features distinguished the JTPA program from its predecessor, the Comprehensive Employment and Training Act (CETA), as well as from other social programs:

- the extension of formal authority for program administration to private-sector representatives (or Private Industry Councils)
- the introduction of performance standards based on financial (or budgetary) incentives
- a highly decentralized administrative structure allowing substantial discretion at state and local levels for developing programs and using performance incentives.

Because of these unique features, JTPA has been the subject of a significant and still growing body of evaluation research. The more sophisticated quantitative studies have used a large-scale data set collected for the National JTPA Study, supplemented by other quantitative and qualitative data, to investigate the influence of the performance standards system on program administration and on the program's employment and earnings impacts. Increasing attention, however, has also been directed at the governance of JTPA programs, that is, the formal structures of control and accountability that assign responsibility for achieving program goals to various levels of government and the private sector.

With previous JTPA research as a foundation, we further investigate the effects of program governance and management on participant employment and earnings. We take advantage of hierarchical, time-varying data from the National JTPA Study (i.e., the availability of individual-level data on client characteristics, program participation, and outcomes and of site-level structural information for the sixteen sites in the National JTPA Study, collected for three different years). We use these data to identify the separate contributions to program outcomes of administrative structures, management strategies, and client characteristics. Our research is designed not only to further explain JTPA program outcomes within a governance framework but also to provide insights for the study of governance and public management that can be gained with theory-based empirical research that employs multilevel, multisite data sets and from the cumulative findings of numerous studies conducted over a long period of time.

The chapter begins with a description of the JTPA program and its evolution, as well as a summary of previous studies of the program. The following section describes the conceptual framework that guided the design of our empirical research. We then describe our empirical models, data, and statistical methods, in particular how we have operationalized structural and management variables. Next we interpret and summarize our results. Finally, we discuss the implications of these findings for future research on governance and public management.

The Job Training Partnership Act (JTPA)

The U.S. Department of Labor (USDOL) was assigned responsibility for implementing JTPA in the effort to increase earnings for low-income individuals and reduce welfare dependency. Federal funds for the main component of JTPA (Title IIA) are allocated to states in proportion to the size of their unemployed and economically disadvantaged resident populations.[3] States subsequently allocate 78 percent of their Title IIA funds to geographically distinct service delivery areas (SDAs) using the federal allocation formula. Services provided under Title IIA include vocational (classroom) training, on-the-job training, basic (or remedial) education, job-search assistance, work experience for youth, and other services such as counseling, job-readiness activities, case management, and supportive services. The remaining Title IIA funds are to be used by the states to provide technical support to SDAs, to finance programs for "hard-to-serve" clients, and to award incentive bonuses to high-performing job-training agencies.

The USDOL provides specific policy direction to the states, but the interpretation of many important legislative provisions and the major responsibility for program administration and service delivery lie with state and local job-training agencies. Key program tasks and processes involved in the administration and delivery of job-training services at federal, state, and local levels are depicted in figure 3.1 and discussed further in the section on governance below.

Key Features of Governance

The main features of JTPA governance were inspired by a belief that quasi markets rather than traditional bureaucracy might be a more reliable way to ensure that the program's goals were met. These features included a broad role for the private sector, an emphasis on performance standards and goals rather than traditional command-and-control compliance with procedural mandates, and the decentralization of authority over program implementation to state and local agencies so that administrative regimes could reflect local preferences.

Private-Sector Role

By law, all JTPA service delivery areas are supervised by a Private Industry Council (PIC), which must include a majority of private-sector representatives.[4] PICs typically include representatives from local industries, businesses, organized labor, community-based organizations, and education institutions. Eligible participants are sometimes included as well. These councils, in conjunction with state and local

FEDERAL   *U.S. Department of Labor*
GOVERNMENT
LEVEL   Distributes federal employment and training funds to states; estab-
                      lishes and transmits target population and performance standard re-
                      quirements; monitors state-level JTPA operations

↓

STATE   *State government employment*
GOVERNMENT   *and training bureaucracy*
LEVEL
                      Establishes state-level target population goals and performance
                      standards based on federal guidelines; develops models to measure
                      JTPA program outcomes and maintains records on all JTPA program
                      participants; distributes federal funds and any additional state em-
                      ployment and training funds and incentive monies to local service
                      delivery areas; translates and develops regulations on the expendi-
                      ture of funds by local agencies; monitors local agency operations

↓   ↓   ↓

LOCAL LEVEL   *Service delivery area   Service delivery area   Service delivery area . . .*

                              Local administrative agencies and/or
                          Private Industry Councils/Workforce development boards

                      Each sets target population and performance goals in conjunction
                      with state-level requirements; develops training plans and solicits
                      contractors through requests for proposals to fulfill training objec-
                      tives; distributes funds through contracts with service provider or-
                      ganizations to deliver program services and also provides services
                      directly through local offices; monitors service providers

                              Contractual arrangements
                      ↓   ↓   ↓

                      Service provider   Service provider   Service provider . . .

                      Each sets a program budget, develops training opportunities and
                      determines costs per client (program service plan); screens appli-
                      cants and selects clients; delivers program services; reports program
                      outcomes to local administrative agency and seeks reimbursement
                      of program costs

FIGURE 3.1   *JTPA Program Administration and Service Delivery*

government representatives, make two main decisions that determine the governance structure of service delivery areas and the degree of power sharing within them: (1) the choice of administrative entity, or the organization responsible for overseeing program operations, and (2) the grant recipient, or the organization that receives JTPA program funds from the state and manages the programs on a daily basis. In some cases, the grant recipient and administrative entity are distinct; in other cases, PICs fulfill both of these roles (program features that will be shown to influence program outcomes). The sequential process by which SDA administrative structures are determined is depicted in figure 3.2.

Performance Standards

In the 1984 program year, the USDOL established the first performance standards, which included measures of participants' "entered employment" rate (i.e., job placement rate), and hourly wage and weekly earnings at the termination of program participation; cost per entry into employment (or per "entered employment"); welfare recipients' entered-employment rate; the entered-employment rate for youth; and cost per entered-employment for youth.[5] Ignoring potential inconsistencies, the USDOL intended the entered-employment rate standards to promote the development of employment-oriented programs, the hourly wage and weekly earnings standards to encourage high-quality training, and the cost standards to promote cost-effective service delivery. Performance standards adjustments made through a regression-based model were developed to mitigate the potential for "cream-skimming," that is, selecting program participants who would contribute to high levels of *measured* program performance but who would also succeed in the labor market without program participation.

State and Local Discretion

States and localities have been given substantial discretion to design their own performance incentive policies and training service strategies for achieving performance goals. States are allowed to modify and add to the federal performance standards and to develop their own systems for monitoring and rewarding (or sanctioning) local job-training agencies following annual performance

Service delivery area boundaries are established primarily by the state government and typically circumscribe one of the following: a city, county, metropolitan area, multicounty area, or state. The jurisdiction of the Private Industry Council (PIC) is the service delivery area. After the designation of service delivery area boundaries, the following decisions determine the governance structure of the SDAs.

1. Choose administrative entity	→	2. Select grant recipient	→	3. Select service providers
choice set:		*choice set:*		*choice set:*
• Private Industry Council • Local elected official (LEO)/public entity or chief executive officer CEO/for-profit firm		• Private Industry Council • Local elected official/ public entity or chief executive officer/ for-profit firm		• direct provision • contract out to for-profit, non-profit, or public organizations

↓

possible power-sharing arrangements:

• PIC and LEO or CEO are equal partners
• PIC is subordinate to LEO or CEO
• LEO or CEO is subordinate to PIC

FIGURE 3.2 *Fundamental decisions in establishing the governance structure of a JTPA Service Delivery Area (SDA)*

reviews. Six percent of the federal government's JTPA appropriation to the states is designated for bonuses or budgetary awards (i.e., discretionary training dollars) to SDAs based on their performance. The local job-training agencies, in turn, maintain sole authority over 78 percent of federal training funds (see Dickinson et al. 1988, and the discussion below).

Included in the legislation creating the performance standards system were provisions to ensure access to services for the most disadvantaged. The legislation requires 90 percent of all participants to be "disadvantaged" and an equitable distribution of services among "substantial segments" of the eligible population.[6] Because JTPA service delivery areas are able to serve, on average, less than 5 percent of their JTPA-eligible populations with the funding available in a given program year, local program administrators have considerable flexibility in selecting and enrolling program applicants.

Variations in Program Administration

Considerable differences in management structures and performance incentive policies have evolved in the more than 600 local
SDAs. The structure and form of JTPA program administration at
the local level may reflect factors such as state-level administrative
policies, the size of the local service delivery area or jurisdiction,
the size and composition of its JTPA-eligible population, urban versus rural location, and local political preferences. Figure 3.2 depicts
two primary choice sets that define an array of mutually exclusive
possibilities for the role of the PIC, local elected official (LEO), and
the chief executive officer (CEO) in program administration (see
also table 3.1), although not all of these possible combinations of
structural or power-sharing arrangements, are, in reality, probable.

A third dimension of program structure, as shown in figure 3.2,
involves the choice of service providers and the types and terms of
contracted services. With respect to program design and contract-

TABLE 3.1

Possible combinations of structural/power-sharing arrangements in JTPA
SDAs

1a PIC is administrative entity *(22)*[a]
1a2a PIC is grant recipient *(19)*
1a2ai   PIC and CEO/LEO are equal partners *(7)*
1a2aii PIC is subordinate to CEO/LEO
1a2aiii CEO/LEO is subordinate to PIC *(12)*
1a2b LEO or CEO is grant recipient *(3)*
1a2bi   PIC and CEO/LEO are equal partners *(3)*
1a2bii PIC is subordinate to CEO/LEO
1a2biii CEO/LEO is subordinate to PIC
1b LEO/public entity or CEO/for-profit firm is administrative entity *(26)*
1b2a PIC is grant recipient *(0)*
1b2ai   PIC and CEO/LEO are equal partners
1b2aii PIC is subordinate to CEO/LEO
1b2aiii CEO/LEO is subordinate to PIC
1b2b LEO or CEO is grant recipient *(26)*
1b2bi   PIC and CEO/LEO are equal partners *(18)*
1b2bii PIC is subordinate to CEO/LEO *(5)*
1b2biii CEO/LEO is subordinate to PIC *(3)*

[a]Numbers represented among 48 cases included in this study; these numbers will be discussed following the introduction of the data in the section on "Structural and Management Considerations."

ing, some administrative entities provide training services directly to participants, while others contract with local service providers. Some of these local agencies may choose to use performance-based contracts and develop their own performance incentive systems, while others may elect not to use any performance-based contracts.

Performance incentive policies at state and local levels may vary in other ways. A majority of states encourage competition among local service delivery areas by making performance bonuses received by one service delivery area dependent on their performance relative to the other SDAs. The stringency of performance requirements instituted by states differs in a number of ways as well, including the minimum number of performance standards SDAs must meet to qualify for incentive bonuses; the minimum number of standards they must fail in order to be classified as "failed to meet"; the level of performance at or above state performance standards that local service delivery areas must attain to qualify for incentives; whether extra bonuses are awarded for extraordinary performance; and the threshold above which local service delivery areas no longer receive additional rewards for improving performance. In addition to the actual performance levels required, the weights accorded by states to the various performance standards in determining bonuses also vary.

Previous Research on JTPA

The JTPA performance standards system has attracted substantial scholarly interest, especially by researchers interested in assessing the influence of performance standards on program outcomes. Two main policy questions concern whether performance-based administration is more effective than traditional bureaucratic control, and whether an emphasis on measured performance induces agencies to change program priorities and primary work processes in ways that influence program outcomes (either positively or negatively).

In 1986 Orfield and Slessarev interviewed JTPA program directors in Illinois and concluded that the performance standards system was generating unintended consequences. Specifically, they reported an "overwhelming emphasis on placement rates and low-cost training" among local service delivery areas, with program administrators and service providers screening for education levels (i.e., cream-skimming) to produce low-cost placements. Studies involving larger samples of SDAs, conducted by the National Commission for Employment Policy (NCEP), corroborated some of these findings. States that sought to exceed performance standards and that placed more weight on cost standards discouraged services to hard-to-serve eligible recipients, provided less basic-skills training, and reduced the average length of program participation for adults. The studies also reported that states with performance standard adjustment policies and explicit policy goals for the hard-to-serve tended to encourage services to these groups and to provide services of higher intensity. Not all of the service delivery areas they studied emphasized achieving high performance levels, however, suggesting the presence of other factors that influence management decisions about performance objectives as well as service delivery.

The findings of these studies led the federal government to change the legislated performance standard requirements in 1988 and to de-emphasize their role in federal and state JTPA program performance evaluations. The principal changes—an end to mandatory use of cost-per-placement standards and a shift toward measuring outcomes 90 days after participants left the program rather than at placement—were intended to encourage local job-training agencies to focus less on facilitating low-cost training and more on providing higher quality training that would promote employment retention. These policy changes contributed to some of the variation we now observe in performance incentives policies across service delivery areas.

In 1987 a three-year experimental evaluation involving sixteen local service delivery areas in sixteen states—the National JTPA Study—was initiated, setting the stage for a subsequent outpouring of academic research focused on assessing the impact of JTPA programs on participants' employment and earnings. Conducted by the Manpower Demonstration Research Corporation (MDRC) and Abt Associates, the study obtained information about local program operations and administrative structures and incentive policies at the sixteen sites. However, this information was not formally linked to individual-level data on program outcomes in the experimental evaluation.

In the early 1990s, eighteen-month and thirty-month impact findings of the National JTPA Study experimental evaluation were released. Small yet statistically significant average earnings effects were found for adult men and women, while average earnings effects for male youth were negative and statistically significant. The size (and sign) of the estimated earnings effects varied substantially across the sixteen sites, although Orr et al. (1994) reported that statistical tests for differences in effects among sites were not statistically significant. They conducted an "exploratory analysis" to identify local factors that might have influenced program effects at the sites, giving consideration to characteristics of the programs, labor market conditions, and the types of clients served. They reported, however, that almost none had a statistically significant effect on earnings.

The National JTPA Study also included a nonexperimental component led by James Heckman and colleagues. Although the primary focus of this research was on comparing the estimates of program effects generated by nonexperimental and experimental analyses, they also examined program implementation at the study sites and how organizational factors might relate to program outcomes and effects. Information obtained through interviews with caseworkers and program administrators was combined with econometric work to analyze the influence of JTPA performance standards in applicant acceptance, service assignment, and participant termination decisions, as well as the implications for program outcomes (Heckman, Smith, and Taber 1996; Heckman and Smith 1995a; Courty and Marschke 1997; Heckman, Heinrich, and Smith, 1997; Heinrich, forthcoming.) In similar research using data on state performance incentive policies from an earlier (1983–87) period and from the National Longitudinal Survey of Youth, Cragg (1997) also investigated the potential for moral hazard problems, finding that more stringent performance incentives encouraged training providers to enroll individuals with high levels of measured performance but low value added (in terms of earnings).

In one of the few studies that operationalize management-administrative structure variables and relate them to program outcomes, Jennings (1994) and Jennings and Ewalt (1998) studied the effects of administrative coordination patterns on JTPA program outcomes. Using data collected in surveys of state program directors linked to JTPA Annual Status Report data on program performance, they analyzed the relationships between increased levels of coordination and program performance, and administrative consolidation of state JTPA and employment service agencies and program performance. Jennings and Ewalt's regression findings lend support to their hy-

potheses that both increased coordination and administrative consolidation have significant, positive effects on program outcomes.

A Multilevel Model of JTPA Performance

The evolution of JTPA research suggests growing interest in getting
inside the "black box" of state- and local-level program implementation in order to understand how administrative discretion—in the
selection of program participants, the structuring of administrative
and service delivery arrangements, and the use of performance incentives—influences JTPA program outcomes and effects. Although
there is considerable variation in JTPA program outcomes by site in
the National JTPA Study, an aggressive attempt has not yet been
made to assess the potential contributions of governance and management factors in explaining this variance.

Although there are only sixteen sites in the National JTPA Study
(of over 600 SDAs in fifty states), an advantage of using these data
compared with state- or locally aggregated data is the availability of
individual-level data on client characteristics, training services received, and program outcomes. In addition, as described above,
there is also year-by-year variation in the state- and site-level variables, including the performance incentive policies. This variation
facilitates analyses by both site and year and triples the number of
study observations at this level. In our research, we employ various
econometric methods, including hierarchical linear modeling, to
take full advantage of the information available at both individual
and site levels.

We also draw on the "reduced form" model of governance presented by Lynn, Heinrich, and Hill in chapter 1 to frame our analyses:

$$O = f (E, C, T, S, M),$$

where: O = outputs/outcomes (individual-level and/or organizational outputs/outcomes); E = environmental factors; C = client at-
tributes/behavior; T = treatments or primary work/core processes; S
= organizational structure; and M = managerial roles and practices.

Using the data from the National JTPA Study and other sources
(see appendix A for a detailed description of the primary data
sources), we were able to construct measures for each of these classes
of variables. The measures relating to C, T, and O are fairly straight-

forward, as are the ones relating to E (in this case, economic conditions and other local area characteristics). The main conceptual and empirical challenges were encountered in modeling structural and management considerations and constructing appropriate variables.

Structural and Management Considerations

The JTPA program allows state and local public managers substantial discretion in defining their own administrative structures and in designing and managing key program processes (see figure 3.3), including the extent of authority or control that PICs would have over these program functions within each SDA. Returning to the array of possible combinations of structural power-sharing arrange-

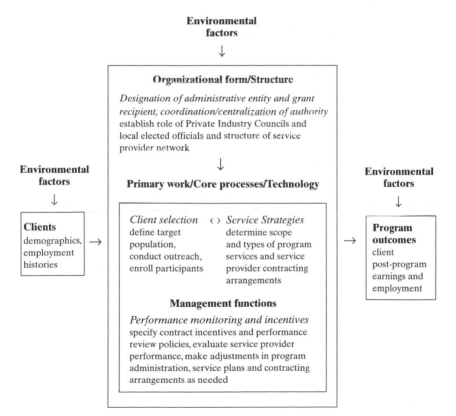

FIGURE 3.3 *Schematic model of governance components in the design and implementation of JTPA programs at the local level*

ments (table 3.1), it is evident that when the PIC was the administrative entity, it was also typically the grant recipient (chi-square = 12.34) in nineteen of the twenty-two cases.

In examining the degree to which power and authority are shared among entities involved in program administration, more diverse patterns of relationships are observed. For example, among the nineteen cases in which the PIC was both the administrative entity and the grant recipient, it was formally an "equal partner" with an LEO or CEO in seven of these. The LEO or CEO, however, was more likely to be subordinate to the PIC when the PIC was both the administrative entity and the grant recipient (as it was in the other twelve of these cases). When the LEO or CEO was both the administrative entity and the grant recipient, equal partnership with the PIC in program administration was more likely (in eighteen of these twenty-six cases). These initial findings suggest that when the PIC was the administrative entity, it was more likely to have consummate authority over program administration; that is, power or control appeared to be centralized in these SDAs.

The extent of PIC administrative authority or control also seemed to be related to the structure of service provider networks at these sites. When the PIC was the administrative entity and the grant recipient, over 41 percent of services were delivered by for-profit providers, compared with about 18 percent when the PIC was not the grant recipient. In addition, a significantly higher percentage of contracts with local service providers were performance based when the PIC was the administrative entity (34% compared with 14% when the PIC was not the administrative entity). In general, SDAs that granted a larger role in program administration to the private sector seemed slightly more likely to "contract out" and significantly more likely to allocate funds to for-profit organizations than SDAs in which a public entity was the dominant actor.

We do not assert causality among the choices of organizational-administrative structures in service delivery areas and the types of administrative policies and incentives that are adopted at both state and local levels to motivate performance. However, we find associations among them that we do not believe are spurious.

- When private-sector representatives assume more formal authority through the role of PICs as administrative entities and recipients of federal job-training funds, they appear to place more emphasis on measured performance and to adopt administrative practices (e.g., more performance-based contracting and contracts with for-profit organizations) that also demand accountability for results. Although we are unable to determine the direction of these relationships, it is possible that PICs negotiate for more formal and real authority in local service delivery areas—or that local elected officials defer more to them—when state-level administrative policies also emphasize performance attainment (e.g., by making the bonus award system competitive and offering extra bonuses for extraordinary performance).

- SDAs with a larger administrative role for local public officials and less control by the PICs delivered more JTPA program services directly (versus contracting out) and were less likely to use performance-based contracts.

Statistical Methods and Variable Selection

We analyze two levels of data: (1) *individual-level* data, which include measures of JTPA client characteristics (demographics and employment histories) and indicators for the types of training services they received ($N = 9,621$ total observations), and (2) *site-level* data, which include variables describing the administrative structures in the sixteen service delivery areas, performance incentive policies they face, their service delivery or contracting strategies, and the unemployment rate and regional indicators. In the past, linear regression techniques were limited in their ability to recognize and maximize the information contained in data with nested or hierarchical structures. The extent to which hierarchical linear modeling (HLM) improves statistical estimation compared with the ordinary least squares (OLS) approach depends on the potential for and strength of multilevel or cross-level effects in the data and the corresponding amount of variation in the dependent variable to be explained at the different levels of analyses. When significant cross-level effects or intraclass correlations are present, the assumption of independence of observations in the traditional OLS approach is violated. Preliminary (unconditional HLM) analyses of our data (i.e., JTPA participant earnings and employment outcomes) produced statistically significant intraclass correlation coefficients, and although the between-site proportion of the total variance in outcomes was still small (approximately 3%), we chose to use hierarchical linear modeling to test our hypotheses about how local JTPA governance structures and management policies (i.e., variables measured at the site level) influence participant program outcomes (occurring at the individual level.)[7]

All six components of our empirical model of governance were included in our hierarchical linear models as either level I or level II predictors or as the dependent variable (client outcomes or O). Our individual-level (level I) data included all available measures of client characteristics (C) (gender, age, race, educational attainment, marital status, family composition, and employment and earnings history) and indicators for training services received (T). The level II measures of environmental factors (E) or local economic conditions (i.e., regional indicators and the unemployment rates at the sites in each of the three years under study) were also fairly straightforward (Appendix B describes the variables used in our empirical models).

Our choices for clients' earnings outcomes (the dependent variables) warrant some explanation. Although data were available from the National JTPA Study for experimental impact estimates, a number of missing observations for several of the sites made yearly calculations of earnings effects problematic. More important, the design of the JTPA performance standards system and incentive policies, as well as the types of program outcome information continuously available to program administrators, suggests that participants' employment and earnings levels are more likely to be the goals of managers than are program impacts. For example, the performance standards used during the 1987–89 period and continuing today measure participants' earnings and employment levels or rates at termination (through 1988) and in the first quarter following termination, and program administrators are typically only able to access up to four quarters of participants' earnings data after the program for additional performance reviews. Although we believe evaluating the influence of management and structural factors on program effects is also an interesting question (and one that we are pursuing as well), it raises a different set of issues about the design of management and performance incentive policies—more prescriptive than explicative—given the construct of the current JTPA system. As Heckman, LaLonde, and Smith (2000) suggest in their extensive review of the "methodological lessons" of job-training program evaluations, there is no inherently appropriate method or choice of estimator; researchers, they say, "should be guided by the economics underlying the problem, the data that are available or can be acquired, and the evaluation question being addressed" (p. 2).

Within our array of other potential site-level (level II) predictors, there were some highly correlated variables, as suggested in our exploratory data analyses. Given the potential for multicollinearity at this level, we carefully tested different combinations of these S and M variables. We monitored changes in the coefficient values and examined the residuals of the estimated models to determine the best specification. The governance structure within the SDAs (S) was represented primarily by the following two variables: an indicator for "PIC is the administrative entity," and a variable indicating whether the PIC and CEO or LEO shared authority over program administration as equal partners. Although other important decisions are involved in establishing the governance structure of SDAs (see figure 3.2), we found strong, statistically significant relationships among these particular elements.

Two other important dimensions of management and structure at the site level include the design of service delivery arrangements and performance incentive policies. Although the influence of structural relationships might be reflected to some extent through the "PIC is the administrative entity" variable, we also include a variable measuring the percent of services provided directly by the administrative entities. In selecting measures for the management dimension (M)—the performance standard policies—we focused primarily on variables (or policies) that were common in their use across the sites and that included some year-to-year variation over the three years as well. One of these variables—the minimum number of standards that sites must meet to qualify for performance bonuses—was included to approximate the stringency of performance incentive requirements faced by local program administrators. A second variable indicated whether states required administrative entities to use any performance bonuses received in services to hard-to-serve groups; we speculate that this constraint on the use of performance bonus funds might reduce the power of these incentives for local program administrators. A third measure used was the weight placed on the entered-employment rate performance (or job placement rate) in determining performance bonus awards by the state. The expected effect of this variable on program administration and outcomes is not wholly clear; however, greater weight accorded to job-placement rate performance might encourage more intensive efforts to secure employment for as many clients as possible and improve outcomes, or it might encourage service providers to focus more on the numbers and less on the quality of job placements, compromising overall program effectiveness. We also chose to include a measure of the percentage of performance-based contracts used in the SDAs because we believe this variable reflects the degree of competition and the strength of performance incentives operating at the site level.

In summary, our multilevel, empirical model of JTPA program performance includes seven site-level measures intended to explain the role of governance and management factors in producing JTPA client earnings and employment outcomes (in addition to the numerous individual-level predictors and other site-level, environmental factors described earlier). A central question we now address is: How well do these variables explain the variance observed in outcomes across the sites, and what do their estimated effects tell us about the influence of these administrative structures and management policies on client outcomes?

Model Specifications

In hierarchical linear modeling (HLM), each of the levels in the hierarchical data structure is formally represented by its own submodel. Each submodel specifies the structural relations occurring at that level, as well as the residual variability observed at that level. In modeling participants' earnings outcomes following participation in JTPA programs, the level I submodel is specified as follows:[8]

$$Y_{ij} = \beta_{0j} + \beta_{1j}X_{1j} + \ldots + \beta_{nj}X_{nj} + r_{ij}, \tag{1}$$

where Y_{ij} is a measure of a participants' postprogram earnings; the subscript j denotes the site (or service delivery area) and allows each site to have a unique intercept and slope for each of the level I (individual characteristic) predictors (X_{1j} to X_{nj}), and the residual, r_{ij}, is assumed to be normally distributed with homogeneous variance across sites.

In the level II submodel, we assume fixed effects of each site-level variable, W_{1j} to W_{nj} (i.e., describing administrative structures, performance incentive policies, contracting practices, and economic conditions at the sites) on each level I (X_{1j} to X_{nj}) predictor of participants' earnings outcomes. Our exploratory analyses showed, for example, that the relationship between administrative structure and the effects of client characteristics on outcomes is fairly constant across sites and years. We therefore specify our level II submodel, a variation of the random-intercept model, as:

$$\beta_{0j} = \gamma_{00} + \gamma_{01}W_{1j} + \ldots + \gamma_{0n}W_{nj} + u_{0j}$$

$$\beta_{1j} = \gamma_{10} \ldots \beta_{nj} = \gamma_{n0} \tag{2}$$

In equation 2, the fixed relationships between the site-level variables and the effects of client-level predictors on earnings outcomes are shown as $\beta_{1j} = \gamma_{10} \ldots \beta_{nj} = \gamma_{n0}$, while β_{0j} varies randomly across level-II units. Combining the level I submodel (eq. 1) and the new level II submodel (i.e., substituting eq. 2 into eq. 1), we obtain the following model, our final specification:

$$Y_{ij} = \gamma_{00} + \gamma_{01}W_{1j} + \ldots + \gamma_{0n}W_{nj} + \gamma_{10}X_{1j} + \ldots + \gamma_{n0}X_{nj} + u_{0j} + r_{ij}. \tag{3}$$

In estimating this hierarchical linear model (eq. 3), we obtain coefficient values for all level I (X_{1j} to X_{nj}) and level II (W_{1j} to W_{nj}) predictors that account for the interrelationships among these variables and indicate the direction and significance of their effects for participants' earnings.

Hypotheses

Previous studies suggest the types of relationships we should expect to observe between some of the governance variables and program outcomes or performance. Based in part on the work of Jennings and Ewalt (1998) and Heckman, Heinrich, and Smith (1997), we suggest two main hypotheses:

H1   Increased levels of coordination or centralization of authority in providing employment and training services will increase program performance.

H2   A more outcomes-oriented approach and a stronger empha-
      sis on performance requirements in administration will be
      positively related to measured program performance.

Meyer, Scott, and Strang (1987) described centralization as the
state where "resources relevant to a focal organization stem from
the same source and are integrated in some clear way" (p. 187). In
the context of JTPA programs, we speculate that greater centralization of authority and program resources and integration of service
delivery processes might be facilitated when PICs serve as the administrative entity and also receive the grant to operate JTPA programs.[9] Figure 3.3 shows that the administrative entity and grant
recipient together have authority over all of the primary work processes (or core program functions), including client selection, the
determination of service strategies and service provider contracting
arrangements, and performance monitoring and incentive policies.
With W_{1j} and W_{2j} as the two variables representing the governance
structure within the SDAs (W_{1j} = "PIC is the administrative entity"
indicator, and W_{2j} = indicator that the PIC and CEO or LEO share
authority equally over program administration), our theory sug-
gests that we should expect the coefficient (γ_{01}) of W_{1j} to be positive
(and statistically significant) and the coefficient (γ_{02}) of W_{2j} to be
negative.

Pertaining to our second hypothesis, Heckman, Heinrich, and
Smith (1997) describe how the emphasis on professional accountability and managerial discretion in JTPA programs at the local level
allow for considerable variation in administrative practices and the
use of performance incentive policies across SDAs. The two JTPA
service delivery areas they studied adopted contrasting approaches
to program implementation. In one, the goal of exceeding performance standards was emphasized in all aspects of program operations, including contracting, participation selection, and service
delivery; in the other, performance standards were given minimal
attention and caseworkers' social service norms guided decision
making in these key program processes. Reviewing the performance
of these SDAs, as measured against federal- and state-established
performance standards, Heckman, Heinrich, and Smith found that
the first (performance conscious) SDA consistently exceeded its
performance requirements and was a high-level performer, while
the other failed to meet minimum performance requirements in

some years and was at risk for federal reorganization (the strongest penalty for poor performance). Based on the findings of their research, we propose a corollary to Hypothesis 1:

C1   Local service delivery areas that (1) face more stringent performance incentive policies (in terms of their requirements for qualifying for performance bonuses and the actual values or weights placed on performance standards) and that (2) reinforce these policies locally through performance-based contracting systems will achieve higher performance levels, as measured in terms of earnings outcomes for participants.

In testing H2 and C1, we examine the direction and significance of the effects of our other site-level incentive policy-management variables (W_{3j} through W_{7j}). For example, we expect a positive relationship between client outcomes and the minimum number of standards SDAs must meet to qualify for performance bonuses and the weight accorded the entered-employment rate (i.e., positive signs on the coefficients γ_{03} and γ_{04}). We anticipate, however, that requiring performance bonuses in serving the hard-to-serve will dilute these incentives and be negatively related to client outcomes (i.e., a negative sign on the coefficient γ_{05}). In addition, C1 suggests that the coefficient (γ_{06}) of the variable measuring the percentage of services provided directly by the administrative entity (rather than contracted out) is likely to be negative in sign, while the percentage of performance-based contracts used should be positively related to client outcomes (i.e., a positive sign on the coefficient γ_{07}).

It is important to point out that shorter-term program outcomes, such as those used in the JTPA performance standards system during the period of this study, have been shown to correlate poorly, and some even negatively, with longer-term program outcomes and effects (Heckman and Smith 1995a; Barnow 1999). Therefore, it is possible that the relationships between these management variables and program outcomes might vary depending on the specific participant outcome measures that are included in the models.

Empirical Results

Table 3.2 presents the results of two hierarchical linear models of JTPA participants' earnings in the first quarter after the program

TABLE 3.2

Hierarchical linear model of JTPA participants' earnings outcome

Predictors - Level I (individual level)	Earnings in first post-program quarter		Earnings in first post-program year	
Intercept	190.55	(0.40)	1117.10	(0.76)
Gender (1 = male)	517.88	(6.51)	2144.18	(7.76)
Age 22–29 years	369.75	(3.98)	1455.00	(4.51)
Age 30–39 years	240.91	(2.36)	1000.99	(2.82)
Age 40 and over years	53.84	(0.42)	397.21	(0.89)
Black	−235.16	(−2.29)	−1079.14	(−3.04)
Hispanic	−109.56	(−0.90)	−699.64	(−1.66)
Divorced, widowed or separated	87.89	(1.02)	325.55	(1.09)
No high school degree	−350.57	(−4.52)	−1424.55	(−5.29)
Some post high school education	360.81	(3.58)	1046.91	(2.99)
Welfare recipient at time of application	−293.05	(−3.71)	−1006.49	(−3.67)
Children under age six	63.58	(0.76)	496.51	(1.70)
Employment-unemployment transition in year before enrollment	−295.66	(−3.92)	−862.80	(−3.30)
Earnings in year before enrollment	0.09	(9.70)	0.33	(10.59)
Received classroom training	100.36	(1.22)	125.71	(0.44)
Received on-the-job training	388.36	(3.58)	1195.17	(3.17)

Predictors - Level II (site level)				
PIC is the administrative entity	446.41	(3.60)	1737.40	(4.59)
PIC and LEO/CEO are equal partners	−472.55	(−2.00)	−1933.65	(−2.61)
Percent of services provided directly by adminstrative entity	−548.28	(−1.45)	−2618.57	(−2.26)
Percent of performance-based contracts	−650.32	(−1.91)	−2719.45	(−2.60)
Weight accorded to employment rate standard	4260.41	(3.21)	15887.75	(3.93)
Minimum number of standards sites must meet to qualify for performance bonuses	21.13	(1.10)	22.25	(0.39)
Requirement that performance bonuses must be used to serve highly disadvantaged groups	−242.70	(−2.02)	−866.66	(−2.30)

TABLE 3.2
(Continued)

Predictors - Level II (site level)	Earnings in first post-program quarter		Earnings in first post-program year	
Southern region	433.03	(1.49)	2035.83	(2.24)
Midwestern region	535.74	(2.90)	1936.15	(3.33)
Western region	825.04	(2.22)	3215.92	(2.76)
Unemployment rate	11725.86	(2.67)	49955.52	(3.71)
Model predicting power– percent of variation explained by model	6% individual-level; 86% between-site variation		13% individual-level; 97% between-site variation	

Coefficient value followed by t-ratio in parentheses

ended and first year after their discharge from the program. The estimated effects of the level I (X_{1j} to X_{nj}) and level II (W_{1j} to W_{nj}) predictors on earnings outcomes, accounting for their interrelationships, are shown in Table 3.2. The coefficient values of the predictors (γ_{01} to γ_{n0}) and their *t*-ratios are displayed in the cells. The *t*-ratios indicate that nearly all of the level I and level II variables are statistically significant.

The direction of the effects of individual-level predictors observed in these models are all consistent with prior JTPA research (see Orr et al. 1994; Heinrich 1998) and our own expectations. Males ages 22–39 years with some post-high-school education and recent earnings achieved the highest earnings levels. In contrast, minorities, high school dropouts, welfare recipients, and those with less stable earnings histories experienced lower earnings in the first quarter and year following the program. Those clients who participated in on-the-job training activities experienced significantly higher earnings levels than those who received classroom training or less-intensive training services, such as job search and counseling (i.e., the omitted category).

Structure and Performance

Examining the site-level coefficient estimates, we observed a number of statistically significant results. Earlier, we suggested that when private-sector representatives assume more formal authority through the role of the PICs as administrative entities and recipients of federal job-training funds, they appear to emphasize measured performance and to adopt administrative practices that demand accountability for results. We also hypothesized that a more outcomes-oriented approach and stronger emphasis on performance requirements would be positively related to program performance. The large, positive, and highly significant effect on participants' earnings when the PIC was the administrative entity seems to provide some support for these arguments. For example, when the PIC is the administrative entity, participants earn, on average, $1,737 more in the first year following the program. In contrast, when the structure of the administrative entity is such that the PIC and CEO or LEO are equal partners in program administration, participants earn, on average, $1,934 less in the year following program discharge.

These two findings might also be interpreted as indirectly supporting our hypothesis on the influence on client outcomes of more centralized authority or control in JTPA program administration. We argued that greater centralization of program resources and service delivery processes might be facilitated when PICs serve as the administrative entity (and also receive the grant to operate JTPA programs), contributing to improved program performance. The results clearly show that significantly higher earning levels are realized, on average, by participants when the PIC is the administrative entity and is not an equal partner with local elected officials.

The percentage of JTPA program services provided directly by the administrative entity is also highly significant and negatively related to program outcomes. Our exploratory analyses showed that when PICs were given a larger role in program administration, fewer services were provided directly by the administrative entity and a higher percentage of contracts were with for-profit organizations. In this context, we view this result as consistent with the other findings discussed above that suggest that giving PICs more authority contributes positively to earnings levels. However, we also believe it suggests an important distinction between the effects of a more centralized administrative structure and those of more centralized service provision. For example, it may be more important that the administrative entity that receives the training grant and maintains full authority over spending decisions also has primary control over selecting service providers than that it controls service mix through direct provision. In the area of job training, it is likely that having a diverse range of services available to the heterogeneous population served outweighs the advantages of direct provision by a single entity.

Contrary to our expectations about the role of performance requirements in increasing accountability and improving program outcomes, we observed a negative and statistically significant coefficient on the variable measuring the percentage of performance-based contracts. One explanation for this result is that this measure of performance-based contracting might be insufficient to characterize adequately the types of incentives included in these contracts. For example, Dickinson et al. (1988) found that SDA administrative entities used a variety of strategies to build performance expectations into their contracts; some made adjustments for services to targeted, hard-to-serve groups; and the stringency of the performance requirements in service provider contracts might have also varied substantially. The weight given to the entered-employment rate standard, arguably one of the most prominent performance standards for JTPA program administrators and staff, is positively and significantly related to participants' earnings outcomes. Of all the performance incentive policies, the weight accorded this standard in performance evaluations had the largest effect on participants' earnings (contributing, on average, $1,875 to participants' earnings in the first year following termination from the program). The minimum number of standards that SDAs must meet to qualify for performance bonuses is also positively related to participants' earnings outcomes, although this relationship is not statistically significant. In addition, we find that requiring performance bonuses to be used to serve highly disadvantaged groups—a constraint that may reduce the power of these performance incentives—is negatively related to participants' earnings levels.

Finally, the models show a positive and statistically significant relationship between the site unemployment rate and participants' earnings outcomes. An explanation for this apparent anomaly might exist in Dickinson et al.'s (1988) examination of the effects of unemployment rates. Specifically, they found that when labor markets were tight, SDAs had a more difficult time recruiting clients, and applicant pools "consisted of individuals with unstable work histories, basic skills deficiencies, and multiple personal and family problems" (p. 119). They also found that program administrators were unprepared to handle this clientele and that many simultaneously experienced funding declines owing to the federal allocation formula that factors in the unemployment rate. In the light of this argument, we suggest that a positive relationship between client earnings and the local unemployment rate might be realistic, particularly if program services were less effective for clients during better economic times (something we are unable to measure and control for in our models).

Structure versus Management

Overall, we believe that one of the most significant governance findings of the client earnings outcome models is the positive relationship between the role of the PIC as the administrative entity and program performance. It is important to know, however, whether this observed relationship occurs mainly because of the advantages of more centralized control of authority over program administration when the PIC is the administrative entity (a structural or S component of our governance model) or whether it is primarily because PICs are more likely to demand accountability for results through more rigorous performance incentive policies (a management or M component of our governance model).

No previous studies have attempted to separate empirically these effects of a strong, authoritative role for the PICs in program administration (the structural component) and the types of performance incentive and contracting policies that they employ (the management contribution). To separate these effects, we use the results of our most precisely estimated earnings outcome model—participants' earnings levels in the first year following the program—to evaluate the evidence for these two hypotheses.

The effects of management (performance incentive and contracting) policies on JTPA participants' earnings in the first year following the program, across the four main administrative structures observed in the National JTPA Study sites, are compared in table 3.3. To compute the effects of these policies on earnings outcomes, we used the estimated coefficients on the performance incentive and contracting policy variables in the hierarchical linear model of participants' earnings in the first year following the program (see table 3.2). These coefficient values were multiplied by the average values of the performance incentive-contracting policy variables for each of three SDA administrative structures to obtain their estimated effects on participants' earnings. In the final row of table 3.3, the combined policy effects for each type of administrative structure—or the sum of the effects on earnings of the five performance incentive-contracting policy variables—are shown in boldface.

With the exception of the variable indicating the percentage of performance-based contracts used at the sites, all of the estimated policy effects on earnings were in the anticipated direction. The results for the first three performance incentive variables confirm that policies that strengthen performance incentives and requirements contribute positively to client outcomes. The results for the contracting policy variables, on the other hand, suggest countervailing influences at work; while earnings are enhanced when a greater percentage of services are contracted out rather than provided directly, the use of performance-based contracts is negatively related to participants' earnings after they have left the program.

Examining the combined policy effects, there is little difference in the effects of these policies on earnings outcomes between PICs that share administrative authority equally with an LEO or CEO (−$22) and PICs that have more authority in program administration and are not equal partners (−$2). Somewhat surprisingly, when the PIC was not the administrative entity, the performance incentive policies and contracting practices appeared to be employed most effectively to enhance program performance. The use of a smaller percentage of performance-based contracts but a larger weight on the entered-employment rate standard gave these categories of SDAs the edge in terms of performance.

To evaluate the overall effectiveness of these three types of local administrative structures, however, the effects of the two structural (S) variables on participants' earnings also had to be computed and combined with the policy variable (M) effects. Table 3.4 shows these computations and the large, statistically significant effects of these structural variables on participants' earnings levels. The final row of this table, which reports an overall measure of the effectiveness of administrative structure and performance incentive-contracting policies on earnings levels, shows that when the PIC is the administrative entity and does not share authority equally with an LEO or CEO, participants attain significantly higher earnings. Furthermore, these superior earnings achievements are realized almost entirely

TABLE 3.3

A comparison of the effects of management/performance incentive policies on JTPA participants' earnings in the first postprogram year, across four administrative structures

	Service delivery area (SDA) administrative structure							
Performance incentive and contracting policy variables	PIC is the administrative entity and is *not* an equal partner with the LEO/CEO (N=10)		PIC is the administrative entity and is an equal partner with the LEO/CEO (N=12)		PIC is *not* the administrative entity but is an equal partner with LEO/CEO (N=18)		PIC is *not* the administrative entity and is *not* an equal partner with the LEO/CEO (N=8)	
HLM coefficient estimates (in parentheses)	*Average value of variable*	*Estimated effect on earnings ($)*	*Average value of variable*	*Estimated effect on earnings ($)*	*Average value of variable*	*Estimated effect on earnings ($)*	*Average value of variable*	*Estimated effect on earnings ($)*
Minimum number of standards SDAs must meet to qualify for performance bonuses (22.25)	6.2	136	3.5	77	5.4	120	1.0	22
Performance bonuses must be used for services to hard-to-serve groups (−866.66)	.25	−217	.30	−260	.17	−147	0.00	0

TABLE 3.3 (continued)

| | Service delivery area (SDA) administrative structure | | | | | | | |
| Performance incentive and contracting policy variables | PIC is the administrative entity and is *not* an equal partner with the LEO/CEO (N=10) | | PIC is the administrative entity and is an equal partner with the LEO/CEO (N=12) | | PIC is not the administrative entity but is an equal partner with LEO/CEO (N=18) | | PIC is *not* the administrative entity and is *not* an equal partner with the LEO/CEO (N=8) | |
HLM coefficient estimates (in parentheses)	Average value of variable	Estimated effect on earnings ($)	Average value of variable	Estimated effect on earnings ($)	Average value of variable	Estimated effect on earnings ($)	Average value of variable	Estimated effect on earnings ($)
Weight accorded entered-employment rate standard in evaluating performance (15,887.75)	.102	1621	.120	1,9C7	.122	1,954	.129	2050
Percentage of contracts that are performance-based (−2,719.45)	.360	−979	.313	−843	.140	−381	.149	−405
Percentage of services provided directly by the administrative entity (−2,618.57)	.215	−563	.345	−903	.264	−691	.330	−864
Combined policy effects (totals)	—	**−2**	—	**−22**	—	**855**	—	**803**

TABLE 3.4

The effects of JTPA service delivery area administrative structure and management/performance incentive policies on JTPA participants' earnings in the first postprogram year

Organizational structure variables	Service delivery area (SDA) administrative structure			
	PIC is the administrative entity and is *not* an equal partner with the LEO/CEO (*N*=10)	PIC is the administrative entity and is an equal partner with the LEO/CEO (*N*=12)	PIC is not the administrative entity but is an equal partner with LEO/CEO (*N*=18)	PIC is *not* the administrative entity and is *not* an equal partner with the LEO/CEO (*N*=8)
HLM coefficient estimates (in parentheses)	*Estimated effects of administrative structure on earnings ($)*			
PIC is the administrative entity (1,737.40)	1,737	−197	−1,934	0
PIC and LEO/CEO are equal partners (−1,933.65)				
Combined performance incentive and contracting policy effects (estimated)	−2	−22	855	803
Overall measure of effectiveness of administrative structure and performance incentive and contracting policies	**1,735**	−219	−1,079	803

due to the structural role assumed by these PICs rather than the performance incentive and contracting policies they adopted.

Conclusion

Our hierarchical linear models performed quite well in explaining the variance in JTPA participant earnings outcomes at both the individual and the site levels. Although the model statistics indicated that there was significant unexplained variation in participants' earnings outcomes after participating in the program, most of this variation occurred at the individual level, as one would expect for a social program such as JTPA.

Many factors affect individuals' success in the labor market following JTPA program participation, particularly as long as a year after. Factors include the dynamics of family relationships and child care responsibilities, relationships with employers and coworkers, acquiring additional education and job-related skills, and many other environmental influences. We are satisfied that our models could explain approximately 13 percent of the individual-level variation in JTPA participants' earnings in the first year after leaving the program. These results are consistent with the performance of models estimated by other researchers (see Jennings and Ewalt 1998; Heinrich 1998).

More encouraging for the study of governance is the fact that we were able to account for virtually all (up to 97%) of the variation in earnings outcomes between the sites we studied. Statistical tests showed that there was no significant variation in these outcomes that remained to be explained by our models. With the structural and management variables we included in our models, we were able to explain almost fully the link between governance and performance in JTPA programs as measured by the earnings outcomes.

The administrative implications of these results are clear. First, structure is important (and so, too, is management to the extent that managers choose the structural arrangements governing program operations, as is true at the state level of JTPA administration).[10] Reorganizing and restructuring SDA governance toward granting PICs full authority over JTPA program operations could improve participant earnings levels significantly, that is, increasing earnings by as much as 25 percent of average earnings after the program. Alternatively, requiring PICs to share power equally with political executives in local political coalitions has a similarly large effect on program outcomes in the opposite direction.

Why might centralization of authority have such a strong positive effect on program outcomes? According to a paradox attributed to Amartya Sen (for a discussion, see Miller 1992), delegation of administrative authority to more than one subordinate entity leads either to incoherent behavior or to inefficiency with respect to a priori preferences, the more so when subordinate entities have specialized (or different) functions. One solution, in principle, is incentive schemes that align preferences, but as Miller shows, such incentive compatibility may prove impossible to attain to the extent that there are multiple, conflicting goals and information asymmetries, as there are in JTPA. Another solution is "leadership," that is, centrally directed coordination, information management, and conflict resolution. Although we have not shown directly how this occurs, our results suggest that PICs, with their tendency toward a more focused, less politicized view of program goals, improve coherence in program administration.

The work of Milward and Provan (1998) in studying mental health services organizations also suggests the importance of coordination and stability in structural and contractual arrangements when public or social services are delivered via interorganizational networks. They find that when mental health services networks are coordinated by a "core" agency with direct, unitary control over funding (e.g., as in the role of PICs with centralized authority), they achieve better results. In addition, they discuss the concept of "stability" in terms of property rights; if property rights are clearly specified and the parties have confidence that a "new regime" is unlikely to enter and change the distribution of property rights, incentives to cooperate will be higher. In the context of JTPA, an administrative entity sharing power equally with a local political regime, which may undergo frequent change and challenge established administrative arrangements, might find it more difficult to develop cooperative and productive relationships with service providers and other local organizations involved in JTPA service delivery.

Our second major finding is that managers drive performance, as well. Defining management as we have (i.e., as choosing the policies guiding program operations, such as reliance on performance-based contracts, emphasizing the relative importance of entered employment and earnings outcomes, and targeting services to disadvantaged groups) suggests that management decisions can have significant effects on earnings levels. The management action with the largest, significant (and positive) influence on earnings outcomes is the decision to emphasize job placements in program administration more strongly. Other research (Orfield and Slessarev, 1986; and Heinrich forthcoming), as well as anecdotal evidence from JTPA programs, suggests that the job placement rate is one of the less ambiguous and more strongly emphasized performance goals. In Heinrich's case study of an Illinois SDA, the number that JTPA intake staff and caseworkers always had on their minds was the job placement rate. The comparative simplicity of this goal in terms of managers' and caseworkers' ability to monitor performance and make programmatic decisions that might affect job placement rates may explain, in part, the emphasis it is given, and it may also aid the coherence (at multiple organizational levels) with which this goal is pursued.

Other management policies or variables, such as the minimum number of standards SDAs must meet to qualify for performance bonuses and the requirement that performance bonuses be used for services to hard-to-serve groups, had much weaker effects on program outcomes. We find these results consistent with our argument above given that the implications of these policies for managers of daily program operations are much less clear. Although different SDAs must satisfy different numbers of minimum standards to obtain bonuses, the stringency of those standards (i.e., their actual values) may also vary depending on the types of clients the SDAs serve and the vagaries of the performance standards policies adopted by their state-level JTPA agencies. In addition, we suggested earlier that requiring SDAs to expend performance bonuses on serving hard-to-serve groups might actually weaken the overall incentive system, making attaining performance bonuses less attractive to program managers. The extent to which the constraint on performance bonus expenditures dampens incentives might also vary across SDAs, depending on the size of their hard-to-serve population as well as economic and other factors.

We argue that these same types of administrative-incentive policy complexities might also explain our somewhat paradoxical finding that the use of performance-based contracting is negatively related to program outcomes. As suggested earlier, our current measure of performance-based contracting might be insufficient to characterize adequately the types of incentives incorporated into these contracts, which sometimes include adjustments for services to hard-to-serve groups and may vary substantially in terms of their rigor. These findings point to the importance of gathering very explicit and detailed documentation of the types of performance incentives and requirements encountered and implemented by program administrators when evaluating their effects on program outcomes. We also recognize, however, that this type of information may be highly sensitive for program administrators, given the potential for variations in these types of policies or requirements across contractors. Heinrich (1999) was only able to obtain such detailed data for a single JTPA service delivery area (not affiliated with the National JTPA Study), and while working with this local SDA over a five-year period and under a special contract.

In summary, we find that a strong emphasis on getting people into jobs on the part of a Private Industry Council along with clear authority over program administration will produce significantly higher earnings levels and greater rates of job placement in the first year following participation in the program than the other SDA administrative models that we have observed at the sixteen sites and across the three years of the National JTPA Study. We must note several qualifications to these relatively unambiguous findings. First, program administrators may, notwithstanding such findings, choose equity over efficiency. That is, they may choose to sacrifice overall earnings and employment achievements in favor of ensuring that the least advantaged groups enjoy high priority in service delivery and, presumably, a higher share of a smaller aggregate outcome.

Second, it is important to reiterate that we estimated the effects of structure and management policies on participants' earnings and employment outcomes in the first year following participation, not their long-term earnings and employment impacts. Using the experimental data collected in the National JTPA Study, Heckman and Smith (1995a, 1995b) and Barnow (1999) have shown that shorter-term program outcomes may be weakly (and even negatively) correlated with program effects over time. We used the NJS data to compute program outcomes as far out (or after program termination) as possible, without losing substantial numbers of data points that would have compromised our examination of the variation in site-level outcomes. Our outcome measures fall between program outcomes at termination and average long-term effects analyzed by these researchers and do not compare with the experimentally estimated effects, which are constructed using control groups and do not produce individual-level estimates.

Finally, despite the success of our models in identifying significant variables at both individual and site levels, the power of these models in explaining individual outcomes is still not especially high. As we noted earlier, this result is to be expected when working with individual-level data and a relatively limited array of client characteristics, compared with all the potential intervening factors when examining outcomes in a period *after participation in the program*. These same challenges are typically encountered in evaluating individual-level outcomes for other social programs, including other training programs, welfare-to-work initiatives, and drug abuse treatment programs. We have no reason to believe that these unobserved characteristics are correlated with observed structural and management variables, and therefore, that our estimates are necessarily biased. We believe we can be confident in the mean effects of results we have presented but not, of course, in the effects for any particular individual at any particular site.

References

Barnow, Burt. January 1999. Exploring the relationship between performance management and program impact: A case study of the Job Training Partnership Act. Working paper. John Hopkins University Institute for Policy Studies.

Bryk, Anthony, and Stephen Raudenbush. 1992. *Hierarchical linear models: Applications and data analysis methods.* London: Sage.

Courty, Pascal, and Gerald Marschke. January 1997. Empirical investigation of gaming responses to performance incentives. Working paper. Department of Economics, University of Chicago.

Cragg, Michael. April 1997. Performance incentives in the public sector: Evidence from the Job Training Partnership Act. *Journal of Law, Economics, and Organization,* 13: 147–68.

Dickinson, Katherine, Richard West, Deborah Kogan, David Drury, Marlene Franks, Laura Schlichtmann, and Mary Vencill. 1988. *Evaluation of the effects of JTPA performance standards on clients, services, and costs.* Report no. 88-17. Washington, D.C.: National Commission for Employment Policy Research.

Heckman, James, Carolyn Heinrich, and Jeffrey Smith. May 1997. Assessing the performance of performance standards in public bureaucracies. *American Economic Review,* 87: 389–96.

Heckman, James, Robert LaLonde, and Jeffrey Smith. 2000. The economics of econometrics and active labor market programs. In *The handbook of labor economics,* vol. 3, edited by Orley Ashenfelter and David Card. Amsterdam: Elsevier Science Publishing Company.

Heckman, James, and Jeffrey Smith. 1995a. The determinants of participation in a social program: Evidence from JTPA. Unpublished paper, Department of Economics, University of Chicago.

————. 1995b. The performance of performance standards: The effects of JTPA performance standards on efficiency, equity, and participant outcomes. Unpublished paper, Department of Economics, University of Chicago.

Heckman, James, Jeffrey Smith, and Christopher Taber. 1996. What do bureaucrats do? The effects of performance standards and bureaucratic preferences on acceptance into the JTPA program. In *Advances in the study of entrepreneurship, innovation, and economic growth,* vol. 7: *Reinventing government and the problem of bureaucracy,* edited by Gary D. Libecap. Greenwich, Conn.: JAI Press, pp. 191–217.

Heinrich, Carolyn. October 1998. Aiding welfare-to-work transitions: Lessons from JTPA on the cost-effectiveness of education and training services. Working paper no. 3. University of Chicago and Northwestern University, Joint Center for Poverty Research.

————. 1999. Do government bureaucrats make effective use of performance management information? *Journal of Public Administration Research and Theory,* 9 (3): 363–93.

————. Forthcoming. The role of performance standards in JTPA program administration and service delivery at the local level. In *Performance standards in a government bureaucracy: Analytical essays on the JTPA performance standards system,* edited by James J. Heckman. Kalamazoo, Mich.: W. E. Upjohn Institute.

Jennings, Edward. 1994. Building bridges in the intergovernmental arena: Coordinating employment and training programs in the American states. *Public Administration Review,* 54 (1): 52–60.

Jennings, Edward, and J. Ewalt. 1998. Interorganizational coordination, administrative consolidation, and policy performance. *Public Administration Review,* 58 (5): 417–28.

Meyer, John, W. Richard Scott, and David Strang. 1987. Centralization and school district complexity. *Administrative Science Quarterly,* 32: 186–201.

Miller, Gary. 1992. *Managerial dilemmas: The political economy of hierarchy.* New York: Cambridge University Press.

Milward, H. Brinton, and Keith Provan. 1998. Governing service pro-
    vider networks. Paper presented at EGOS 14th colloquium, Maas-
    tricht University, The Netherlands.
Orfield, Gary, and Helene Slessarev. 1986. *Job training under the new
    federalism: JTPA in the industrial heartland.* Report to the Subcom-
    mittee on Employment Opportunities, Committee on Education and
    Labor, U.S. House of Representatives.
Orr, Larry, Howard Bloom, Stephen Bell, Winston Lin, George Cave, and
    Fred Doolittle. 1994. *The National JTPA Study: Impacts, benefits, and
    costs of Title II-A programs.* Bethesda, Md: Abt Associates Inc.

Endnotes

*The research for this chapter was funded by a grant from the Pew
Charitable Trusts.

1. The JTPA program operated under its authorizing legislation
    through 1999. Since that time it has been administered under the
    authority of the Workforce Investment Act of 1998, although the
    program administrative structures will remain largely the same.
2. Sections 141(c) and 106 (a), The Job Training Partnership Act,
    Public Law 97-300, October 13, 1982.
3. Funding for Title IIA at its peak reached $2 billion. One-third of
    the funds received by states depends on the relative number of un-
    employed individuals in the state, another one-third depends on
    the relative excess (defined as over 4.5%) number of unemployed
    individuals, and the final one-third depends on the number of eco-
    nomically disadvantaged persons (as defined by the act.)
4. The private sector's involvement in federal job-training programs
    increased during the 1970s and was made formal by the 1978
    CETA Reauthorization Act, which established the Private Sector
    Initiatives Program that eventually evolved into the Private In-
    dustry Councils. The Workforce Investment Act of 1998 gives the
    PICs a new name—Workforce Investment Boards—and maintains
    the private-sector majority in the composition of these entities.
5. In 1988 USDOL changed these performance standards to mea-
    sures of post-program outcomes (i.e., employment and earnings
    outcomes evaluated three months after participants' termination
    from the program) and discontinued its use of cost standards.
6. Section 141(c), The Job Training Partnership Act, Public Law
    97-300, October 13, 1982.
7. Bryk and Raudenbush (1992) describe in further detail the ad-
    vantages of using hierarchical linear modeling techniques over

ordinary least squares methods when data are hierarchically structured.

8. We follow the terminology of Bryk and Raudenbush (1992) to make it easier for our readers to refer back to this book for additional information on HLM methods. We do not center our data as they do in their examples, as the nature of our data suggests that using the "natural X metric," or raw data, is most appropriate.

9. Among the sixteen local JTPA sites in our study, when the PIC was the administrative entity, in all but one of these cases it was also the grant recipient.

10. Politics undoubtedly influence JTPA structural and administrative arrangements. Political variables are unlikely to influence systematically our dependent variables, however. Thus we believe our coefficient estimates are unbiased (although we cannot test this directly).

Appendix A
Description of Data Sources

1. National JTPA Study (NJS)

The U.S. Department of Labor commissioned the National JTPA Study in 1986, fulfilling a congressional mandate that required a study of the effectiveness of programs operating under the Job Training Partnership Act of 1982. Sixteen local service delivery areas (SDAs) agreed to participate in the study, which included both experimental and nonexperimental evaluation components. (See appendix B for the names of the sixteen sites.) Data were collected during the three-year study (beginning in November 1987 and continuing through September 1989), through random assignment of JTPA applicants to "treatment" and "control" groups. Treatment group members were allowed access to JTPA program services, while control group members were prohibited from enrolling in the program for a period of eighteen months after random assignment. Approximately 20,000 treatment and control group members, who applied to Title IIA adult or youth programs, were included in the study. In our research, we focused on the 9,621 JTPA participants who were treatment group members in the NJS. The Manpower Demonstration Research Corporation (MDRC), Abt Associates Inc., and their subcontractors, including the National Opinion Research Center (NORC), conducted the evaluation.

2. Training service plans of the sixteen NJS sites for program years 1987–89

All JTPA administrative entities are required to prepare annual training service plans that document: (1) the composition of the Private Industry Council (PIC), (2) the structure of the administrative entity and its service delivery arrangements, (3) the types of program services that will be offered and anticipated wage and employment outcomes of the training recipients, (4) the types of supportive services that will be made available, (5) coordination agreements with other government, nonprofit and for-profit organizations, (6) performance monitoring plans, and (7) basic information on budget allocations. The SDA's administrative structure is documented through formal, signed agreements that specify the relationships between the PIC and CEO or LEO, the designated administrative entity, and the grant recipient. We used the information contained in these agreements to create our variables that describe the organizational structure of the sixteen NJS service delivery areas.

3. Performance incentive policy documentation from the sixteen NJS sites

Detailed information was collected directly from the sixteen NJS sites on the performance incentives policies adopted in the states in which they operated, as well as the performance incentive policies they implemented at the local level. The state-level performance incentive policy information was verified by comparing it with data in the JTPA Annual Status Report (JASR) data system. The local-level performance incentive policy information was also confirmed through copies of policy documentation and interviews with program administrators at the sites. These data were coded and combined into a single database.

Appendix B
Description of Variables Included in Empirical Models

Variables[a]	Mean	Standard deviation
Demographic Characteristics		
Gender (male)	0.363	N.A.[b]
Age 22–29	0.302	N.A.
Age 30–39	0.246	N.A.
Over age 40	0.122	N.A.
Black	0.263	N.A.
Hispanic	0.160	N.A.
Divorced, widowed, or separated	0.253	N.A.
High school dropout	0.448	N.A.
Post high school education	0.153	N.A.
Employment → unemployment transition in preprogram year	0.627	N.A.
Welfare recipient	0.518	N.A.
Parent of child(ren) under age 6	0.260	N.A.
Earning Employment Histories		
Gross earnings in preprogram year ($)	2485.87	3895.46
Zero earnings in preprogram year	0.336	N.A.
Treatment Training Services Received		
Received classroom training	0.668	N.A.
Received on-the-job training	0.147	N.A.
Earnings and Employment Outcomes		
Earnings in first postprogram quarter ($)	1767.63	2058.26
Earnings in first postprogram year ($)	7076.69	7428.53
Employed 3 months after program termination	0.598	N.A.
Employed 12 months after program termination	0.623	N.A.
Regional and Economic Indicators		
South	0.250	N.A.
West	0.250	N.A.
Midwest	0.313	N.A.
Unemployed rate	0.064	N.A.
Service Delivery Area Structure Management Polices		
PIC is the administrative entity	0.458	N.A.
PIC and CEO/LEO share administrative and authority equally	0.583	N.A.
Percent of services provided directly by the administrative entity	0.280	N.A.
Percent of performance-based contracts	0.233	N.A.
Minimum number of standards an SDA must meet to qualify for performance bonuses	4.479	2.744

continued on next page

Variables[a]	Mean	Standard deviation
Administrative entity required to use performance bonuses in service to hard-to-serve groups	0.313	N.A.
Weight accorded entered employment rate standard	0.118	0.052

[a] Values based on observations of 9,621 JTPA participants; see next page
[b] N.A., Not applicable

Total participants

Eastern sites	
Jersey City, New Jersey	806
Providence, Rhode Island	763
Marion, Ohio	629
Southern sites	
Heartland, Florida	286
Coosa Valley, Georgia	786
Jackson, Mississippi	592
Corpus Christi, Texas	654
Midwestern sites	
Decatur, Illinois	256
Fort Wayne, Indiana	1,675
Northwest Minnesota	246
Cedar Rapids, Iowa	231
Springfield, Missouri	536
Omaha, Nebraska	698
Western sites	
Larimer County, Colorado	564
Oakland, California	582
Butte, Montana	317
All sites	9,621

Driving Caseloads Down: Welfare Policy Choices and Administrative Action in the States

Edward T. Jennings, Jr. and Jo Ann G. Ewalt

The Personal Responsibility and Work Opportunity Reconciliation Act (PRWORA) of 1996 eliminates the federal entitlement to welfare support. It replaces Aid to Families with Dependent Children (AFDC) with the Temporary Assistance for Needy Families (TANF) program. The name change symbolizes the central thrust of welfare policy change—assistance is to be temporary. Reflecting the dominant political majority's view that welfare had become dysfunctional, fostering dependency among the poor, the new law makes cash support a short-term measure to meet a family's needs until the head of the household can join the labor force and the family can support itself without public assistance.

There are two basic arguments about what will shape the outcomes of welfare reform. The policy design camp asserts that the end of welfare dependency can be brought about only by dramatic, broad, and deep changes in policy (Murray 1984; Mead 1997; Hayward 1998). When lawmakers, according to this school of thought, enact policies that reorient the system from one that encourages dependency to one that encourages self-sufficiency, behavior—of some type—will follow. According to another group of students of the welfare system, changes in policy will have little effect unless the culture of the welfare system changes. This is the administrative argument—what happens in welfare reform will be determined by the actions of administrators and street-level bureaucrats (Nathan

1993; Meyers, Glaser, and MacDonald 1998). Administrators can set the tone, provide direction, and use the tools of control to shape action at the street level. They can send the message, but case managers and service providers have to follow through on that message.

Our analysis incorporates these two schools of thought and assesses the relative impact of policy choices and administrative action. Whether implementation works depends on the policy choices made by states, the commitment of administrators to reform, the goals established by state-level administrators, the steps they take to change the culture of state welfare agencies, and the behavior of case managers as they interact with recipients. Of course, outcomes are also likely shaped by contextual factors, such as the condition of the economy, the availability of jobs, the characteristics of recipients, and the availability of rich civic networks to aid the transformation.

We explore the translation of federal law into state action. We look at the policy choices of state officials, the priorities and goals of state assistance programs, the actions administrators take to implement reform, and the outcomes of those choices and actions. Our exploration is grounded in theories of policy implementation and studies of the implementation of earlier welfare reform initiatives.

In the first chapter, Lynn, Heinrich, and Hill suggest that the outcomes of public programs are potentially shaped by five sets of variables: environmental factors, client characteristics, treatments, structures, and managerial roles and actions. Our model of welfare reform implementation includes environmental, treatment, and managerial variables. We were less successful at capturing client or structural characteristics.

PRWORA and TANF

Public welfare (in this case, cash assistance in the form of AFDC) has been under attack for years. Critics believe that it fosters dependency and undermines important social values of work and family. As more women entered the workforce and more children were born to unwed mothers, criticism of the program escalated. On the one hand, it was hard to justify a program that allowed poor mothers to stay home with their children while other women went to work. On the other hand, despite a lack of conclusive findings about the effects of welfare on unwed pregnancies, the growth in the rolls paralleled a startling increase in unwed pregnancies.

States experimented with program variations throughout the 1980s and 1990s in search of approaches that would encourage education, discourage pregnancy (including unwed pregnancies) while receiving welfare, and encourage movement from dependency to work. Numerous accounts of those welfare-to-work experiments have documented differences between two reform approaches (Behn 1991; Mead 1997). The first could be called the human capital approach. This approach attempts to improve the employability of welfare recipients by shoring up their basic education, improving their literacy, helping those who need it acquire a high school equivalency degree, and providing skills training or vocational education. The basic idea is to improve the educational attainment of recipients so they have sufficient human capital to obtain and move ahead in self-supporting jobs.

In contrast to this is the work-first approach (Hayward 1998). Under this approach, clients are encouraged to take a job, whether it offers self-sufficiency or not. Recipients, it is argued, must accept responsibility for their own well-being and contribute to their family's needs. Advocates of this approach argue also that welfare recipients often had bad experiences with the educational system and had failed to achieve in the past. Thus by first having an opportunity to succeed at work, clients might subsequently seek out educational opportunities that would allow them to achieve still more.

Whatever the merits of the two approaches, work-first won out in the end. Conservative Republicans in Congress and the New Democrats in the White House agreed on a welfare reform plan that dramatically changed existing policy. They replaced AFDC, an entitlement program, with PRWORA and its TANF program—a block grant to states to support public assistance activities. The new program includes a number of incentives for states to move recipients off the rolls. It also includes a variety of restrictions, including time limits on the receipt of benefits. TANF is designed to encourage states to move recipients quickly into work. It sets sharp limits on the use of education and training as tools to move clients toward self-sufficiency.

In the two-and-a-half years since the adoption of PRWORA, welfare rolls have declined dramatically across the United States. This has led many advocates of reform to herald the success of the more stringent new approach (e.g., Hayward 1998). The family caseload declined by 34 percent from August 1996 to September 1998, falling from 4.4 million cases to just under 2.9 million cases. In some states, the decline was especially dramatic. Wisconsin, a leader in the new approach to welfare, saw its rolls plummet from 65,400 families to 10,200—a drop of 84 percent. Hawaii, on the other hand, saw a much more modest drop of 24 percent over that same period, from 22,100 cases to 16,700 cases. In fact, measured from January 1993, just before the rolls surged, Hawaii's family caseload had fallen only 7 percent by September 1998, while Wisconsin's plunged 87 percent.

What accounts for the overall dramatic decline? Can we attribute it to PRWORA? How do we account for the widespread variation among the states? We hope in this chapter to shed light on these questions.

States as Implementers

Different actors attribute different goals to PRWORA and TANF. Those that stand out most sharply are self-sufficiency for clients, a reduction in the welfare rolls, and reduced spending for welfare. When a group of midwestern officials sat down to discuss the goals of welfare reform, they suggested both short-term and long-term goals. These members of the Midwest Welfare Peer Assistance Network (WELPLAN 1998) determined that the short-term or immediate goals of reform are a decrease in welfare dependency and an increase in self-sufficiency, improved economic well-being for the recipients, and enhanced parental responsibility. Long-term or more indirect goals include improved child well-being, improved parent-adult well-being, stronger families, and community involvement.

Whether TANF can accomplish this complex array of goals, or any subset of these goals, depends on the actions that states take to implement the program. States will make policy choices and undertake administrative actions to execute those choices. Despite its focus on a more restrictive welfare agenda, PRWORA grants considerable flexibility to states. As with AFDC, states determine benefit levels in the TANF program. Within the limits of federal policy, they can choose to be more or less restrictive in the way they treat clients. State officials decide how they will move clients off welfare and meet the participation and time-limit requirements put in place by the legislation. Thus there is much potential for interstate variation in the TANF program.

In designing their TANF programs, states find that one set of policy choices they face relates to program eligibility and benefits, time limits, and work requirements (Gallagher et al. 1998). In addition, of course, states can set varying payment levels for dependent families. As they make decisions regarding these matters, states make their programs more or less restrictive. The choices make it either easier or more difficult for participants to continue to receive cash assistance. The choices include the following:

- the level of assets a family can have while remaining eligible for assistance;
- the level of income a family can have while qualifying for assistance;
- diversion assistance payments to avoid placing recipients on welfare;
- eligibility for two-parent families;
- time limits on benefits;
- work exemptions based on the age of the youngest child;
- sanctions for failing to comply with work requirements;
- length of time at which work requirements are imposed;
- earnings disregards, or the amount clients can earn while receiving cash benefits;
- family caps, or limits on benefits for children born while a family is receiving assistance; and
- child support pass-through (giving child support payments to custodial parents or passing all or some of the funds on to the state).[1]

These restrictions are the focus of our analysis. We want to understand the consequences of state policy choices. In terms of the concepts identified in the Lynn, Heinrich, Hill chapter, these are the treatments of the program. We also want to understand what mediates between these policy choices and the ultimate outcome of the program. Our theoretical assumption is that policy design and the administration of welfare are critical forces in the transformation of policy into outcome.

Theory of Policy Impact

Although the restrictiveness of policy is likely to be a critical feature of state implementation of TANF, it alone is not likely to determine the outcomes. Whatever the policy choices of state officials, those choices must be translated into action. As numerous implementation studies have demonstrated, there is often a considerable gap between policy choices and policy outcomes (Pressman and Wildavsky 1984; Bardach 1977; Goggin et al. 1990; Matland 1995). The translation of policy choices into administrative actions is seldom automatic. In the welfare arena, it is often a substantial challenge (Meyers, Glaser, and MacDonald 1998). Administrators must interpret policy. As they do so, they establish goals, priorities, and theories of action. Those, in turn, shape their behavior. Critical to policy success is administrative commitment to the goals of policy. In the welfare arena, this is easy enough to see. If welfare administrators are not committed to the new regime, they are unlikely to take forceful and effective action to translate policy into outcomes.

Commitment alone is insufficient. For commitment to affect outcomes, administrative leaders must convert it into organizational action. They must communicate policy goals and objectives, priorities, and desired actions down through the organization. They must convince those at the service delivery level to commit to the policy goals and effectively pursue them. Thus they must transform the culture of the organization. To do this, they can take advantage of sanctions, incentives, training, and education directed toward the staff who directly implement the program.

As we think about that challenge of implementing welfare reform and the factors that affect outcomes in the states, we are drawn to theories of policy implementation and welfare culture. The two traditions overlap, with implementation theories identifying a broad range of factors that shape policy effects and welfare culture theory drawing attention to the welfare office and its role in program administration. As Matland (1995) points out in his recent review of implementation studies, diverse approaches characterize the literature (Bardach 1977; Elmore 1982; Goggin et al. 1990; Sabatier and Mazmanian 1979; Van Meter and Van Horn 1975; Hjern 1982). Scholars have identified an almost endless array of factors that can affect program implementation. O'Toole (1986), for example, recorded more than 300 variables that had been identified in different studies.

There is more order than this diversity suggests, however. Scholars have identified two contrasting general orientations: top-down and bottom-up (Matland 1995; Sabatier 1986; Goggin et al. 1990). The top-down orientation emphasizes implementation as viewed by hierarchical superiors. It sees the key implementation issue as the extent to which policy implementation mirrors the goals and preferences of authoritative decision makers. Implementation is seen as shaped by policy design and the actions of principals to enforce compliance. Success is defined as correspondence between goals defined at the top and actions taken in the field. The bottom-up perspective views implementation from the orientation of the field. If we want to understand implementation, we have to understand "the view of the target population and the service deliverers" (Matland 1995, p. 148). From this viewpoint, hierarchical superiors have limited control over what actually happens in policy implementation. Furthermore, it is legitimate and appropriate for policy targets and service providers to turn policy to their own ends.

We draw from this the lesson that the designs of policymakers in Washington or in state capitals are only part of what will affect the outcome of welfare reform in the field. This is consistent with studies of organizational culture in welfare reform, which have found that the actions of case managers and service providers are critical determinants of the outcomes of reform (Meyers, Glaser, and MacDonald 1998; Corbett 1994; Pavetti and Duke 1998; Ewalt 1998). Ewalt frames the issue this way: "There exists within the social work profession a code of ethics grounded in the belief that the proper role of the social work profession is to see to it that—at the very least—recipients get all of the resources to which they are entitled. To the extent that this may conflict with policy reforms which emphasize work over income maintenance, and more recently focus on work rather than education, it is not surprising that over the past few years talk has turned to 'reforming the culture of welfare'" (pp. 98–99).

Meyers and her colleagues (1998) found in a study of California's Work Pays demonstration program of the early 1990s that policy reforms were not fully implemented by street-level bureaucrats. Caseworkers continued to focus on claims processing and allocating resources to clients. This emphasis was poorly aligned with the new policies aimed at changing the services and message delivered to the clients. In contrast, Corbett's (1994) study of three Job Opportunities and Basic Skills (JOBS) programs that succeeded in changing the behavior of both clients and caseworkers found two things to be critical: changes in institutional structure to emphasize the importance of work and continuous messages to caseworkers that work outcomes were to be the major force moving the program.

This kind of change at the service delivery level depends heavily on administrative leadership. In fact, several studies have suggested that administrative action is critical to the success of welfare reform. Behn (1991), Nathan (1993), Mead (1996), and Meyers and her colleagues (1998) have pointed out the critical role of managers who can marshal resources, project a vision of change, guide administrative systems, and provide leadership in the transformation of welfare systems. Corbett (1994), Meyers, Glaser, and MacDonald (1998), Lurie (1996), and Ewalt (1998) have indicated the importance of the local welfare office culture in pursuing new approaches to welfare. Brodkin (1995) has pointed out the critical role of administrative capacity.

Implementation, however, is seldom solely a matter of administrative action. Matland (1995) points out that the character of policy implementation is shaped by the degree of ambiguity and the degree of conflict. In addition, policy design and the political and social environment in which it is implemented shape policy outcomes. The economic environment, for example, is likely to be critical to the success of welfare reform. Significant declines in unemployment levels have accompanied the dramatic drop in welfare rolls nationally in the mid- to late 1990s. We could reasonably expect interstate variations in employment opportunities to affect interstate variations in welfare roll reductions.

The implementation literature, then, draws attention to policy design, political and social environment, economic context, characteristics of the target population, and administrative action as key factors shaping policy success. These are, in effect, the treatment, environmental, and managerial roles and actions variables noted in the introduction. The success of policy depends on the goals and priorities administrators establish, the actions they take, and the response of policy targets. Mediating the link between policy design and executive action, on the one hand, and target response, on the other, is the behavior of service providers. If a top-down perspective is to work (and welfare reform is certainly top down in orientation), then steps must be taken to transform organizational cultures in the field, where the action takes place. It is a classic principal-agent problem (Moe 1984).

Thus we begin with the hypothesis that the decline in welfare under TANF is a function of the restrictiveness of state policies. Those states that adopt more stringent controls should see their rolls decline more. That basic relationship, however, should be mediated by the commitment of implementers and the actions they take to implement the new policies. The communications perspective of Goggin and his colleagues (1990) informs us, for example, that the link between policy and implementation success depends on successful communication of policy goals and objectives. As we look at the array of findings from implementation studies, we hypothesize that several factors will critically affect the link between policy choices and policy outcomes. These factors are the goals and objectives established by administrators, the actions they take to pursue the goals and objectives, and their efforts to establish a new culture in the organization.

Because the outcomes of welfare reform will turn on such a complex array of factors, we cannot hope to analyze everything. Instead, we adopt a selective approach, focusing on three critical dimensions of reform implementation: the fit between policy choices and administrative goals, the fit between administrative goals and organizational processes, and the fit between administrative actions and policy outcomes. Our assumption is that goal-setting at the state level must be translated into action at the local level. There are a number of steps administrators can take to accomplish this. Crucial to implementing more restrictive welfare policy that seeks to reduce the welfare rolls is the creation of a new culture in the welfare bureaucracy. Communicating that culture is one of the most important steps administrators can take to make it a reality.

Four general hypotheses about the implementation of welfare reform guide our analysis:

H1   Policy design affects outcomes. In particular, more stringent state policy designs lead to greater reductions in the welfare rolls.

H2   The fit of administrative goals with policy design affects outcomes. When administrative goals emphasize priorities aimed at reducing the rolls, the rolls are more likely to decrease.

H3   The reduction in rolls depends on administrative strategies and actions. When strategies and actions are consistent with a work-first philosophy and restrictive policy choices, there will be a greater decline in the rolls.

H4   Promoting a work-first culture in the organization will lead to greater reductions in the rolls. State agencies that try to promote the work-first philosophy to their local agents will see greater reductions in the rolls.

Two classes of variables identified by Lynn, Heinrich, and Hill as factors shaping policy performance are not included in our analysis. We lack information on client characteristics, something that clearly could influence outcomes. We also lack information on structural variations among the states. Under ideal conditions, we would have information about these aspects of the structure of the program.

Study Design

This study proceeds in three phases. First, we examine state TANF administrators' perceptions of the importance of various goals, objectives, and activities to their welfare reform programs. Next, we examine the relationships between state policy choices and state policy goals, between goals and strategies and action, and between each of these and caseload reductions. Our aim is to identify those goals and strategies that mediate between policy choices and outcomes. Finally, we present a multivariate model of program outcome, with percent of caseload reductions as the dependent variable, using as explanatory variables state policy restrictiveness, goals, strategies, and administrative actions.

Although much data exists on welfare caseload levels and state program provisions, little is known about the goals, strategies, and administrative activities of state TANF agencies. To study empirically the relationships among caseload reductions, the policy priorities of the states, and the actions administrators are taking to implement TANF, we have cooperated with the Council of State Governments in a survey of state government administrators. The survey, conducted between June 1998 and January 1999, asked TANF administrators to rate the importance that their state places on specific goals for welfare reform, management strategies to implement welfare reform, and administrative activities necessary to implement TANF. Forty-four states responded to the survey (88 percent return rate).[2]

An important focus of the survey was the attempt to gauge state efforts to alter the culture of the welfare office. We provided TANF administrators with policy options that reflect institutional culture change and that have theoretical links to successful reform implementation. In addition, we provided a number of policy options that reflect a commitment to human capital models of welfare programs (e.g., concern for clients' financial well-being and increasing opportunities for remedial education). We expect states that emphasize such policies will be less likely to focus strongly on culture change and will be less successful in reducing welfare rolls, at least in the short term.

In addition to our survey, we draw on several other sources of information. The Urban Institute has compiled information about state TANF plans, including the variety of policy choices states have made with respect to TANF. We use that information to categorize state actions as more or less restrictive. We use data on the social and economic characteristics of the states from U.S. Bureau of the Census publications and web sites. We also use information on state caseloads from the Internet site of the Administration for Children and Families of the U.S. Department of Health and Human Services.

State Goals

Patton and Sawicki (1993, p. 187) define policy goals as "formally and broadly worded statements about what we desire to achieve in the long run." The statutory language of PRWORA provides goals for the TANF program. Among these are ending adult clients' dependence on government benefits by promoting job preparation, work, and marriage; preventing and reducing the incidence of out-of-wedlock pregnancies; and encouraging the formation and maintenance of two-parent families. Building on the law's explicit goals, as well as those implied by the act, state TANF administrators were asked to rate the importance of the following program goals:

- Changing the attitudes of clients
- Self-sufficiency for clients
- Changing the behavior of clients
- Avoiding penalties for failing to meet federal participation guidelines

- Reducing teen pregnancy
- Addressing recipients' financial needs
- Helping clients find jobs that pay a living wage
- Monitoring former recipients' status
- Reducing the welfare rolls
- Reducing welfare expenditures
- Earning federal bonus payments for placing recipients in unsubsidized work
- Earning federal bonus payments for reducing out-of-wedlock births

Implementation Strategies

The welfare reform literature points to a number of strategies that should be linked to successful efforts to reduce the level of welfare dependency in a state. Among these are efforts to address administrative needs, clients' transitional needs, and office culture (including offering incentives and setting performance standards). State welfare administrators were asked to rate the importance of these strategies in implementing welfare reform. We expect that through their emphasis on these program elements, TANF administrators will demonstrate commitment to welfare reform goals. As noted previously, we also included strategies that support the human capital model so that we could compare states' relative emphasis on welfare reform and traditional welfare services. The strategies are as follows:

- Provide transitional child care
- Provide transitional health care
- Change attitudes of welfare staff
- Develop effective coordination among agencies
- Enhance relations with private-sector employers
- Work with legislature on implementing laws
- Enhance transportation assistance
- Change the way clients are processed
- Set performance standards for employment training providers
- Develop employment opportunities for clients
- Improve client assessment protocols
- Improve job placement skills of staff
- Reconfigure or install database

- Improve job training
- Enhance local welfare office autonomy
- Improve remedial education
- Pursue new opportunities to contract out services
- Develop incentives for staff to increase job placement rates

Administrative Activities

Commitment to policy goals must be linked to specific organizational activities if the goals are to be achieved. Although the distinction between the strategies described above and administrative activities is a subtle one, the primary thrust of the administrative activities is a very specific and immediate action (telling clients that welfare is about work and not about benefits, for example), rather than a longer term programmatic change (such as enhancing relations with private-sector employers). Administrative activities include those designed to communicate the goals and strategies to staff and to translate goals into desired outcomes. TANF administrators were presented thirty-six specific activities relating to (1) an emphasis on new work expectations for clients; (2) efforts to change office culture; and (3) administrative changes suggested by new client expectations and office culture issues. The activities falling under each activity include the following:

Emphasis on new client expectations for work
- Set realistic self-sufficiency plans
- Monitor clients' work activities more closely
- Immerse in work immediately
- Say welfare is about work, not benefits
- Change first client contact
- Enforce strict sanctions
- Target all clients for work
- Increase scrutiny of applications
- Reward clients who retain employment

Efforts to change office culture
- Redefine staff roles
- Maintain ongoing communication with staff about policy implementation
- Allow special training for managers

- Change procedures for processing clients
- Reorient front-line workers from eligibility to case management
- Get governor's public support
- Set new performance expectations for staff
- Offer special staff training—interacting with clients to emphasize work
- Produce special promotional materials for local offices
- Offer special staff training—overcoming clients' barriers to work
- Conduct regular staff meetings to develop staff support
- Produce informational memos and brochures for staff on policy goals
- Identify specific outcomes for each welfare office
- Reward staff successful in placing clients in work
- Set explicit goals for job-placement rates for staff
- Make public service announcements about welfare reform
- Redesign work space for "up front" emphasis on work

Administrative actions to support work emphasis and change in office culture
- Engage in ongoing communication with service providers regarding policy goals
- Set performance standards for employment and training service providers
- Maintain ongoing communication with staff regarding caseload
- Monitor clients who move off welfare
- Maintain ongoing communication with service providers regarding caseload
- Collect child well-being indicators
- Reward service providers whose clients retain employment
- Locate welfare staff and service providers in close proximity to each other
- Contract out case management
- Contract out data and records system

State Welfare Program Provisions

States vary considerably in the choices they have made for TANF policy. Building on the Urban Institute data on state programs

(Gallagher et al. 1998), we identified twenty choices that, considered together, represent state programmatic decisions. We divided these variables into stringent and nonstringent categories.[3] We then added the scores for the twenty program decisions to obtain a score of relative state program stringency or restrictiveness. Stringency involves the degree of restriction that the policy choice places on clients. We then examined states' restrictiveness scores in relation to their emphasis of various policy goals, strategies, and implementation activities.

Policy Outcomes

Ultimately, the most important questions about public policy implementation relate to program effects. There are numerous possible effects or outcomes of welfare reform that one could study. We focus on reductions in the rolls for four reasons: (1) the size of the welfare system and the number of people on the rolls were key targets of much of the welfare reform movement; (2) many of the reforms (e.g., time limits, work requirements) are clearly designed to reduce the rolls; (3) achieving other welfare reform goals, such as self-sufficiency, is likely to lead to reductions in the rolls; and (4) it is the one outcome measure for which data are currently available for the fifty states.

We use data on state caseloads from the Administration for Children and Families of the U.S. Department of Health and Human Services to examine the extent to which percentage reductions in caseload levels from January 1996 to June 1998 are linked to the goals, objectives, and administrative activities of state TANF directors and the programmatic choices of state welfare plans.

Findings

We first report on the goals, objectives, and activities TANF administrators find most important to welfare reform in their state. The relative emphasis welfare directors place on these implementation elements is then linked to both caseload reductions and state welfare program provisions. Finally, the contributions of programmatic features and program goals, strategies, and activities are analyzed in a multivariate model of welfare program outcome.

State TANF Goals, Strategies, and Activities

Most respondents believed all goals were at least somewhat applicable to their reform efforts. TANF administrators vary, however, in the relative importance they attributed to the goals.[4] Three goals emerge for almost all of the administrators as critical or very important for state reform: changing the attitudes of clients; clients achieving self-sufficiency; and changing the behavior of clients. These are consistent with the thrust of the new welfare, which uses a set of incentives, sanctions, and support services to move clients toward self-sufficiency. Also ranked as critical or very important by three-fourths of administrators is avoiding penalties for failure to meet federal participation requirements. Given the priority with which PRWORA treats the teen pregnancy issue, it is interesting that although most respondents say reducing teen pregnancy is an important goal, over a quarter of them do not emphasize it highly.

Two long-cherished goals of welfare reform fare relatively poorly. Only 66 percent of respondents emphasize ensuring that recipients' financial needs are met or helping recipients find jobs that pay a "living wage." Although the only way to know whether welfare reform is enhancing the well-being of clients is to monitor their progress once they leave the rolls, only 57 percent of TANF directors say monitoring clients is an important goal of welfare reform in their state. Thus the financial needs of clients do not receive the same level of attention as efforts to change the clients. This fits with the thrust of contemporary reform.

Despite some variation, what we find most striking in these results is the widespread support for the central theory of contemporary welfare reform: self-sufficiency brought about by changes in the attitudes and behavior of recipients. Among administrators, the view that the goal of welfare reform is to reduce the size of the welfare system receives only moderate support. It is not perceived as the primary goal of reform, even though many reformers clearly had that as a primary goal.

Among reform strategies, transitional child care and health care are viewed by all administrators as critical to the success of welfare reform. This is in keeping with expectations that clients moving from welfare to work are entering low-wage jobs that generally provide little or no health insurance or other "family friendly" support services. On the other hand, fewer than three-quarters of TANF directors say enhancing transportation assistance for clients is a priority. Almost all TANF directors report strong support for changing the attitudes of their staff. Other objectives designed to address office culture receive considerably less emphasis. Changing the way clients are processed is rated as important by 73 percent of directors, improving staff job-placement skills is a priority for 59 percent, while enhancing local autonomy[5] and developing incentives for staff to increase job-placement rates are emphasized by only 46 percent and 21 percent of respondents, respectively.

Reflecting the demand that welfare reform has created for agencies to work together, 91 percent of TANF administrators say developing effective coordination among agencies is critical to reform efforts. Because the preferred outcome of welfare reform is moving from welfare to unsubsidized employment, it is also not surprising that 89 percent of administrators say enhancing relations with private-sector employers is a top priority. However, only 70 percent of administrators emphasize staff development of employment opportunities for clients. Of course, this could be because unemployment is quite low and jobs are relatively easy to find in most settings.

Improving job training and remedial education services—two mainstays of the human capital model—receive limited emphasis by TANF directors. Nor are large majorities of administrators emphasizing better client assessment protocols, perhaps because the new theory of welfare constrains both the time clients can spend in the program and the services they can receive. In fact, it is somewhat surprising that these objectives receive the level of support they do given that PRWORA clearly discourages education and emphasizes work.

Administrators also rated the importance that various activities related to emphasizing work and to office culture play in state welfare reform efforts. Turning first to the importance TANF directors place on activities designed to emphasize client work, we see that the most interesting findings involve those actions that receive the least emphasis. Rewards to clients for maintaining employment are not supported. Targeting all clients for work also appears to gain more support in the literature than in practice. In addition, administrators report that they do not believe increasing the scrutiny of applications for TANF benefits is a particularly critical activity. Although personal responsibility and accountability are recurring themes of welfare reform, almost 30 percent of administrators say strict enforcement of sanctions for noncompliance is not an important activity.

As might be expected given PRWORA's time limits and its focus on constraining education and training, the activity most often cited as critical is developing realistic self-sufficiency plans. Explicit messages about the need for work and lessening the emphasis on benefits are seen as important by 84 percent of TANF directors. On the other hand, administrators generally do not emphasize explicit job-placement goals for staff or desired outcomes for each welfare office. Although ongoing communication and special training about welfare reform policy are considered critical, more specialized sessions on overcoming client barriers or enhancing staff support for reform policy receive much less support. Over one-fourth of administrators do not report emphasizing setting new performance expectations for staff or for employment training for service providers. Administrators seem to be focused primarily on redefining staff roles, communication and training specific to new program policies, changing the procedure for dealing with clients (which implies a change in staff procedure as well), and reorienting front-line workers from eligibility to case management activity.

The literature on the culture of welfare suggests that contracting out is one way to implement culture change quickly, but very few administrators indicate contracting out is an important aspect of their state's reform. Co-location of welfare staff and service providers is also not widely supported. One-half of the administrators say monitoring former clients is important, while only 44 percent say collecting information on child well-being is a critical activity for welfare reform. Although this may reflect administrators' realistic assessment of the resources available for such tasks, it is a troublesome indication of the potential lack of valid evaluation data that practitioners and scholars will face.

Policy Goals, Strategies, and Program Choices

We have hypothesized that policy choices should be linked to the goals, strategies, and activities states emphasize. Table 4.1 examines these relationships. In particular, we expect that states with the most restrictive policy choices will be those that emphasize goals and strategies designed to move clients quickly off welfare and into

TABLE 4.1

Correlation coefficients of state policy goals with policy restrictiveness

State Welfare Reform Goals, Objectives, and Implementation Activities	Restrictiveness of State Policy
Goals	
Reduce welfare rolls	$-.28^a$
Reduce teen pregnancy	$.30^b$
Strategies	
Change attitudes of welfare staff	$.29^b$
Improve remedial education	$.38^c$
Work with legislature on implementing laws	$.34^b$
Implementation Activities	
Emphasis on client work	
Increase scrutiny of applications	$.30^a$
Changing Office Culture	
Redefine staff roles	$.25^a$
Governor's public support	$.25^a$
New performance expectations for staff	$.29^a$
Explicit job placement goals for staff	$.29^a$
Administrative Support – Work, Culture	
Co-locate staff and service providers	$.38^c$
Contract out data records system	$.30^b$

[a] Significant at .10.
[b] Significant at .05.
[c] Significant at .01.
N = 44. Cell entries are Pearson correlation coefficients.

work. We also expect that state strategies and implementation activities will be related to policy choices.

It appears that the importance that state administrators place on many of the goals, strategies, and activities is not related to a state's policy restrictiveness. For most of these items, there are no significant correlation coefficients. Two program goals relate to policy choices: support for reducing teen pregnancy is positively related to restrictiveness; and emphasis on reducing the size of welfare caseloads is negatively related to policy stringency. Earlier we noted widespread support for the central theory of contemporary welfare reform, that is, self-sufficiency brought about by changes in the attitudes and behavior of recipients. Thus because there was little variation in the broad program goals reported by administrators, it is not surprising that most goals are not closely linked to actual programmatic choices. It is interesting, however, that those administrators who explicitly emphasize a reduction in the welfare rolls are the ones whose states have instituted less stringent welfare policies.

Several strategies and activities designed to move clients into work expeditiously are moderately related to the welfare program decisions states have made. These include changing the attitudes of welfare staff, increasing the scrutiny of applications, redefining staff roles, co-locating welfare and service provider personnel, and setting new performance expectations and explicit job placement goals for staff. The governor's support for welfare reform is also positively related to program restrictiveness. Two items are a bit puzzling: Improving remedial education and contracting out data records systems are also moderately related to the restrictiveness of state policy. Again, states that have instituted programs that constrain client options may be facing a caseload that consists largely of the hardest to serve. For these clients, some sort of basic remedial education—although not supported by federal welfare legislation—may be seen as increasingly important. In addition, contracting out has often been considered a way to streamline administrative functions and increase efficiency. Those states with the most restrictive policies are most likely to look outside their welfare organizations for records management.

Although only a small number of administrative activities relate to restrictiveness of policy, we also sought to determine whether there are clusters of activities that might be important in understanding administrative response and policy outcomes. To assess this, we created two additive indices of welfare implementation activities. These indices were constructed using the activities that support a new emphasis on client work and that support efforts to change office culture. This step is important because we cannot include all of these activities as individual components in a multivariate model. Thus the indices conserve degrees of freedom while permitting us to assess the overall contribution that culture change and work emphasis make to caseload reductions. The Cronbach coefficient alpha for the index reflecting an emphasis on client work is 0.76; alpha for the index of activities to change office culture is 0.79.[6]

We first examined the correlations between percent reductions in family caseloads from January 1996 to January 1998 and state TANF

TABLE 4.2

Correlation coefficients of state welfare activities with state policies and caseload reductions

State Welfare Reform Activity Indices	State Policy Restrictiveness	Percent Reductions in State Caseloads, January 1996 to January 1998
Emphasis on client work	.16	.30[b]
Changing office culture	.27[a]	−.09

N=44. Cell entries are Pearson correlation coefficients.
[a] Significant at .10.
[b] Significant at .05.

directors' emphasis on welfare policy goals, strategies, and activities. None of the welfare reform goals or strategies is significantly correlated with caseload reductions, although a few are close. This is not unexpected given that TANF administrators reported that most goals were important to their programs.

We then turned to the relationship between caseload reductions, state policy choices, and our newly constructed measures of focus on client work and office culture change in order to duplicate the above analysis using these two indices. Table 4.2 reports the correlations of the client work and office culture indices with state policy and caseload reduction. The correlation between caseload reductions and the work index is 0.30, while the culture index is not significantly related to reductions in the caseload. An emphasis on changing the office culture is correlated with state policy restrictiveness at a level of 0.27. Although not reported in table 4.2, the two welfare activity indices—work and culture—are correlated at 0.51.

Policy Choices, Priorities, Actions, and Outcomes

Our ultimate interest, of course, is whether a combination of state policies, goals, and administrative actions affects outcomes. Thus the final phase of the analysis is a multivariate model of state outcomes. Drawing on relationships previously described, we estimate an ordinary least squares regression model of family caseload reductions as follows:

$$Y = \beta_0 + \beta_1 G + \beta_2 S + \beta_3 W + \beta_4 C + \beta_5 P + \beta_6 E + \varepsilon$$

where Y = percent reduction in family caseloads from January 1996 to June 1998; G = state goals; S = state strategies; W = implementation activities index emphasizing client work; C = implementation activities index emphasizing changing office culture; P = state policy decisions (the restrictiveness of state welfare programs); E = environmental factors (socioeconomic conditions in the state); and ε = an error term.

This model builds on our theoretical understanding of the effect of state policy design and implementation on policy outcome. As hypothesized earlier, we expect that more stringent welfare policy will lead to greater reductions in welfare rolls. When administrative goals and strategies emphasize work-first priorities, the rolls should be more likely to decline. Finally, we expect that states that use implementation activities to emphasize client work and to change the culture of the welfare office to promote work will experience greater caseload reductions.

We estimate two versions of this model. In one, we seek to remain true to the model and include state goals and strategies as well as the work and culture indices. The second estimation reflects an effort to find a better-fitting model, one that takes into account independent variables that have an effect on caseload declines while controlling for other factors, but that omits state goals. As noted, there is little variation in the support states give to various welfare implementation goals; thus these items are not very powerful contributors to caseload reduction. We include as a control variable in both models the percent of caseload reductions from January 1993 to January 1996, the period prior to TANF implementation. In addition, we look at several socioeconomic measures of the local environment. In preliminary analyses, we examined standard socioeconomic indicators for 1995, including median family income, poverty rate, percent of one-parent families, unemployment rate and female employment rate, percent minorities, percent of population living in metropolitan areas, percent of adults age 25 and older without a high school diploma, and gross state product. Most of these variables are not significant in the multivariate models.

Estimations included are by no means the only variable sets that could have been used. The two we present are selected for the relative strength of their explanatory power, as well as for the specific implementation tools they include. Depending on the variables used, different mixes of goals, strategies, and environmental con-

trols could have been included. As we will discuss shortly, however, several patterns emerge from the data analysis that remain
consistent regardless of the model specification. Table 4.3 provides
the ordinary least squares regression estimation of the contributions
of state policy, administrators' program goals, strategies, and work
and culture change activities to policy outcome.

The restrictiveness of state policy (our proxy for state policy
choices) is a strong influence on caseload reductions. In addition,
when state administrators emphasize the goal of changing client behavior, it has the effect of reducing the rolls. Similarly, placing a priority on developing employment opportunities is related to

TABLE 4.3

*OLS regression estimates of the impact of state welfare policy, goals, and
implementation activities on caseload reductions*

Variable	Regression Coefficient	Standardized Coefficient	Standard Error	*t* Statistic
Intercept	31.77	.000	15.834	2.006
Reductions in family caseloads 1993–1996	.12	.075	.183	.636
State policy choice ("restrictiveness")	2.78[a]	.499	.683	4.077
State goal: changing client behavior	11.20[b]	.222	5.946	1.884
State strategy: developing employment opportunities	10.41[c]	.297	4.123	2.525
State activities: changing office culture	−.88[a]	−.569	.217	−4.075
State activities: emphasis on client work	1.21[a]	.497	.311	3.877
1995 state median income	−.0006	−.194	.0003	−1.638

Dependent variable is percent reduction in family caseload. F = 6.824 (*p*=.000). Adj. R^2
= .49.
[a]Significant at .001.
[b]Significant at .10.
[c]Significant at .01.

caseload reductions. The two indices measuring administrative activities to change office culture and to emphasize work have significant but contrary effects. States that emphasize activities that promote client work report greater caseload reductions. However, states that place more importance on changing office culture experience smaller caseload reductions than do states where culture change is not reported to be an important activity. Of the control variables, median family income has a negative effect on caseload reductions.

This is consistent with many of our expectations, but there are some surprises. Policy choices make a difference, as do administrative priorities and actions. Conversely, an emphasis on changing the culture of the welfare office is inversely related to drops in the caseload. This finding is counterintuitive; the literature suggests that this activity should relate to stronger policy implementation. Perhaps the causal arrow actually runs in the opposite direction here. That is, states with modest caseload reductions may be those most concerned with the behavior of staff. An alternative explanation views this as a matter of focus. It is possible that agencies concerned with changing the culture of their offices are diverting their attention from clients. Because they focus on staff rather than clients, their efforts to move clients from the rolls suffer.

The level of previous caseload reductions has no effect. Although we might expect wealthier states to have greater capacity to move recipients toward self-sufficiency, that is not what has happened. The higher a state's median family income, the smaller the caseload reduction. Wisconsin is the dramatic exception, with one of the highest median income levels ($40,955) and highest caseload reductions (82.7%).[7] What this suggests is that the poorest states are most eager to reduce the rolls, reflecting historic patterns and political orientations. For example, median family income correlates at the 0.56 level with the 1997 Wright-Erikson-MacIver (1987) measure of state liberalism, with poorer states showing greater conservative ideology.

As noted, our second estimation of the model includes those variables that provide the greatest degree of explained variance. In fact, the estimation is very similar to the first equation, as can be seen in table 4.4. State policy led to a reduction in family caseloads from 1996 to 1998. That is, the more restrictive a state's welfare policy, the greater the reduction in the caseload. In addition, states that

TABLE 4.4

OLS regression estimates of the impact of state welfare policy, strategies, and implementation activities on caseload reductions

Variable	Regression Coefficient	Standardized Coefficient	Standard Error	*t* Statistic
Intercept	−.28	.000	13.195	−.021
Reductions in family caseloads 1993–1996	.11	.075	.176	.661
State policy choice ("restrictiveness")	2.50[a]	.448	.678	3.685
State strategy: developing employment opportunities	8.68[b]	.248	4.070	2.129
State strategy: changing way clients are processed	10.49[b]	.292	4.500	2.331
State activities: changing office culture	−1.09[a]	−.704	.226	−4.838
State activities: emphasis on client work	1.52[a]	.625	.325	4.661
Percent of adults without high school	.80[b]	.287	.330	2.415

Dependent variable is percent reduction in family caseload. $F = 7.376$ ($p = .000$). Adj. R^2 = .51.
[a]Significant at .001.
[b]Significant at .05.

placed greater emphasis on developing employment opportunities and on changing the way clients are processed had significantly greater reductions in family caseload.

As was the case in the first model, implementation activities are also significantly related to outcome. States that emphasize client work experienced greater caseload reductions, while states emphasizing culture change had significantly lower reductions in caseloads. Earlier caseload reductions are not significantly related to reduced rolls in either model. The greater a state's proportion of adults who lack high school degrees, the higher the reduction in the rolls. As we discussed with respect to median income, what this suggests is that states with the greatest strain on social services are those most eager to reduce the rolls.[8]

As in the first model, the standardized coefficients suggest that although policy choices are a very important influence on caseload reductions, state focus on changing office culture and emphasizing client work are the most important factors affecting caseload declines.[9] In both models, implementation goals, strategies, and environmental factors have roughly the same influence on caseload reduction.

Conclusion

We set out to examine how federal law is being translated into state action with respect to the implementation of TANF. In that context, we examined the policy choices states have made, the self-reported priorities and goals of state TANF administrators, the self-reported importance of specific activities to implement TANF, and the linkage choices, priorities, and goals and actions of policy outcomes. Our findings suggest that there are links among policies, goals, actions, and outcomes. Although the links are not as strong as they might be, we find evidence that the importance that administrators attach to clusters of administrative activities makes a difference. We draw attention to six general sets of findings.

- The link between state policy restrictiveness and administrative policy goals is weak. State program administrators have not developed policy goals that are consistent with the restrictiveness of state policy choices. In fact, there is a negative relationship between the restrictiveness of policy and the importance policymakers attach to reducing the rolls. In general, administrative goals do not seem to fit policy choices. This would align with other studies that have found that administrators do not appear to be acting in ways consistent with policy. This reflects, however, at least in part, widespread agreement on goals among state administrators.
- Variables do not cluster into neat sets of goals and strategies. We had expected that the priorities attached to goals would

show a clustering around certain items (e.g., reduction in rolls with reduction in expenditures), but this did occur. Nor did we find a clustering of items involving state strategies.

- Administrative activities reveal consistent patterns. There are consistent patterns in the degree to which state administrators emphasize activities focused on client work and changing office culture. This suggests that when we move beyond general statements about strategy and look at specific patterns of activity, states are developing consistent approaches to program outcome.
- The link between policy choices and outcomes is strong. Those states that have experienced the greatest reduction in their caseloads are those that have instituted the most restrictive policies. This supports the contention of some reformers that the key to welfare system change is the proper policy design.
- There is a systematic link between the importance that administrators attach to various types of administrative action and reductions in the caseloads. State activities that emphasize client work consistently are linked with reductions in the rolls. This fits with the fact that states in which administrators place priority on the goal of developing employment opportunities also experience welfare roll reductions in the multivariate models. Conversely, states in which administrators attach greater importance to changing the culture of the welfare office have smaller reductions in welfare rolls in the multivariate analysis.
- A model that incorporates policy design, administrative goals, and administrative actions explains about one-half of the variance in the reduction of caseloads among the states. Administrative activities make the most difference, followed closely by the restrictiveness of state policy.

We do not have data on many aspects of program design for the states. We do not know, for example, which procedures they have put in place to handle applicants and current recipients. Nor do we know how well state goals, priorities, and strategies have been transmitted to the service delivery level. Our measures are self-reported indications of administrators' emphasis on various program goals and strategies. For example, although we have tried to catalog the commitment of state administrators to change the culture of the welfare offices in their states, we have no information on whether that message has been received at the service delivery level. That suggests a logical next pathway for analysis. Moreover, to fully understand the impact of state policy choices, goals and priorities, implementation action, and administrative emphases on policy outcomes we must be able to measure the other important outcomes of TANF. Critical in this respect will be measuring client well-being. In that regard, the little emphasis states appear to be placing on collecting child well-being data and on monitoring clients who leave the rolls is disappointing.

In line with the conceptual framework offered by Lynn, Heinrich, and Hill in this volume, our analysis suggests that treatments, the environment, and managerial roles and actions all have some bearing on the outcomes of welfare reform. Consistent with their theme, we have provided a focus on the outcome of a program and have assessed the effects of multiple variables on this outcome. Although our analysis is unable to encompass client characteristics and important aspects of structure, it moves beyond a simple consideration of environment and policy to take into account the administrative milieu in which welfare reform is implemented. This is an important step for studies that purport to explain the outcomes of government policies.

References

Bardach, Eugene. 1977. *The implementation game: What happens when a bill becomes a law.* Cambridge, Mass.: MIT Press.

Behn, Robert. 1991. *Leadership counts: Lessons for public managers from the Massachusetts welfare, training, and employment program.* Cambridge, Mass.: Harvard University Press.

Brodkin, Evelyn Z. 1995. Administrative capacity and welfare reform. In *Looking before we leap: Social science and welfare reform,* edited by R. Kent Weaver and William T. Dickens. Washington, D.C.: Brookings Institution.

Cohen, Jacob, and Patricia Cohen. 1983. *Applied multiple regression/correlation analysis for the behavioral sciences.* 2d ed. Hillside, N.J.: Lawrence Erlbaum.

Corbett, Thomas. 1994. Changing the culture of welfare. *Focus,* 16 (Winter).

Elmore, Richard. 1982. Backward mapping: Implementation research and policy decisions. In *Studying Implementation,* edited by Walter Williams. New York: Chatham House.

Ewalt, Jo Ann Gomer. 1998. *An analysis of the Job Opportunities and Basic Skills Program in Kentucky: Determinants of component choice.* Dissertation. Lexington: University of Kentucky.

Gallagher, L. Jerome, Megan Gallagher, Kevin Perese, Susan Schreiber, and Keith Watson. March 1998. One year after federal welfare reform: A description of state Temporary Assistance for Needy Families (TANF) decisions as of October 1997. Preliminary edition. Washington, D.C.: The Urban Institute.

Goggin, Malcolm, Ann Bowman, James Lester, and Laurence O'Toole, Jr. 1990. *Implementation theory and practice: Toward a third generation.* New York: Harper Collins.

Hayward, Steven. 1998. The shocking success of welfare reform. *Policy Review,* 87 (January–February): 6–11.

Hjern, Benny. 1982. Implementation research—The link gone missing. *Journal of Public Policy,* 2 (3): 301–08.

Lurie, Irene. 1996. A lesson from the JOBS program: Reforming welfare must be both dazzling and dull. *Journal of Policy Analysis and Management,* 15 (Fall): 572–86.

Matland, Richard A. 1995. Synthesizing the implementation literature: The ambiguity-conflict model of policy implementation. *Journal of Public Administration Research and Theory,* 5 (April): 145–74.

Mead, Lawrence. 1996. Welfare policy: The administrative frontier. *Journal of Policy Analysis and Management,* 15 (Fall): 587–600.

———. 1997. Optimizing JOBS: Evaluation versus administration. *Public Administration Review,* 57 (March/April): 113–23.

Meyers, Marcia, Bonnie Glaser, and Karin MacDonald. 1998. On the front lines of welfare delivery: Are workers implementing policy reforms? *Journal of Policy Analysis and Management,* 17 (Winter): 1–22.

Moe, Terry M. 1984. The new economics of organization. *American Journal of Political Science,* 28 (February): 739–77.

Murray, Charles. 1984. *Losing ground: American social policy 1950 – 1980.* New York: Basic Books.

Nathan, Richard. 1993. *Turning promises into performance: The management challenge of implementing workfare.* New York: Columbia University Press.

O'Toole, Laurence, Jr. 1986. Policy recommendations for multi-actor implementation: An assessment of the field. *Journal of Public Policy,* 6 (2): 181–210.

Patton, Carl, and David Sawicki. 1993. *Basic methods of policy analysis and planning.* Englewood Cliffs, N.J.: Prentice-Hall.

Pavetti, LaDonna A., and Amy Ellen Duke. 1998. Increasing participation in work and work-related activities: Lessons from five state welfare reform demonstration projects. Washington, D.C.: The Urban Institute, <http:aspe.os.dhhs.gov/hsp/isp/15xs.htm>

Pressman, Jeffrey, and Aaron Wildavsky. 1984. *Implementation*. 3d edition. Berkeley: University of California Press.

Sabatier, Paul. 1986. Top-down and bottom-up approaches to implementation research: A critical analysis and suggested synthesis. *Journal of Public Policy,* 6 (1): 21–48.

Sabatier, Paul, and Daniel Mazmanian. 1979. The conditions of effective policy implementation: A guide to accomplishing policy objectives. *Policy Analysis,* 5: 481–504.

Van Meter, Donald, and Carl Van Horn. 1975. The policy implementation process: A conceptual framework. *Administration and Society,* 6: 445–88.

WELPLAN. January 1998. Welfare reform: How will we know if it works? Midwest Peer Assistance Network, Family Impact Seminar, Washington, D.C.

Wright, Gerald, Robert Erikson, and John MacIver. 1987. Public opinion and policy liberalism in the American states. *American Journal of Political Science,* 31 (November): 980–1001.

Endnotes

1. A description of the program choices states have made in implementing TANF, as well as summary statistics and coding decisions made in transforming several of these variables to binary data, is available from the authors.

2. States not included in the analysis are California, Hawaii, Massachusetts, New Hampshire, Oregon, and South Dakota. Between January 1996 and September 1998, these states had family caseload reductions of 27 percent, 24 percent, 31 percent, 39 percent, 50 percent, and 44 percent, respectively. The national average was 37 percent. Given that one-half of our missing states' caseload drops are below this level and one-half are above, we do not believe these missing data present serious nonresponse bias problems. The survey instrument is available from the authors.

3. Ibid.

4. TANF administrators' rankings of goals, objectives, and activities are available from the authors.

5. We did not distinguish those states with local control of welfare programs from those with a centralized administration. Thus it is likely that some states reported that increasing local autonomy is not important because the system is already under local management.

6. We attempted to construct indices for state welfare program goals and strategies, but the reliability of those measures was insufficient to justify using them.

7. Wisconsin was removed from the model to check for its influence. The results were essentially unchanged.

8. Other socioeconomic factors that appeared to have significant, negative impact on caseload reductions include poverty rates and percent of the population living in metropolitan areas.

9. Standardized coefficients can be unreliable, particularly when sample size is small and independent variables are highly correlated (Cohen and Cohen 1983). Our sample, however, encompasses 88 percent of the population, and independent variables are not significantly correlated. In addition, variance inflation factor diagnostics show that multicollinearity is not a problem. Finally, in the preliminary models we examined, the relationships reported here were found consistently. Therefore, we interpret the standardized coefficients as an indication of the most important explanatory variables.

Examining the Effect of Welfare-to-Work Structures and Services on a Desired Policy Outcome

Jodi R. Sandfort

In the arena of social services, it has long been recognized that most important governance decisions occur not in centralized offices of the federal bureaucracy but in state, regional, and local offices of service agencies (Brodkin 1997; Gueron and Pauly 1991; Ingram 1990; Milward and Provan 1993). The decentralized nature of service delivery, however, has made it challenging to study how management decisions and implementation conditions of publicly supported programs affect citizens. Some scholars have looked at front-line operations, seeking to understand the forces that motivate street-level staff and direct their behavior (Brodkin 1997; Lipsky 1980; Meyers, Glaser, and MacDonald 1998). Others have examined organizational technology, trying to understand better how services are provided to diverse clientele with complex problems (Hasenfeld and English 1974; Savage 1987; Glisson 1992). Others have tried to understand how relationships among organizations form implementation networks at local or regional levels that influence the outcomes that programs try to attain (Hjern and Porter 1981; Provan and Milward 1995; O'Toole 1997). Still others have looked at state-level variation in policy and practices, examining how these broad program parameters are connected to state-level outcomes (Jennings and Ewalt, this volume; Mettler 2000).

Taken together, this research suggests that to understand the dynamics of governance in decentralized service delivery systems, we must proceed on multiple tracks. Descriptive studies that document the variation in front-line practices, organizational service technology, local implementation networks, and state policy are important. Yet with the increasing public demand to understand the effects of public programs, scholars also must develop empirical models that explore how these multiple levels of state action are related to desired ends.

At an empirical level, this charge is challenging. As others in this volume have noted (Roderick, for example), it requires extensive data collection, the development of new theoretical models, and innovative methods. Many intermediary steps are required to respond to the charge put forth by Lynn, Heinrich, and Hill (in this volume) and O'Toole and Meier (in this volume) to specify adequately the important links between environmental factors, client characteristics, service technologies, delivery structures, management actions, and the intermediate and ultimate outcomes these factors are designed to affect.

This chapter is an initial attempt to grapple with some of these challenges by examining the delivery of welfare-to-work programs in one state. Although much has been made about the "devolution" of public policymaking and management resulting from the federal welfare reform in 1996, there has always been considerable variation in the administration of welfare programs in this country (Wiseman 1993). Initial accounts of the implementation of recent reforms suggest that this variation is only growing through what is termed "second-order devolution" (Holcomb et al. 1998; Nathan and Gais 1998). Increasingly, localities are experimenting significantly in how they deliver welfare services. Such local variation is found in Michigan, the site of my investigation. Drawing on data gathered from all welfare-to-work programs in the state, I explore the effect of local variation on an important intermediate policy goal—having welfare recipients combine welfare and work. The exploratory model presented teases apart the various levels of government action involved in implementing welfare-to-work programs. My primary research question, however, is whether county variation in service delivery structures and service technology has a quantifiable effect on the proportion of a county's welfare caseload that moves into the workforce. To investigate this, I use a more rigorous estimation technique than has been used in prior welfare research.

Conceptual Framework and Prior Research

Social policy implementation occurs on multiple levels. Although the federal government provides general policy parameters and resources, states establish many of the policies, procedures, and administrative rules in most public welfare programs. Jennings and Ewalt (in this volume) explore how variations in state policies, implementation strategies, and goals are related to changes in the welfare caseloads.[1] Rarely, however, within an individual state does one public, state-administered bureaucracy hold primary responsibility for implementing a social program. Instead, social services are often delivered through decentralized structures that involve multiple state agencies and various public and private organizations at the local level (Hjern and Porter 1981; Provan and Milward 1995; Smith and Lipsky 1993). Within these local organizations, variation in service technologies is great when the state is merely contracting for services and providing little oversight (DeHoog 1984; Kramer 1994).

To understand better how the administration and implementation of social services are related to policy outcomes, a first step is to disentangle these various levels of service delivery in our empirical models. Earlier scholars of policy implementation (Berman 1978; Palumbo and Calista 1990) have suggested distinguishing between program implementation at the macro and micro levels. "Macro-implementation" factors are the actions of federal or state governments that establish the general parameters within which social programs are to be carried out. They might include funding levels, administrative authority, regulation, or administrative rules. "Micro-implementation" factors refer to the actions taken by the organizations charged with delivering public programs, including establishing routines, monitoring front-line practices, and adopting various service technologies. The model proposed by Lynn, Heinrich, and Hill (in this volume) expands on this general orientation to separate some of the various elements that may connect government action to government outcomes. Their basic model presents program outputs or outcomes as a function of environmental factors (E), client characteristics (C), service technologies or treatments (T), structures (S), and managerial actions (M). Structures relate to the elements of macro-implementation, while service technologies denote the forces of micro-implementation.

This specification is much more complete than what has been used by prior welfare and welfare-to-work research that sought to understand the relationship between program delivery and policy outcomes. In these studies (Mitchell, Chadwin, and Smith Nightingale 1980; Mead 1983, 1985, 1997), most scholars have used variables denoting managerial, structural, and service conditions to investigate political questions, without placing these factors in a large conceptual framework. For example, although Mead (1997) explores whether counties' administrative conditions affect policy outcomes, he does not provide any justification for the specification of his predictive models.

In the analysis presented here, I develop a multivariate model that includes important factors in the macro- and micro-implementation process in Michigan's welfare system. Other research of this type suggests that the factors important to implementing a particular program cannot be determined a priori from economic, interorganizational, or organizational theories. In these cases, empirical models are better generated inductively from in-depth knowledge of field conditions (Hjern and Porter 1981). The variables included in this model were identified as qualitatively significant through investigations of welfare service delivery in Michigan (Sandfort 1997; Seefeldt, Sandfort, and Danziger 1998). This analysis was conducted to discern if any quantifiable impact could be documented. I then adopted the basic framework of Lynn, Heinrich, and Hill to broaden the discussion of this model and the results of the analysis.

Research Context

During the 1996 national debates over welfare reform, Michigan emerged as an exemplar of substantive welfare reform. Like other states, Michigan had taken advantage of the waiver of federal AFDC regulations in the early 1990s and instituted a series of program and policy changes. These early choices set Michigan on a path that stresses clients' combination of welfare and work rather than simply reducing the welfare rolls. The state did not adopt policies that divert potential clients from the welfare rolls or institute shorter time limits than required by federal legislation; instead, the state implemented many changes in eligibility rules and program operation in the early 1990s designed to "make work pay." Examples include larger disregards of earned income and eliminating the restrictions on the amount of time certain families could work. Although the state instituted sanctions for clients who did not comply with new work or job-search requirements, the implementation of sanctions has been minimal throughout the state.[2] In Michigan, the policy "carrots" to encourage work have been larger than the "sticks" requiring recipients to leave the rolls.

In 1994 Michigan moved from a welfare-to-work model that stressed education to a quick-labor-force-attachment model, called Work First. Work First programs focus on moving welfare recipients into the labor market rather than making them self-sufficient. As a technical manual designed to help states implement a Work First approach summarizes, "Any job is a good job. The best way to succeed in the labor market is to join it, developing work habits and skills on the job rather than in a classroom" (Brown 1997, p. 4). As in many other states (Nathan and Gais 1998), administrative responsibility for the new program was shifted from the state's public welfare agency to a new economic and workforce development agency.

Suddenly many diverse organizations were involved in Michigan's welfare system. County offices that were part of the public welfare bureaucracy retained their roles of determining and reevaluating eligibility for public assistance programs. A decentralized, quasi governmental system previously responsible for the Job Training Partnership Act (JTPA) was given authority to issue contracts for Work First to private and public organizations. Minimal program oversight was granted and, as a consequence, there is considerable variation in how each Work First operator tries to move recipients into jobs (Sandfort 1997; Seefeldt, Sandfort, and Danziger 1998).

The combination of these policy and administrative changes allowed Michigan to apply for Temporary Assistance for Needy Families (TANF) funds after the passage of federal welfare reform and in October 1996 to become one of the first states to receive these funds. The data examined here were gathered from all Michigan counties during this first year of operation under the new TANF program. Although the results are not strictly generalizable to other states because of the diversity of implementation conditions, this analysis suggests that the structures and services developed by implementing agents—at both state and local levels—may have a quantifiable effect on policy goals.

Research Methods

This chapter presents a cross-sectional examination of eighty-two counties in Michigan during the first year following the passage of the Personal Responsibility and Work Opportunity Reconciliation Act (PRWORA)—from October 1996 to September 1997. Wayne County was excluded because initial exploration of this data set showed that it was an outlier on the independent variables included in this model. Detroit is in Wayne County, and in 1994 the county had a population of 2.1 million. The large population makes the service delivery context of the county unique. The county has, for example, twenty-six welfare-to-work providers and twenty-seven public welfare offices. The state itself separates Wayne County administrative data from that of other counties because of its unique characteristics.

Although prior research (Mitchell, Chadwin, and Smith Nightingale 1980; Mead 1985, 1988, 1997) uses administrative data from the employment-training system, such data do not provide reliable information in Michigan, particularly concerning the structural and service technology factors of primary importance here. Instead, the county-level data set used in this analysis was assembled from a number of sources. Data from the U.S. Census and other government sources are used for a number of the environmental control variables, such as geography, unemployment rate, and poverty rate. Administrative data from the public welfare system are used for one independent measure of client characteristics and for the dependent variable examined. (See appendix A for a detailed definition of all variables.)

The measures of structural conditions and service technology, which are the focus of this analysis, are from telephone interviews conducted during fiscal year 1997 with the managers of local public welfare and welfare-to-work programs. We interviewed ninety-eight managers, who oversee all local public welfare offices in the state. Thus we had a 100 percent response rate in this population. In addition, we conducted interviews with 106 local managers of welfare-to-work programs, with a response rate of 93 percent. The phone interviews were structured and open-ended, lasting between 45 and 60 minutes. Managers were asked uniform questions on a range of topics, including organizational conditions, service technology, and interagency collaboration efforts. The results of these interviews were composed in a word processing file, checked for accuracy, and then transferred to a qualitative software analysis package, *QSR-Nudist* (Hannibal and Gahan 1998; Richards and Richards 1994). The software facilitated our efforts to apply codes systematically and check for consistency. The results of this initial exploration were presented in a descriptive policy report (Seefeldt, Sandfort, and Danziger 1998). For the analysis presented in this volume, I summarized the data from these interviews county by county, using quantitative variables. Lessons from the qualitative analysis informed the interpretation of the quantitative results.

The data and model were not originally developed with the Lynn, Heinrich, and Hill model in mind. As a result, not all factors in their basic model are fully specified in this investigation. For example, because counties are the unit of analysis, it is difficult to operationalize managerial actions (*M*), particularly because the implementation structures for services in each county are not coordinated by one managerial actor. Instead, these structures are created by multiple organizations functioning under different administrative authorities and various mandates.

Because this analysis was primarily concerned with whether the structures of a county's service delivery (*S*) or the service technology (*T*) used in welfare-to-work contracts are related to a county's ability to move recipients into the workforce, the environmental factors (*E*) in this model are used merely as control variables. Resembling the models used in prior research (Brasher 1994; Mitchell, Chadwin, and Smith Nightingale 1980; Mead 1985, 1997), the environmental measures include geography, local economic conditions, and demographic characteristics of the county. Specific variables are the type of county (rural or urban), unemployment rate, proportion of jobs in the manufacturing sector, poverty rate, proportion of the population with a high school degree, and proportion of the population that is single-mother families.

Similarly, I use client characteristics (*C*) as a control variable, largely because data limitations prohibit specifying this construct adequately . Although the state collects extensive information from welfare recipients to determine eligibility and benefits payments, this information is unavailable as county-level data. Only variables denoting clients' race are routinely published. In this analysis, a variable to denote the proportion of a county's cash assistance cases that is white is included in the multivariate model. Additional information to denote the human capital characteristics of the welfare caseload, such as level of education, work experience, or work level, would be desirable.

Table 5.1 presents some descriptive information about these control variables. Ten of the eighty-two counties examined in this analysis are characterized as urban. The average county unemployment rate was 6.4 percent, and 17 percent of the jobs were in the manufacturing sector. The average poverty rate was 14.8 percent. In an average county, 75 percent of the adults had a high school degree and 12 percent were single-mother families. Eighty-four percent of the welfare recipients in the average county were white.

The main independent factors from the Lynn, Heinrich, and Hill model explored are those depicting the county's implementation

TABLE 5.1

Means and standard deviations of model variables

Variable	Mean	Standard Deviation
Environmental controls		
Urban	0.1220	0.3292
Unemployment rate	6.4408	2.6416
Manufacturing	0.1722	0.0812
Poverty rate	14.8573	3.9807
High school diploma	0.7494	0.0557
Female-headed family	0.1242	0.0269
White	0.8442	0.1829
Service delivery structure		
Project Zero	0.0488	0.2167
Work first providers	1.4756	1.4421
Nonprofit agency	0.7868	0.3628
Specialized contractor	0.0854	0.2811
Service Technology		
Immediate job search	0.2189	0.4016
Job seeking skills	0.7791	0.3992
Soft skills	0.2185	0.3845
Problem management skills	0.4130	0.4708
No job search assistance	0.3224	0.4450
Focused job search assistance	0.5362	0.4724
Workshops	0.7689	0.4099
Working recipients	0.4312	0.0783

Source: Computed by author.

structure (S) and service technology (T). In Michigan, the structures of local implementation are established by state and local administrators. The specific variables included describe a county's unique public welfare services and the types of organizations selected to operate the welfare-to-work program. Specifically, they denote whether the county was a Project Zero site,[3] the number of Work First operators in the county, the frequency of nonprofit organizations, and whether special Work First contracts were given in the county to serve special populations of clients. Four counties were designated as Project Zero sites.[4] The average number of Work First providers in a county was 1.5, with the number varying from 1 to 12.[5] In an average county, 79 percent of the welfare-to-work organizations were private nonprofit agencies, 18 percent were schools, and 2 percent were private for-profit firms. In seven counties, special Work First contracts existed to serve populations with particular barriers to entering the workforce, such as pregnant women or non-English-speakers.

I relied extensively on information gathered through management interviews to construct variables regarding service technology or treatment (T). Because each county has multiple welfare-to-work providers, these dimensions are summarized at the county level as the proportion of providers in that area that use various service technologies. In particular, I explore the effects of immediate job search, skill-building workshops, and different types of job-search assistance provided to clients. As table 5.1 reflects, in an average county, 22 percent of the providers required welfare recipients referred to their program to engage in a job search immediately. In contrast, 77 percent of the programs in an average county required clients to attend workshops on topics such as résumé preparation or workplace behavior. In an average county, 53 percent of the programs offered focused job-search assistance to help clients find a job, including employing a staff member to develop potential jobs for clients with local employers or bringing local employers on-site to meet with potential employees. Thirty-two percent of the providers in an average county provided no such job-search assistance.

I use a logit regression estimation technique for grouped data that provides generalized or weighted least squares estimates for the dependent variable (Zellner and Lee 1965). This model is appropriate when the available data are, in reality, mean values for the underlying population. Although micro-level data from a statewide sample of welfare recipients would be desirable in order to explore how environmental factors, client characteristics, implementation structures, and service technologies contribute to individuals' ability to find employment or leave welfare because of work, such data are not available. Instead, this analysis considers aggregate data that represent these factors at the county level.

In the welfare policy arena, the desired outcomes of policy are often hotly debated. Some policy advocates assert that the system should be focused on supporting welfare recipients so that they can ultimately earn enough to lift their families out of poverty. Others consider a decline in the number of families receiving cash assistance as an adequate outcome. Both goals are embedded in the 1996 federal welfare reform provisions. Michigan resembles many other states in that it has chosen to focus its policy efforts on getting welfare clients into the labor force quickly. This approach, combined with the numerous policies adopted to "make work pay," has resulted in the state defining a more intermediate outcome as a policy success: increase the proportion of the cash assistance caseload combining welfare and work. As a result of this focus, the outcome of interest examined here is the ability of the welfare system to move recipients into the labor market; it is operationalized as the percentage of the county caseload that combines welfare and work in an average month. The average monthly proportion of clients reporting earned income during fiscal year 1997 was 43 percent, a rate considerably higher than the national average.[6]

Multivariate Results

I first examine the relationship between the economic and demographic characteristics typically thought to influence the likelihood of welfare recipients combining welfare and work. I then consider whether the variation in county service delivery structure is related to that outcome. Finally, I add to the model variables denoting the service technology adopted by organizations in a county. The results of these multivariate analyses are displayed in tables 5.2 and 5.3.[7]

As table 5.2 reveals, the statistically significant environmental and client variables in this model are county unemployment rate

TABLE 5.2

Effect of environmental controls on the proportion of a county's welfare caseload working

Environmental Controls	
Urban	−0.0343
	(0.0732)
Unemployment	−0.0309[a]
	(0.0183)
Manufacturing	−1.2059[b]
	(0.3757)
Poverty	0.0155
	(0.0114)
High school degree	0.6854
	(0.7806)
Female-headed family	2.1544[a]
	(1.2407)
White	0.9946[b]
	(0.1720)
Sample size (n)	82
Adjusted R^2	0.4767

[a] $p < .10$.
[b] $p < .01$.
Numbers in parentheses are standard errors.
Source: Computed by author.

and the proportion of manufacturing jobs in the county. Both have a statistically discernible, negative impact. The proportion of single-mother families in the county is positively related to the outcome and reflects the largest magnitude of any coefficient in this initial model. Finally, the proportion of the cash assistance caseload that is white has a positive relationship. This variable has a large *t*-statistic relative to the other factors. The strength of this relationship undoubtedly reflects omitted variable bias. As noted earlier, because of data limitations, this variable is the only one that reflects the demographic characteristics of the welfare caseload. Data providing more details about the demographic characteristics of welfare recipients, such as proportion with a high school diploma or average work experience, are unavailable on a county-by-county basis in Michigan. As a result, the proportion of the caseload that is white captures not only the effect of race on the likelihood that a

TABLE 5.3

Effect of service delivery structure and service technology on the proportion of a county's caseload that is working[a]

Predictors	1	2	3	4
Service Delivery Structure				
Project Zero	0.5602[d]	0.5474[d]	0.5517[d]	0.5604[d]
	(0.1370)	(0.1387)	(0.1347)	(0.1310)
Work First providers	−0.0152[b]	−0.0156[b]	−0.0194[c]	−0.0257[d]
	(0.0084)	(0.0084)	(0.0085)	(0.0087)
Non-profit agency	−0.0532	−0.0538	−0.0217	−0.0459
	(0.0631)	(0.0633)	(0.0642)	(0.0623)
Specialized contractor	0.6036	0.0616	0.0974	0.0831
	(0.0593)	(0.0600)	(0.0612)	(0.0590)
Service Technology				
Immediate job search		−0.0829	−0.1343[b]	
		(0.0677)	(0.0697)	
No job search assistance		0.0062		
		(0.0721)		
Focused job search			−0.1113[b]	−0.1535[c]
assistance			(0.0611)	(0.0635)
Workshops				0.1901[d]
				(0.0694)
Sample size (n)	82	82	82	82
Adjusted R^2	0.5825	0.5800	0.5995	0.6197

[b] $p < .10$.
[c] $p < .05$.
[d] $p < .01$.
[a] The above models include control variables not shown for environmental factors outside of the control of program implementers.
Source: Computed by author.

welfare recipient will be working but also unmeasured characteristics in the welfare population in each county.

These control variables were maintained in the models as I explored my central question about whether service structures and technology affect county-level outcomes. Table 5.3 reports the results of this multivariate analysis. Participation in the Project Zero pilot is a statistically significant positive predictor in the first model, which includes only variables related to service delivery structure. The number of Work First providers in the county is negatively related to the outcome, although the magnitude of the marginal effect of this coefficient is very small. Neither the practice of issuing specialized contracts to serve hard-to-employ clients nor the proportion of the contractors that were nonprofit is statistically related to the outcome.

The next series of models seeks to uncover whether the types of service technologies adopted by welfare-to-work organizations in a county are related to the proportion of welfare recipients who are working. As mentioned earlier, Michigan's Work First approach to welfare-to-work is focused on quick labor force attachment. Within these parameters, managers and staff in local programs make decisions on two dimensions of service technology: whether to provide upfront service before clients begin looking for work and whether to provide support while clients are actively searching for employment. It is conceivable that local economic conditions might influence the type of service technology adopted by a program; for example, tight labor markets might inspire programs to offer workshops to hone clients' job-search skills before they seek employment, or programs may be less likely to offer ongoing job-search assistance in robust markets. An earlier analysis of these data revealed, however, that local unemployment rates were not correlated with the particular service technology adopted by Work First programs (Seefeldt, Sandfort, and Danziger 1998). In fact, frequently there is significant variation in the service technology used by Work First providers in the same county, even though they share the same local economic environment. As explained earlier, the variables in these models are operationalized as the intensity of each service approach because of this variation within each county.

Columns 2–4 of table 5.3 demonstrate how different service technologies are related to the outcome in the multivariate model. In the second column, I examine instances in which clients are required to do their own independent job search immediately on referral to the program and are given minimal support while searching. When including environmental control and macro-implementation variables, this service technology has no statistically discernible effect on the outcome. In the third column, I investigate programs that offer moderately more support to welfare recipients searching for employment. These programs still require clients to immediately begin job search but they then provide focused job-search assistance in the form of on-site information sessions with local employers, "job clubs" that provide peer support, or a staff member who actively cultivates local job leads. As the table shows, both components of service technology have a negative effect on the proportion of a county's caseload that is reporting earned income. In fact, assuming this model is correctly specified, when the proportion of a county's providers using immediate job search increases by one percentage point, the proportion of the caseload that is working decreases by 3.3 percentage points. Similarly, when the proportion of a county's Work First providers using focused job-search assistance techniques increases by 1 percentage point, the proportion of the caseload working decreases by 2.8 percentage points.[8]

Last, I examine the relationship between programs that provide both initial workshops on job-search techniques before clients begin to look for employment and those that provide ongoing support while clients are searching for employment. Of the three approaches, this combination offers the most assistance to welfare recipients searching for employment. As the last column in table 5.3 reflects, workshops prior to job search are positively related to outcomes. Holding all other factors constant, when the proportion of a county's Work First providers that offer workshops increases by one percentage point, the caseload that is working increases by 4.7 percentage points. As in the previous model, focused job-search assistance is negatively related to this policy outcome. Assuming this model is correctly specified, the proportion of a county's welfare population that is working decreases by 3.8 percentage points with every one-unit increase in the proportion of Work First providers offering this type of assistance.

In analysis not presented here, variables representing various workshop topics were substituted for the more general workshop variable listed in column 4. The proportion of the providers offering workshops on specific job-seeking skills—interview techniques, résumé preparation, application completion, and constructing cover letters—was a statistically significant positive predictor of the proportion of welfare recipients combining welfare and work. Some Work First programs, though, provide instruction in other topics. Because managers and staff believe that understanding the rules of the workplace is important for finding jobs in the low-wage labor market (Holzer 1996; Moss and Tilly 1996), some programs include workshops on "soft skills," such as the importance of proper dress, punctuality, and general workplace behavior. In the models used for this analysis, however, these types of programs have a statistically significant negative effect on the proportion of a county's welfare caseload that is working.

Still other programs run workshops that seek to improve clients' problem management skills. Because of the challenges of problem management and of low-self esteem (Herr, Wagner, and Halpern 1996; Pavetti and Duke 1995), these programs attempt to increase clients' abilities to function more effectively. For example, they may do simulations that help clients think through what they would do if their babysitter cancels during their second week of work, or they use role-playing to help clients value their skills as parents, or they offer exercises designed to increase their motivation for work. In the models used for this analysis, the proportion of these types of workshops offered in a county is a statistically significant, positive predictor of the proportion of welfare recipients reporting earned income.

In all of the models, the two variables denoting service delivery structure remain statistically significant. The number of Work First providers in the county is consistently a negative predictor of the proportion of working clients. In all models, however, the magnitude of the coefficient is quite small.[9] In contrast, counties designated as a Project Zero pilot site have statistically significant positive relationships of sizable magnitude. In fact, if the model used in this analysis is correctly specified, being a Project Zero site increases by 13.4 to 13.7 percentage points the proportion of a county's caseload that is working, holding all other factors constant. In the county with the mean outcome, this would entail a 32 percent increase in the proportion of the caseload that is working.

Discussion and Implications

This exploratory analysis was undertaken for two purposes. First, it was intended to add to our understanding of the various elements of program implementation in the devolved welfare system. With eligibility for cash assistance recipients limited, there is a growing array of techniques being used to move welfare recipients into the labor market. With this increased variation, the importance of both service delivery structures and service technologies in moving welfare recipients into work should be empirically explored. The second purpose for this analysis is to illustrate how one could disentangle the various levels of service delivery in human service programs and, using the framework of Lynn and his colleagues, relate them to program and policy outcomes.

As would be expected, there are many forces beyond the influence of implementing agents that predict how many welfare recipients in a county report earnings from work. Geography, economic conditions, and demographic characteristics are all significant factors that influence how a county stands on this policy goal. What this analysis reveals, however, is that other factors related to the implementation of public policy also play a statistically discernible role.

In the multivariate analysis, the county's designation as a Project Zero site and its number of Work First providers were consistently statistically significant predictors. The Project Zero finding is particularly striking because of the relatively large magnitude of its marginal effect. From July 1996 to June 1997, the counties selected to participate in Project Zero were focused on reducing to zero the number of welfare recipients who were not employed at least twenty hours a week. To meet this goal, sites were given additional resources to address clients' child care and transportation barriers, and three of six sites offered mentoring services (Seefeldt, Sandfort, and Danziger 1997). The Project Zero sites also were the pilot for a substantial reorientation of the public welfare office. These counties were the initial implementation sites for Michigan's new classification of front-line welfare workers as "Family Independence Specialists." Although not fully implemented during this first year, the idea was to transform front-line staff from mere eligibility workers to more professional case managers who would help families move into employment. At a minimum, when clients applied for assistance in a Project Zero site, they were given a clear message about the importance of finding work and relying on cash assistance only temporarily.

Unfortunately, there are no data with which to explore which of these services within the Project Zero intervention is related to the effect examined here. It is not possible to tell whether it is increased child care and transportation, the mentoring program, the altered role of front-line workers, or the interactions in the public welfare office that stressed work. This analysis does show, however, that the environment created by this pilot program had a statistically detectable influence on the proportion of the county's caseload that was working, even when controlling for other environmental factors.

The consistently negative, albeit small, effect of the county's number of Work First providers reveals that more providers do not move larger proportions of the welfare caseload into employment. This is probably because of the complexity introduced into the system by more programs. In the decentralized Work First system, each service organization has a contractual relationship with the administrative entity responsible for welfare-to-work programs in the county; there is little communication or coordination among these entities in counties with multiple providers. Furthermore, this administrative organization is distinct from the county's welfare office, which determines and monitors eligibility for public assistance, thereby increasing the complexity of the service delivery structure. Nearly one-third of the welfare-to-work managers report that there is very little communication between their staff and the county welfare office. This communication barrier is more common in counties with more Work First operators and with more complicated service delivery structures.[10] The multivariate analysis presented here suggests that the more complicated the local implementation structure, the less successful a county is in encouraging welfare recipients to combine welfare and work.

This analysis also provides some evidence about the relationship between service technology and the goal of moving welfare recipients into work. Although conventional wisdom abounds, there is relatively little empirical evidence linking Work First service technology to policy outcomes. Building on comparisons of various welfare-to-work program evaluations in the last fifteen years (Gueron and Pauly 1991), the Manpower Demonstration Research Corporation has written a technical assistance guide for states that stresses that workshops and ongoing support while clients are engaged in job search are the "best practices" for Work First programs (Brown 1997). Other analysts conclude that job-search assistance, particularly an individual job developer, is more beneficial than clients' independent job search (Herr, Wagner, and Halpern 1996).

Among the counties in Michigan, independent job search with minimal programmatic support has no impact on the proportion of a county's welfare caseload that finds employment. This is consistent with research suggesting that this is not the most effective method of helping welfare recipients find employment. When investigating the various ways of supporting job search, I find that the proportion of programs with workshop sessions has a positive effect on the percentage of county's welfare caseload that is working. In particular, workshops stressing job-seeking skills—such as interview techniques, résumé preparation, or cover letter preparation—and problem management techniques seem to be especially useful. Again, these findings reinforce conventional wisdom about the types of useful services to include in Work First programs.

One finding of this analysis, however, contradicts widely accepted practices. In our models, the proportion of a county's programs that use job-search assistance—such as on-site employer information sessions, job clubs that offer peer support, or job development staff—is negatively related to the county's working caseload. There are a couple of potential explanations for this finding. In interviews with local Work First managers, a sizable minority voiced their belief that continued job-search assistance was not necessary; these managers argued that clients who do their own search are more committed to the jobs they accept and more able to look for another job when the first one ends. Another potential explanation is that programs offering continued support are not reaching out to employers who are the right match for their clients' skills or employment preferences. In a second wave of data collection for this study, we are gathering more comprehensive information that will allow us to identify more precisely which employers are being targeted and what types of relationships Work First programs cultivate with them. This additional information will allow for more exploration of the potential source of the negative relationship between the intensity of these services and the proportion of a county's caseload that is working.

In examining these results, it is important to remember that this multivariate model is exploratory and restricted by field conditions and data limitations. For example, a potentially important structural variable not included is the amount of financial resources allotted to each county for welfare-to-work services. Also, as pointed out earlier, service technology variables are summarized at the county level as the proportion of the providers who use each approach. Ideally, these measures would be adjusted to reflect the proportion of a county's caseload that receives each approach. Finally, given the federal TANF requirements, other important policy outcomes, such as a county's participation rate in employment activities or the proportion of the caseload employed for 90 days, should be investigated.

Unlike prior research on welfare administration, however, in developing an exploratory, empirical model, this study does draw on both the broad framework developed by Lynn and colleagues and the knowledge of implementation structures developed from field-based research. It was undertaken to investigate whether county variation in the devolved welfare state—particularly in the structure of service delivery or the service technology used by program operators—has any effect on policy outcomes. Although not framed in the same way, the work of other welfare scholars echoes the finding that administrative conditions do influence outcomes in the welfare system (Hasenfeld and Weaver 1996; Mitchell, Chadwin, and Smith Nightingale 1980; Mead, 1983, 1988, 1997; Riccio and Hasenfeld 1996). Future research should strive for better specification of models that tease out how the various links between the types of service delivery choices are related to the desired outcomes. Because delivery of social programs is complex—involving multiple organizations, intricate networks, distinct state policy parameters—this charge will not be easy. It is critical nonetheless to understanding how the mechanics of governance influence the services provided to needy citizens.

References

Berman, Paul. 1978. The study of macro- and micro-implementation. *Public Policy,* 26(2): 157–84.

Brasher, C. Nielsen. 1994. Workfare in Ohio: Political and socioeconomic climate and program impact. *Policy Studies Journal,* 22(3): 514–27.

Brodkin, Evelyn. 1997. Inside the welfare contract: Discretion and accountability in state welfare administration. *Social Service Review,* 71(1): 1–33.

Brown, Amy. March 1997. Work First: How to implement an employment-focused approach to welfare reform. Mimeo, Re: Working Welfare Series. New York: Manpower Demonstration Research Corporation.

DeHoog, R. H. 1984. Theoretical perspectives on contracting out for services; implementation problems and possibilities of privatizing public services. In *Public policy implementation.* Vol. 1, edited by George Edwards. Greenwich, Conn.: JAI Press.

Gallagher, L. Jerome, Megan Gallagher, Kevin Perese, Susan Schreiber, and Kevin Watson. May 1998. *One year after welfare reform: A description of state Temporary Assistance for Needy Families (TANF) decisions as of October 1997*. Washington, D.C.: The Urban Institute.

Glisson, Charles. 1992. Structure and technology in human service organizations. In *Human services as complex organizations*, edited by Yeheskel Hasenfeld. Newbury Park, Calif.: Sage.

Gueron, Judith, and Edward Pauly. 1991. *From welfare to work*. New York: Russell Sage Foundation.

Hannibal, Mike, and Celia Gahan. 1998. *Doing qualitative research using* QSR Nudist. Thousand Oaks, Calif.: Sage.

Hasenfeld, Yeheskel, and R. English. 1974. *Organizational technology: Human service organizations: A book of readings*. Ann Arbor: University of Michigan Press, pp. 279–83.

Hasenfeld, Yeheskel, and Dale Weaver. 1996. Enforcement, compliance, and disputes in welfare-to-work programs. *Social Service Review*, 70 (2): 235–36.

Herr, Toby, Suzanne Wagner, and Robert Halpern. 1996. *Making the shoe fit: Creating a work-prep system for a large and diverse population*. Chicago: Project Match and the Erikson Institute.

Hjern, Benny, and David Porter. 1981. Implementation structures: A new unit of administrative analysis. *Organizational Studies*, 2(3): 211–27.

Holcomb, Pamela, LaDonna Pavetti, Caroline Ratcliffe, and Susan Riedinger. June 1998. *Building an employment focused welfare system: Work First and other work-oriented strategies in five states*. Washington, D.C.: The Urban Institute.

Holzer, Harry. 1996. *What employers want: Job prospects for less educated workers*. New York: Russell Sage Foundation.

Ingram, Helen. 1990. Implementation: A review and suggested framework. In *Public administration: The state of the discipline*, edited by Naomi Lynn and Aaron Wildavsky. Chatham, N.J.: Chatham House.

Kramer, Ralph. 1994. Voluntary agencies and the contract culture: Dream or nightmare? *Social Service Review*, 68(1): 33–58.

Lipsky, Michael. 1980. *Street-level bureaucracy: Dilemmas of the individual in public services*. New York: Russell Sage Foundation.

Mead, Lawrence. 1983. Expectations and welfare work: WIN in New York City. *Policy Studies Review* 2(4): 649–62.

———. 1985. Expectations and welfare work: WIN in New York State. *Polity*, 18: 225–52.

———. 1988. The potential for work enforcement in WIN. *Journal of Policy Analysis and Management*, 7(2): 264–88.

———. 1997. Optimizing JOBS: Evaluation versus administration. *Public Administration Review*, 57(2): 113–22.

Mettler, Suzanne. 2000. State's rights, women's obligations: Contemporary welfare reform in historical perspective. *Women in Politics,* 21(1): 1–34.

Meyers, Marcia, Bonnie Glaser, and Karin MacDonald. 1998. On the front lines of welfare delivery: Are workers implementing policy reforms? *Journal of Policy Analysis and Management,* 17(1): 1–22.

Milward, H. Brinton, and Keith Provan. 1993. The hollow state: Private provision of public services. In *Public policy for democracy,* edited by Helen Ingram and Steven Rathgeb Smith. Washington, D.C.: Brookings Institution.

Mitchell, John, Mark Chadwin, and Demetra Smith Nightingale. 1980. *Implementing welfare employment programs: An institutional analysis of the Work Incentive (WIN) program.* R&D Monograph 78. U.S. Department of Labor. Washington, D.C.: U.S. Government Printing Office.

Moss, Philip, and Chris Tilly. 1996. Soft skills and race: An investigation of black men's employment problems. *Work and Occupations,* 23(3): 252–76.

Nathan, Richard, and Thomas Gais. 1998. Overview report: Implementation of the Personal Responsibility Act of 1996. Working paper, Federalism Research Group. Albany: State University of New York, Nelson A. Rockefeller Institute of Government.

O'Toole, Laurence. 1997. Treating networks seriously. *Public Administration Review,* 57(1): 45–52.

Palumbo, Dennis, and Donald Calista. 1990. *Implementation and the policy process: Opening up the black box.* New York: Greenwood Press.

Pavetti, LaDonna and Amy-Ellen Duke. September 1995. *Increasing participation in work and work-related activities: Lessons from five state welfare reform demonstration projects.* Washington, D.C.: The Urban Institute.

Provan, Keith, and H. Brinton Milward. 1995. A preliminary theory of interorganizational network effectiveness: A comparative study of four community mental health systems. *Administrative Science Quarterly,* 40: 1–33.

Riccio, James, and Yeheskel Hasenfeld. 1996. Enforcing participation mandate in a welfare-to-work program. *Social Service Review,* 70(4): 516–39.

Richards, Thomas, and Lyn Richards. 1994. From filing cabinets to computer. In *Analyzing qualitative data,* edited by A. Bryman and R. Burgess. London: Routledge.

Sandfort, Jodi. 1997. Peering into the black box: A study of the front-line organizations implementing welfare reform in Michigan.

Ph.D. dissertation. University of Michigan, Department of Political Science and School of Social Work.

——. 1999. The structural impediments to human service collaboration: The case of welfare reform. *Social Service Review,* 73 (3): 314–39.

Savage, A. 1987. Maximizing effectiveness through technological complexity. *Administration in Social Work,* 11(3/4): 127–43.

Seefeldt, Kristin, Jodi Sandfort, and Sandra Danziger. 1997. Project Zero: The view from the sites. Ann Arbor: University of Michigan Program on Poverty and Social Welfare Policy, unpublished data.

——. 1998. Moving towards a vision of family independence: Local managers' views of Michigan's welfare reforms. Ann Arbor: University of Michigan Program on Poverty and Social Welfare Policy, unpublished data. Also located at *www.ssw.umich.edu/poverty/report.*

Smith, Steven Rathgeb, and Michael Lipsky. 1993. *Non-profits for hire: The welfare state in the age of contracting.* Cambridge, Mass.: Harvard University Press.

Wiseman, Michael. 1993. Welfare reform in the states: The Bush legacy. *Focus,* 15(1): 18–36.

Zellner, Arnold, and Tong Hun Lee. 1965. Joint estimation of relationships involving discrete random variables. *Econometrica,* 33(2): 382–402.

Endnotes

1. Much of the early evidence about the implementation of the federal Temporary Assistance for Needy Families (TANF) grant programs are descriptions of variation in these state-level factors (Gallagher et al. 1998; Holcomb et al. 1998; Nathan and Gais 1998).

2. During the last three months of fiscal year 1997, for example, a reduction in grants was made on only 0.2 to 0.3 percent of the state's caseload.

3. In 1996 Michigan implemented the pilot "Project Zero" in six sites with the goal of reducing the number of welfare cases without earned income to zero. Additional information about the scope of the initiative is explained later in the chapter. In addition, see Seefeldt, Sandfort, and Danziger (1997).

4. The two other Project Zero sites were in Wayne County, so they are excluded from this analysis.

5. Because of this variation, the variables providing more detailed information about the welfare-to-work organizations in the county were constructed as a proportion. Thus rather than con-

structing a dummy variable to denote the presence or absence of nonprofit welfare-to-work programs, the variable represents the proportion of certain types of organizations in the county. Although it would be desirable to have these variables adjusted for the proportion of the county's caseload served by a particular type of provider, these data were not available systematically for all counties in the state.

6. The most recent national data available are from fiscal year 1995. In that year, Michigan had the second-highest rate (23%) among states of clients combining welfare and work (this included Wayne County, which is not included in this analysis). This rate compared with a national average of 9.5 percent.

7. Like other prior researchers in this area (Jennings and Ewalt, this volume; Mead 1997; Riccio and Hasenfeld 1997), I have elected to use a p-value less than or equal to 0.10 to designate statistical significance in these exploratory models.

8. Because of the estimation model used, the coefficients reported in table 5.3 do not directly reflect the magnitude of the marginal effects. To calculate the magnitude, these coefficients were transformed using the following derived formula: $\bar{y}(1 - \bar{y})\beta$.

9. The marginal effect of this variable is between 0.37 and 0.62 percentage points in all models.

10. In-depth analysis of front-line conditions in two counties reveal impediments to effective interagency collaborations: there are few ways to standardize the message clients receive about policies that encourage work or accurately monitor clients' participation in the Work First program (Sandfort 1999).

Appendix A
Definition of Variables

Outcome of interest (O)

Working recipients | The average monthly proportion of current cash assistance recipients with earned income, October 1996–September 1997

Environmental (E) and Client Characteristics (C)

Urban | 1= urban (when more than 70% of population live in an urban area), 0– rural

Unemployment rate | Average monthly county unemployment rate, October 1996–September 1997

Manufacturing sector | Proportion of jobs in manufacturing sector, 1993 Bureau of Economic Analysis

Poverty rate | Proportion of individuals below federal poverty line, 1994 Current Population Survey

High school degree | Proportion of adult population with high school degree, 1990 census

Female-headed family | Proportion of female-headed families, 1990 census

White | Proportion of cash assistance recipients who are white, June 1997

Service Delivery Structure (S)

Project Zero | 1= counties designated Project Zero program sites, 0= counties not designated Project Zero sites

Work First providers | Number of Work First providers in the county

Nonprofit agency	Proportion of Work First providers in the county that are nonprofit
Specialized contractors	1= counties in which Work First contracts were awarded to serve populations with special barriers to employment such as pregnant women, people with limited English proficiency, and those unable to find work through typical job search techniques. 0= counties in which such contracts did not exist.

Service Technology (T)

Immediate job search	Proportion of Work First providers in the county that had clients immediately search for employment
Job seeking skills	Proportion of Work First providers in the county that provided classroom instruction in resume preparation, application completion, and interviewing techniques
Soft skills	Proportion of Work First providers in the county offering classroom instruction in "soft skills" such as dress, punctuality, and rules of the workplace
Problem management skills	Proportion of Work First providers in the county that offered training to improve problem-solving skills and boost self-esteem
Focused job search assistance	Proportion of Work First providers in the county that offered one or more of the following services: a staff position devoted to job development, on-site visits to employers or an organized peer group to support job search efforts
No job search assistance	Proportion of Work First providers in the county that provided no job search assistance

Workshops

Proportion of Work First providers in the county that offered clients classroom instruction to assist in job search efforts

Management, Organizational Characteristics, and Performance: The Case of Welfare-to-Work Programs*

James Riccio, Howard S. Bloom, and Carolyn J. Hill

Management practices and organizational characteristics are widely believed to have an important influence on the performance of public and nonprofit organizations, but despite much research, their role is not well understood. This chapter describes new research under way by the Manpower Demonstration Research Corporation (MDRC) on how such factors affect the performance of a particular type of public organization: welfare-to-work programs.

This research is distinct in several ways. It measures organizational performance in terms of program effects on individual-level behavioral outcomes (employment, earnings, and welfare receipt) based on a series of randomized experiments implemented across numerous program sites. It attempts to explain the cross-site variation in these effects using a rich set of quantitative data on a host of organization-level factors that prior research suggests ought to be influential. The analysis also controls for site differences in client characteristics and local economic environments and uses a hierarchical modeling approach that accommodates the grouping of sample members by local welfare office. Results from the study are forthcoming from MDRC.

The sections that follow outline the study's theoretical framework and method. They describe its conceptual model, sample and data, key constructs and relevant prior literature, and the statistical estimation procedures used for assessing the determinants of organizational performance. Although this research focuses on welfare-to-work programs, its methods and findings may prove relevant to future inquiries into the influence of management practices and organizational characteristics on organizational performance in other publicly supported institutions.

Background

Broadly speaking, this study is about how to improve the performance of the class of institutions known as human service organizations. As Hasenfeld and English said in their 1974 study (p. 1), these are "formal organizations explicitly designed to process and change people," and they include, among others, schools, employment agencies, welfare agencies, correctional institutions, hospitals, and mental health clinics. Although the place of human service organizations in modern society is relatively secure, public complaints about their failure to perform adequately, and calls for their reform and "reinvention," are as old as the institutions themselves.

Improving the performance of human service organizations is a difficult challenge, in part because rigorous empirical evidence about "what works best for whom" is sorely lacking. If social scientists are to help fill this information gap, they must make considerable progress on at least two challenging fronts: (1) improving the *measurement* of performance, and (2) increasing knowledge about *what drives* performance.

Measuring Performance

Among private, for-profit organizations, one benchmark of success reigns supreme—financial profit. For human service organizations, however, which operate mainly as public or not-for-profit entities, success is much harder to gauge. Part of this difficulty stems from the fact that such organizations usually have multiple goals. For example, schools are expected to develop general literacy, mathematical and critical thinking skills, impart specific knowledge in a wide array of subject areas, and help socialize young people. Correctional institutions often are expected both to incarcerate and to rehabilitate. Many welfare-to-work programs try to increase employment, reduce welfare dependence, reduce poverty, and improve quality of life. Goals may conflict with each other (e.g., reducing welfare may increase poverty), and stakeholders may not agree on the relative priority of the goals. Thus it is difficult, if not impossible, to capture an organization's performance with a universally acceptable "bottom-line" measure of success.

Measuring success is also difficult when the desired outcomes are partly or wholly intangible. For example, standardized tests of student achievement, rates of recidivism among former prison inmates, and quality-of-life questions on surveys of former welfare recipients often fail to do justice to the complex nature of the educational, rehabilitative, and life improvement goals they are intended to reflect.

Even for tangible outcomes that can be measured precisely and objectively, data limited to an organization's own clients are not enough to gauge overall performance because they cannot isolate the organization's unique contribution to those outcomes. This contribution, often referred to as the organization's *impact* or *added value*, is the change in outcomes that it caused to happen. Determining that added value requires not only data on client outcomes but also information on what those outcomes would have been without help from the organization. This latter condition is often called a "counterfactual." Ideally then, the performance of an organization should be measured as the *difference* between its actual client outcomes and their counterfactual.

Such evidence is difficult to obtain, however, especially in real time on an ongoing basis for an operating program. Although the program evaluation literature is replete with alternative methods for assessing program effectiveness (e.g., Cook and Campbell 1979), it is widely acknowledged that the most valid of these methods is a randomized experiment (e.g., Betsey, Hollister, and Papageorgiou 1985). Using this approach, individuals targeted for services are randomly assigned (through a lottery-like process) either to a program group that is offered assistance or a control group that is not. Because the assignment process is random and all sample members have an equal chance of being selected for the program, systematic differences in the measured and unmeasured characteristics of the two groups are eliminated (assuming sufficiently large sample sizes). Thus the subsequent outcomes of the control group accurately reflect what the program group's outcomes would have been without the program, and the difference between the two groups'

outcomes provides a valid estimate of the organization's effects, or
"impacts." For example, if 50 percent of a program group in a welfare-to-work initiative found employment compared with only 40
percent of the control group, the 10 percentage point increase in employment would be the added value attributable to the program.

Because of their ability to provide valid program impact estimates, randomized experiments are now widely used to evaluate
many types of human services and have played an especially prominent role in the evaluation of employment and training programs
(Friedlander, Greenberg, and Robins 1997; Greenberg and Shroder
1997).

Understanding What Drives Organizational Performance (Impacts)

The accumulating experimental evidence on the effectiveness of social programs has been more successful at determining how effective these programs are than at explaining *why* they are or are not
effective. If program performance is to be improved, however, a
better understanding is needed of what accounts for success. This
will require going beyond the design of previous social experiments, which almost exclusively test the effects of whole programs,
not their constituent parts. This limitation is often referred to as the
"black box" problem. What is needed is a way to unpack the black
box in order to determine how impacts are affected by the nature of
the services being tested, the manner in which they are implemented, the types of clients who received them, and the environment within which they are provided.[1]

Multisite experiments that measure program impacts, and the
factors that potentially influence those impacts offer perhaps the
best opportunity for studying what drives program performance
(Greenberg, Meyer, and Wiseman 1994). Such a comparison-of-sites
approach can explain the variation in impacts across sites in terms
of measured differences in the characteristics of these sites and
their samples.[2] Although promising, this approach is not foolproof.
For one thing, even though evidence of each site's performance is
based on a random assignment experiment, the statistical techniques used to estimate the relationships between impacts and site
characteristics are subject to the same uncertainties inherent in any
nonexperimental research (e.g., selection bias). In addition, multisite experiments typically involve very few sites, making it impos-

sible to measure the independent effect on performance of very many factors. Furthermore, if some important factors are left out of the analysis, estimates of the influence of the included factors could be biased.

The present study uses a comparison-of-sites approach to examine the determinants of variation in program impacts across an unusually large number of experimental sites with large samples. It also draws on extensive cross-site data on organizational and client characteristics. These conditions may make it possible to measure the influence of each factor controlling for the other characteristics to an extent that is not feasible in smaller-scale studies with less rich data.

Sample and Data

This study uses data from three major evaluations conducted by MDRC on innovative welfare-to-work programs targeted toward recipients and new applicants of Aid to Families with Dependent Children (AFDC), the nation's former main cash welfare program for poor families. The three evaluations were conducted on California's Greater Avenues for Independence (GAIN) program (in six counties); Florida's Project Independence (in nine counties); and the National Evaluation of Welfare-to-Work Strategies (NEWWS), initiated as a study of the federal Job Opportunities and Basic Skills Training (JOBS) program in seven areas in six states (see, e.g., Hamilton and Brock 1994; Riccio, Friedlander, and Freeman 1994; Kemple, Friedlander, and Fellerath 1995). In some cases, the county welfare department operated the welfare-to-work program directly, often through several local offices, each with its own staff and caseload. Elsewhere, the state welfare agency operated the program statewide directly through local departmental offices or units. Drawing on all three evaluations, this study includes data on seventy-two local welfare-to-work program offices covering twenty-two counties or areas in eight states.[3]

To varying degrees, the programs included in the three evaluations offered welfare recipients a range of work-promoting activities, such as job-search guidance, basic education, vocational education, training, and unpaid work experience.[4] They also provided support services, such as assistance in paying for child care and transportation, to make it easier for recipients to participate in the activities. The recipients were assigned to case managers and other line staff who arranged for them to attend particular activities, helped them gain access to needed support services, and monitored their participation and progress in the program.

Each state's program was part of a new, national effort to transform welfare into a conditional entitlement, under which a person's full welfare grant would be provided contingent on a good faith effort to prepare for work—unless disabilities, severe family problems, or other recognized "good cause" reasons made working untenable. Officially, at least, participation in the programs was mandatory, and a recipient's welfare grant could be reduced as a sanction for failing to comply with this requirement.

All three evaluations used a random assignment research design with similarly defined outcome variables and similar kinds of data on program operations. In each study, recipients who were deemed mandatory for the program were randomly assigned to either a program group or a control group. The latter were not subject to the participation mandate and could not access the special welfare-to-work services. They were free, however, to seek other employment and training assistance on their own in the community.

The welfare recipients in these evaluations were primarily single parents (mostly women) when they entered the sample. Drawing from all three studies, the current study uses a sample of about 84,000 single-parent applicants and recipients in the program and control groups across the seventy-two local welfare-to-work program offices. Sample sizes in each office ranged from about 300 to about 4,700 people.

The data on the performance of the local program offices come from administrative records showing the employment and welfare experiences of the program and control groups for at least two years after random assignment (and up to five years in the California evaluation). Wage and benefit records for employment-related outcomes were obtained from the state agency that administers the Unemployment Insurance system. Welfare payment records were obtained from state or county welfare departments. The evaluations were conducted at different times, with the follow-up data spanning the period from the late 1980s through the mid-1990s.

Each evaluation also includes rich quantitative data on organizational conditions and staff and management practices from surveys of line staff in the welfare-to-work programs. Self-administered questionnaires were completed by almost all staff (approximately 1,500, or roughly twenty per office, on average) who directly interacted with welfare recipients and had responsibility for case management or related functions. The immediate supervisors of these staff also completed questionnaires. Some questionnaire items were repeated in the surveys used in all three evaluations and will allow us to make comparisons across all seventy-two program offices. Other items, however, are unique to one or two of the evaluations, so fewer offices can be compared with these data.

The study also uses data from a variety of other sources. These include information on client characteristics collected by welfare staff prior to random assignment; client survey and program case file data on sample members' participation in employment-related activities; and published data on local economic conditions, welfare grants, and other features of the local context or environment within which the programs operate.

Analytical Framework

The choices made and actions taken by the managers of human service organizations may determine how well those organizations perform. Although their decision-making authority is constrained by laws, regulations, resource limitations, and organizational guidelines, managers typically have substantial influence over how services are provided to clients; the social environment that clients experience within the organization; the training, supports, and rewards used to motivate and guide front-line staff; and the types of people chosen to fill front-line positions. Although it is reasonable to assume that management decisions matter for program performance, the sparseness of the evidence linking specific program features, staff strategies, general organizational characteristics, and managerial processes (over all of which managers have at least some control) to performance leaves managers with little empirical guidance to improve the effectiveness of their institutions.

This study's attempt to "get inside the black box" of welfare-to-work programs to understand what drives their performance is one attempt to help fill this knowledge vacuum. The analysis is structured in accordance with a modified version of the analytical framework presented in Lynn, Heinrich, and Hill in this volume. Specifically, it will determine the extent to which office performance is influenced by organizational and management factors above and beyond the influence exerted by the types of people served by the office or its local context or environment (such as the strength of the job market). This can be expressed as the following reduced-form equation:

Impact $= f$ (service technology, organizational climate, managerial processes, staff characteristics, client characteristics, and program environment)   (1)

The next sections describe the meaning of these constructs, why they are considered relevant to explaining the performance of human service organizations, and which of their aspects are analyzed in the current study. The discussion begins with the independent variables in the equation before turning to alternative forms of the dependent variable. As will be seen, early analyses reveal large and statistically significant variation in program impacts on the dependent variables across offices. This provides a rare opportunity to study what produced this variation.

Independent Variables: Factors That May Affect Performance

The literature on organizations and management in general, and on human service organizations in particular, points to several factors that hypothetically influence an organization's performance. This study examines those listed in table 6.1, which are grouped by the categories represented in equation 1.[5]

Service Technology

A principal focus of this analysis is the primary work—or "service technology"—of welfare-to-work programs. A human service organization's service technology refers to the set of procedures by which it attempts to bring about the desired changes in its clients or their circumstances (see Hasenfeld and English 1974; Lynn, Heinrich, and Hill, in this volume).[6] Much of what constitutes a service technology is carried out through the interactions between front-line staff and their clients—for example, the interactions between teachers and students in the classroom, between doctors and patients in hospitals, and between guards and inmates in prisons. In

TABLE 6.1

Independent variables to be used in the analysis

Construct	Variables
Service Technology	Employment message conveyed by staff
	Personalized attention from staff
	Client monitoring by staff
	Enforcement of participation mandate by staff
	Formal penalty rate
	Staff efforts to "cream" or target certain types of clients
	Client-to-staff ratio
	Client activity patterns
Organizational Climate	Staff perceptions of clients
	Staff relationships with clients
	Staff belief in program's effectiveness
	Staff job satisfaction and morale
Managerial Processes	Agency commitment to program mission
	Provision of training and support to staff
	Recognition of staff's work quality
	Degree of staff discretion
Staff Characteristics	Education level and other demographics
	Experience in the welfare-to-work field
	Prior welfare receipt
Client Characteristics	Prior employment
	Prior welfare receipt
	High school diploma or GED
	Age, gender, race/ethnicity
	Age and number of young children
	Membership in the experimental or control group
Environmental Factors	Unemployment rate
	Employment growth
	Population growth
	AFDC benefit amount
	Food stamp benefit amount
	Control group members' participation in alternative programs

part, an organization's choice of a particular service technology reflects hypotheses about how client change can be accomplished. This technology is usually multidimensional, encompassing an array of staff practices and organizational routines, especially where multiple goals are pursued. For example, a correctional institution may use a combination of individual counseling, group therapy, drug treatment, and varying levels of freedom and privileges in its efforts to reform inmates. A school may combine classroom lectures, group discussions, peer learning, and computer-assisted instruction in pursuit of its educational goals.

Ultimately, the real nature and meaning of an organization's service technology are shaped by how front-line staff (or "street-level bureaucrats") exercise the inherent discretion they have in performing their roles—how they interpret and implement the organization's rules and policies (Lipsky 1980). For example, prison workers may use their discretion to emphasize forms of interaction with inmates that give primacy either to therapeutic goals or to security concerns, and teachers can often decide how much to emphasize test-taking skills versus critical thinking skills. These front-line interpretations and choices may influence an organization's performance because they may shape clients' understanding of a program, their experiences in it, and ultimately, how if at all they change their behavior in response to it.

In this study of welfare-to-work programs, the surveys of front-line staff cover several important aspects of the programs' service technologies, particularly strategies or practices whose importance to a program's success is a matter of some dispute among welfare experts.

One illustration concerns the enforcement of the program's participation mandate. Opinion among experts differs as to the importance of participation mandates to the effectiveness of welfare-to-work programs (e.g., see Mead 1989; Bane 1989; Riccio and Hasenfeld 1996). Some supporters contend, for example, that mandates can be a way to reach recipients who could benefit from the program's services but who might not come forward or participate regularly enough unless compelled to do so. In contrast, critics of mandates argue that they create adversarial relationships between staff and clients that may be inimical to the kinds of value and behavioral changes the program hopes to achieve. Of course, even where a program includes a participation mandate, its implementation may be limited or nonexistent. Staff in some programs may go to great lengths to avoid imposing sanctions except perhaps as a last resort, and rely instead on persuasion to achieve compliance (Riccio and Hasenfeld 1996).

A growing body of evidence shows that welfare-to-work programs in which the participation mandate is strongly enforced can be effective in increasing recipients' earnings and reducing their reliance on welfare (e.g., Riccio, Friedlander, and Freedman 1994; Friedlander and Burtless 1995; Scrivener et al. 1998; Freedman, Mitchell, and Navarro 1999). However, the explicit contribution of enforcement to program performance has been difficult to isolate from other program features, making this aspect of the service technology an important area for further investigation in the present study.[7]

This study is also investigating the influence of several other aspects of service technology that are often presumed by administrators to have a bearing on program effectiveness. One concerns the employment message that staff convey to clients—that is, whether staff encourage them to take a job quickly, even a job that is not particularly desirable, or to be more selective and to take advantage of education and training opportunities in the program in the hope of getting a better job later.[8] A second factor concerns how much staff emphasize personalized attention to clients—that is, trying to gain an in-depth understanding of their personal histories and circumstances and trying to accommodate their individual needs, situations, and preferences in assigning them to other program activities. This can be time consuming for staff and increase agency costs by requiring lower client-staff ratios. Also explored are the effects on performance of how closely staff monitor clients' participation in their assigned program activities, and the degree to which staff engage in "creaming" (i.e., making a greater effort to help clients they believe are the most motivated and have the best chances of succeeding, and reducing their efforts to help other individuals in their caseloads).

Organizational Climate

Complaints from clients of human service organizations—and also from customers of retail and other types of establishments—that the workers "don't care" about them and do not treat them with respect are not uncommon. If such sentiments are widespread, and if clients or customers can turn to other institutions for services, the survival of the "offending" institution may be threatened (Hirschman 1970). For human service organizations, client alienation may make it impossible to achieve people-changing goals even if clients remain involved.

How clients experience and respond to an organization may thus be influenced by features of its social climate, which in this study refers to the shared perceptions among line staff that set the temper and tone of the organization's internal environment.[9] In theory, organizational climate may influence how much clients embrace the organization's goals and service technologies and, in turn, whether they cooperate with or resist the change process. For example, some treatment-oriented correctional institutions try to construct a supportive social environment in which inmates feel understood and respected by staff and believe that staff sincerely want to help them. This climate of support is believed to be essential for gaining inmates' cooperation with counseling and other treatment modalities (Feld 1977; Riccio 1984).

A human service organization's social climate may be reflected in and shaped by a variety of staff beliefs and relationships with clients. This study examines four such factors in welfare-to-work programs, which are described in more detail below: (1) the degree of trust (in the opinion of staff) between line staff and clients; (2) staff beliefs about clients' reasons for receiving welfare and their desire to work; (3) staff beliefs about their program's effectiveness; and (4) staff job satisfaction and morale. All of these factors can influence whether clients come to view the program as a positive, indifferent, or negative intervention in their lives, and this perception may ultimately affect whether the program changes their labor market behavior and welfare outcomes.

Trust between staff and clients. Trust is at the core of the relationship between staff and clients in people-changing organizations. As Hasenfeld (1983) puts it: "Trust represents willingness to put one's fate and welfare into the hands of the other person—a cornerstone of the helping process. . . . Without trust, the client cannot hope to gain the moral commitment of the staff to respond to his or her needs, and the staff cannot hope to gain access to the client's private domain to administer intervention techniques" (p.197; see also Handler 1992). This suggests that in the present study impacts on employment and welfare outcomes will be larger in program offices where a higher proportion of staff believe they have candid, trusting relationships with their clients.

Staff perceptions of clients.   A number of factors may affect whether a climate of trust emerges. Among them are staff beliefs about clients' character and whether they are deemed to be morally responsible for their own predicaments (Hasenfeld 1983). In welfare-to-work programs, staff perceptions of clients range from a belief that recipients are responsible for their own poverty because of a lack of motivation or poor work ethic to a belief that recipients are victims of circumstances beyond their control and have few skills that would make them attractive to employers. Some administrators contend that programs in which there is a climate of acceptance—that is, where staff view recipients more positively and are less likely to blame them—will be more effective in improving recipients' work and welfare outcomes (Riccio, Friedlander, and Freedman 1994; Hasenfeld and Weaver 1996). In essence, expecting that recipients want to work and will do so if given a chance implies a belief that they have "a significant capacity to improve and are amenable to change," an important assumption of people-changing technologies (Hasenfeld 1983, p. 140).[10]

Staff belief in the program's efficacy.   Another potentially important aspect of an organization's social climate is whether staff believe that the program is effective. It is reasonable to expect that the more conviction staff have about the value of the intervention, the more convincing, inspiring, and influential they will be to their clients. Thus by influencing clients' responses to the program, a climate of expected efficacy may enhance a program's actual performance. Although evidence testing this presumption is sparse, Mead (1983) offers some support for it in a study of the Work Incentive (WIN) program (a former welfare-to-work program) in New York City: "In the better offices," he explains, "staff more often really believed that clients could benefit from WIN. In the lower-performing offices, respondents voiced doubt as to whether WIN was a good thing either for registrants or for themselves as employees" (p. 655).

Staff morale and job satisfaction.   Many administrators also believe that when staff are enthusiastic about their jobs and their working environment, job performance is better. Moreover, in staff-client interactions, a climate of enthusiasm might become infectious, helping to secure a positive response by clients to the organization. In contrast, when staff feel alienated from their jobs, they may convey those feelings to clients, who may in turn respond with less engagement.

Although worker morale is a common concern of managers, research demonstrating its relevance to performance is limited. Scott (1998), for example, notes that "several decades of research have demonstrated no clear relation between worker satisfaction and productivity" (p. 65; see also Wilson 1989). The disparity between conventional wisdom and the organizational literature makes it important to investigate whether staff morale matters to the success of welfare-to-work programs.

Managerial Processes

Managing—"figuring out what to do"—is distinguished from front-line work, or "doing it" (Radner 1992, p. 1387). Deciding what to do, however, also implies trying to influence how front-line work is actually done. For example, managers of welfare-to-work programs try to influence how front-line staff implement a service technology (e.g., how strongly to enforce the program's participation mandate) and how these staff try to cultivate the desired internal social climate (e.g., how to foster the development of trusting relationships with clients).

Managerial efforts to direct the work of front-line staff are a form of principal-agent problem, where managers are the principals and front-line staff are the agents (Arrow 1985). These efforts are particularly challenging in human service organizations where staff roles involve significant amounts of discretion and where managers cannot easily monitor how staff perform their assigned functions (Lipsky 1980). For example, a manager has very limited direct control over how counselors in a drug treatment center, employment program, or correctional institution interact with their clients because much of the interaction occurs in private. Thus managers of these street-level bureaucracies must rely on a variety of formal and informal incentives, sanctions, recognition, and other mechanisms to shape line staff behavior, particularly when staff members' own ideologies and interests are not aligned with those of the organization as interpreted by the managers.[11]

One such mechanism can be found in how managers communicate the importance of the organization's mission and the staff's contributions to it. For example, writing from a political economy perspective, Miller asserts that leaders in hierarchies "shape expectations among subordinates about cooperation among employees and between employees and their hierarchical superiors" through "communication, exhortation, symbolic position taking" (1992, p. 217). Case studies of a 1980s welfare-to-work program in Massachusetts (Employment and Training Choices) offer an illustration. In these programs, higher-level welfare administrators (and even the governor himself) energized staff and forged their commitment to the program's mission by clearly and publicly communicating support for the program and the importance of its success (Behn 1991; Nathan 1993). Behn contends that managers who "articulate the agency's mission can help the street level bureaucrats exercise the discretion that the standard operating procedures cannot eliminate" (1991, p. 120).

The current study assesses whether variation in these aspects of management across welfare-to-work program offices helps explain the observed variation in office impacts on employment and welfare outcomes. It uses data from staff surveys on how much importance the front-line staff believed higher-level administrators assigned to the success of the program, and how much discretion staff believed they were permitted to exercise in their work with clients. In addition, the study examines the influence of other management-related factors that might affect how line staff perform their roles, such as staff perceptions of whether high-quality work was recognized and rewarded by managers, and whether staff believed that the organization provided them with adequate training and support to do their jobs well.[12]

Staff Characteristics

Most managers would agree that an organization's performance depends heavily on the skills and quality of the staff. However, given the limited information available at the point of hiring, it is difficult for them to predict how well a given candidate will perform. In welfare-to-work programs, the necessary expertise for many front-line positions is broad. For example, Brodkin (1995, p. 81) argues that caseworkers in such programs "need skills and training equivalent to that of human resources counselors, social workers, teachers, or others in related professions" to prepare them for the complex judgments they face in working with clients. These requisite skills contrast with the relatively straightforward decision making required of eligibility workers who process grant applications and welfare benefit payments. Of course, characteristics such as commitment, judgment, and maturity are critical in case management tasks but are difficult to assess. Therefore, to an important extent, managers' decisions are driven by objective characteristics such as the candidate's prior experience, education level, and professional training in relation to the requirements of the job.

How much, then, do these staff characteristics really matter to a program's success? The current study addresses this question, in part, by determining whether program offices that are more heavily staffed by people with higher education (e.g., those with at least a bachelor's degree) are more effective than offices in which fewer staff have such credentials. The study also considers the importance of hiring staff who hold a master of social work (MSW) degree. Some administrators of welfare-to-work programs may favor such a credential because of social work training in personal and family problem-solving skills. Others are not convinced that professional social work training is essential in a program where employment is a central goal; instead, they favor experience in private-sector businesses or other professions. The current study, therefore, examines whether a program's performance is enhanced when the proportion of staff with MSWs is higher. (Information on other professional degrees is not available.) In addition, it examines whether a higher proportion of staff with prior experience working as an employment counselor in a Job Training Partnership Act (JTPA) or other welfare-to-work or job-training program confers any advantage for program performance.

Client Characteristics

How well a program appears to perform may be influenced by the types of people it serves, and much of the literature on welfare-to-work and job-training programs finds that program effects are often much larger for some subgroups of clients than for others. For example, one study of mandatory, primarily job-search, programs for welfare recipients found that impacts were larger for moderately disadvantaged clients than for those with either few or substantial disadvantages, as defined by their work history and prior reliance on welfare (Friedlander and Burtless 1995). It is also noteworthy that federal performance standards for JTPA programs required that estimates of individual programs' job placement rates be adjusted for a range of participant characteristics, such as gender and level of basic skills, to account for the possibility that some local offices may have lower placement rates, in part because they serve more difficult-to-place people.[13]

Some of the offices in the current study are likely to have a disproportionate share of clients whose behavior and circumstances are harder, or easier, to change. Therefore, to permit a fairer comparison of program effects across offices, and to isolate the independent contribution of the offices' organizational and management conditions and practices on program impacts, cross-office differences in measured client characteristics are controlled for statistically.

Program Environment

How well a program performs may also be affected by the local context within which it operates. As one illustration, the outcomes and impacts of welfare-to-work and job-training programs may be influenced by the strength of the local job market: where jobs are plentiful, it may be easier to attain high job-placement rates.[14] Recognizing this, JTPA performance standards were adjusted to reflect the local unemployment rate and other indicators of the local economy. How program impacts are affected by local economic conditions is less certain. Indeed, a better labor market may make it easier for the control group to find work, which may reduce program impacts. Because of the potential influence of local conditions, we hope to include measures of the local unemployment rate, employment growth, and population growth in the statistical models as control variables.

Welfare and food stamp grant levels, which vary by state, are also important external factors to consider. In a state paying lower welfare benefits, even a low-wage job may pay considerably more than welfare, making work more attractive than in a high-benefit state. Thus state differences in welfare and food stamp grants are included as control variables in the analysis.

Finally, program impacts may be affected by the availability beyond the program of similar services. Some locations are service-rich, with many alternative training programs or support services, whereas in other areas, the supply is much more limited. If these alternative services are as effective as those offered by the program, then all else being equal, program impacts will be smaller in areas where the control group is more highly served. This study, therefore, attempts to control for this variation in service use by using survey data on the extent of the control group's (as well as the program group's) participation in employment and training programs.

Looking Beyond the Average and Separate Effects of the Independent Variables

So far, we have discussed office-level characteristics in terms of average perceptions, attitudes, or behavior. For example, we have discussed average staff perceptions of clients' willingness to work, or of the agency's commitment to the mission of their program. As noted, our study estimates the relationship between these averages and program impacts. In addition, we consider other, and possibly more plausible, ways in which management and organizational characteristics might affect program performance.

Staff consensus.   Some researchers and practitioners posit that, to be effective, organizations require a common set of values and assumptions plus a common sense of mission, sometimes referred to as a "strong culture." For example, Denison contends that a "strong culture, with well-socialized members, improves effectiveness because it facilitates the exchange of information and coordination of behavior" (1990, p. 9). A strong culture helps to define and reinforce the goals of the organization and gives direction to staff actions. In contrast, organizational performance may suffer when staff are divided over what the organization and they should be doing. Thus it is often argued that managers' most important job is to instill commonality of purpose.[15] Therefore, one might expect local welfare offices with a high degree of staff agreement on core issues to be more effective than offices where staff hold opposing views or emphasize different priorities.

To test whether greater staff agreement on core issues leads to better organizational performance, the within-office standard deviation of staff perceptions, attitudes, and behaviors is calculated and included as office-level independent variables in the statistical models.[16] Offices with more staff agreement will have smaller standard deviations. If a "strong culture" is advantageous to an organization's performance, these offices should have larger impacts, on average.

Staff-client social distance.   The analysis also includes measures of the social distance between program staff and their clients. Less social distance may result in greater program-induced employment and earnings gains. For example, less social distance may lead to greater trust and increased communication between staff and clients (Katan 1974). Improved communication might produce a better flow of information and increased motivation by clients to act on what they have learned.

Social distance might play a very different role in clients' use of welfare. More social distance might produce a greater reduction in welfare receipt because staff who differ from their clients in fundamental ways might find it difficult to understand clients' personal circumstances. This in turn might cause staff to rely mainly on threats and sanctions to motivate clients, inducing some clients to stop receiving welfare even if they cannot find a job (a pure welfare deterrent effect). Alternatively, staff who have been on welfare themselves may have less tolerance for some recipients' seemingly lagging efforts to get off the rolls, which also might cause them to take actions that deter future welfare receipt by their clients.

Candidate measures of social distance include the percentage of local office staff who themselves received welfare in the past; the difference between the percentage of staff and clients who are male; and the difference between the percentage of staff and clients who are from particular racial or ethnic groups.

Threshold effects.   It is also important to consider potential nonlinear relationships between office characteristics and office performance. One such nonlinearity is a threshold effect, which is a marked shift in the effect of an office characteristic on office performance when the characteristic exceeds a certain level. For example, there may be no relationship between the strength of the employment message conveyed by program staff and the labor market behavior of clients until the persistence and consistency of this message exceed a certain threshold. Above this level, however, the message may have a pronounced effect on client behavior.[17]

Synergy.   Finally, it is reasonable to expect that some organizational factors may have little independent effect on an organization's performance but a powerful influence when combined with some other organizational practice or condition. For example, a consistent employment message may have little effect on client behavior without a program approach that simultaneously emphasizes strong enforcement of the participation requirement. If both factors are present, however, their combined effect might greatly exceed the sum of their two separate effects. Our analysis tries to account for such synergy by specifying interaction terms for factors that are combined.[18] Because these interactions involve mainly office-level characteristics, their number is limited substantially by the number of offices in the sample and the number of other office-level independent variables in the analysis.

Dependent Variables: Measures and Preliminary Findings

Welfare-to-work programs all aim to increase welfare recipients' employment and earnings and reduce their reliance on welfare. However, not all programs place the same degree of emphasis on employment-related versus welfare-related goals. For example, some programs attach a higher priority to helping clients increase their income and offer more intensive and longer-duration services, even if it means extending their stay on welfare. Others attach higher priority to reducing the welfare rolls to achieve financial savings. Furthermore, success in increasing employment and earnings is not always accompanied by success in reducing welfare payments, in part because a program may cause some people to leave welfare without obtaining a job—for example, to avoid a participation mandate (Gueron and Pauly 1991; Friedlander and Burtless 1995). For these reasons, our study measures program performance—and assesses the factors that influence it—separately for employment-related and welfare-related goals by using a variety of dependent variables rather than a single, composite measure.

Different programs can also produce differences in the timing of impacts. Programs that focus on immediate job search are expected to increase participants' employment and earnings within a relatively short period of time. In contrast, programs that emphasize human capital development through education and training may actually reduce participants' earnings in the short run when participants are enrolled in training while some of their control group counterparts are findings jobs. When the training is completed, however, the new skills learned may help participants obtain better jobs than they would have otherwise, causing them eventually to earn more than the control group.

To account properly for these alternative timing patterns requires follow-up data for as long as possible. As previously noted, the present analysis uses data for the first two years after random assignment for all sample members. This is longer than typical efforts to monitor program performance (Barnow 1999), although it may be too short to assess fully programs that involve extensive training. Three to five years of follow-up data are available on sample members in a subset of offices.

Reflecting the different program goals and potentially different timing of impacts, eight measures are used as dependent variables. These measures fall into two categories. The first category reflects the cumulative experience of sample members during the full two years of follow-up and summarizes any immediate and later program impacts that occur. Four such measures have been constructed: the mean number of quarters employed; mean total earnings; the mean number of quarters of welfare receipt; and mean total welfare payments received. (Longer-term impacts may also be examined for a subset of sites where extended follow-up data are available.)

The second category of outcome measures reflects the experience of sample members during the last quarter of the available follow-up period. Thus it provides an indication of whether impacts are likely to continue beyond this period. Four such measures have been constructed: the percent employed during the quarter; mean earnings; the percent receiving welfare; and the mean amount of welfare received.

Table 6.2 indicates that local office variation is highly statistically significant for all eight potential dependent variables—which means that they represent real differences in true impacts.[19] Consider the results for impacts on mean total earnings and welfare receipt during the two-year follow-up period. Impacts on earnings ranged from a negligible $74 decrease for the local office at the twenty-fifth percentile, to a $587 increase for the office at the fiftieth percentile (the median office), to a $1,280 increase for the office at the seventy-fifth percentile.[20] Likewise, estimated impacts on total dollars of AFDC received ranged from decreases of $230 to $480 to

TABLE 6.2

Distribution of office impacts

Outcome Measure	Estimated Impact for the Welfare Office at the:			Significant Cross-Site Impact Variation[a]
	75th Percentile	50th Percentile (median)	25th Percentile	
Full two-year follow-up period				
Mean dollars earned	$1,280	$587	−$74	Yes
Mean dollars of AFDC received	−$1,070	−$480	−$230	Yes
Mean quarters employed	0.5	0.2	0.1	Yes
Mean quarters receiving AFDC	−1.5	−0.8	−0.4	Yes
Last quarter of period				
Mean dollars earned	$180	$100	−$10	Yes
Mean dollars of AFDC received	−$130	−$60	−$20	Yes
Percentage employed	6.6 %	3.0 %	0.4 %	Yes
Percentage receiving AFDC	−6.8 %	−3.6 %	−1.1 %	Yes

[a]Yes indicates that the variation in impacts across sites is statistically significant at beyond the 0.0000 level based on a chi-square test of their homogeneity (Hedges and Olkin 1985).

$1,070 for the offices at the twenty-fifth, fiftieth, and seventy-fifth percentiles, respectively.

Thus the first requirement for the analyses proposed in this chapter appears to be met: there is indeed a large and statistically significant variation in local welfare office performance. This variation makes it possible to explore the relationships between program performance and the characteristics of offices and their clients.

Estimating the Relationships

Hierarchical or multilevel models (Bryk and Raudenbush 1992) are used to estimate these relationships in a way that properly accounts for the multilevel nature of the data. Specifically, hierarchical models address the fact that individual sample members are grouped within local welfare offices.[21] Doing so is necessary in order to compute appropriate standard errors for parameter estimates, which, in turn, are necessary for appropriate statistical tests of parameters.

Multilevel models can also support a richer conceptualization of the behavior being studied than is possible with simpler models; multilevel models explicitly distinguish between factors at each level of aggregation in the data. In this study, this means focusing first on the factors that affect individual outcomes and impacts within a welfare office, and then focusing on the factors that produce differences in these experiences across offices.

Multilevel models provide yet another important benefit: an ability to estimate how true program impacts vary across sites. Most past multisite experiments have reported how program impact *estimates* varied across sites. However, much of this variation is due to random sampling and measurement error and thus does not reflect differences in true impacts. Hierarchical models can estimate this error (from random individual variation within sites) and separate it from the true variation in impacts. Such models also make it possible to measure the extent to which the variation in true impacts across offices can be "explained" by the characteristics of these offices.

Equations 2, 3, and 4 illustrate the basic two-level hierarchical model used for the present study.[22] This model includes separate regression equations at the levels of individual sample members and local welfare offices.

Level #1 (Individuals)

$$Y_{ji} = a_j + B_j P_{ji} + \sum_k \gamma_k X_{kji} P_{ji} + \sum_k \delta_k X_{kji} + \varepsilon_{ji} \tag{2}$$

Level #2 (Offices)

$$B_j = B_0 + \sum_m \pi_m Z_{mj} + r_j \tag{3}$$

$$a_j = a_0 + \sum_m \lambda_m Z_{mj} + v_j \tag{4}$$

where:

Y_{ji} = the outcome for person i from office j,

P_{ji} = 1 if person i from office j is a program group member and zero otherwise,

X_{kji} = the kth background characteristic for person i from office j,

Z_{mj} = the mth characteristic for office j,

B_j = the true impact for office j, controlling for its client mix,

B_0 = the mean true impact for all of the offices, controlling for their client mixes,

a_j = the true mean outcome for office j, controlling for its client mix,

a_o = the true mean outcome for all of the offices, controlling for their client mixes,

$\gamma_k, \delta_k,$ = individual-level parameters to be estimated,

π_m, λ_m = office-level parameters to be estimated,

ε_{ji} = a random error term for individual outcomes,

r_j = a random error term for office impacts, and

v_j = a random error term for office mean outcomes.

The level 1 equation specifies individual outcomes (employment, earnings, or welfare received), Y_{ji}, as a function of random assignment to the program or control group, P_{ji}, plus a series of interactions between P_{ji} and individual background characteristics, X_{kji}, plus a series of covariates that comprise the individual background characteristics themselves, not as part of interaction terms.

Including covariates in the model is desirable for the purposes of increasing statistical precision. Given random assignment, however, these covariates are not necessary in order to produce unbiased estimates of program impacts.[23] Thus the coefficients for these covariates will not play an important role in the study's findings.

Coefficients for the interactions between background characteristics and the random assignment variable indicate how program impacts differ for different types of clients. These findings are of substantive interest in their own right because they provide information about who benefited most (and least) from the programs being evaluated. In addition—and of greater importance for the present study—they make it possible to estimate how the impact for each office differs from the overall average impact, controlling statistically for measured differences in the local client mix. This office-specific impact difference is represented by B_j in the model. It is this term that forms the basis for studying how local office impacts are related to differences in local office characteristics, controlling for their client mix.

Lastly, note that equation 2 includes an office-specific intercept, a_j. This represents how the average outcome for each office differs from the overall average outcome for all offices. This parameter, however, has limited substantive importance for the present study.

The level 2 model contains two equations, one for the variation across offices in program impacts, B_j, and another for the variation across offices in average outcomes, a_j. Equation 3 for the variation in B_j is the central focus of the analysis. It describes how program impacts vary with the office-level factors, Z_{mj}, such as their service technology, organizational climate, management processes, and economic environment.

The equation for a_j describes how office characteristics are related to average outcome levels, which is only of secondary interest for the present study. Nevertheless, because all three equations must be estimated simultaneously, as a system, it is necessary to include them all.[24]

Conclusion

This chapter has described a research study that aims to "get inside the black box" of welfare-to-work programs and help explain why some programs are more successful than others in increasing recipients' employment and earnings and reducing their reliance on welfare. The study is unusual in being able to measure the variation in performance by drawing on evidence of true program impacts based on site-specific random assignment experiments in a large number of program sites. Moreover, using rare quantitative data on a variety of management and organizational variables, and employing hierarchical modeling techniques, it tests hypotheses about the relative importance of such factors in accounting for organizational performance (program impacts).

We hope to make two contributions. First, we hope with this study to inform welfare-to-work policy by providing evidence about the extent to which certain program and management approaches widely believed to enhance a program's effectiveness really do matter. Second, and more broadly, we seek to illustrate an empirical method for studying organizational performance that can serve as a model for other studies.

References

Arrow, Kenneth. 1985. The economics of agency. In *Principals and agents: The structure of business*, edited by John W. Pratt and Richard J. Zeckhauser. Boston, Mass.: Harvard Business School Press, pp. 37–51.

Bane, Mary Jo. 1989. Welfare reform and mandatory versus voluntary work: Policy issue or management problem? *Journal of Policy Analysis and Management*, 8 (2): 285–89.

Bardach, Eugene. 1993. *Improving the productivity of JOBS programs.* New York: Manpower Demonstration Research Corporation.

Barnow, Burt. 1992. The effects of performance standards on state and local programs. In *Evaluating welfare and training programs*, edited by Charles F. Manski and Irwin Garfinkel. Cambridge, Mass.: Harvard University Press, pp. 277–309.

Barnow, Burt. 1999. Exploring the relationship between performance management and program impact: A case study of the Job Training Partnership Act. Working paper. Baltimore: Johns Hopkins University Institute for Policy Studies.

Behn, Robert. 1991. *Leadership counts: Lessons for public managers from the Massachusetts welfare, training, and employment program.* Cambridge, Mass.: Harvard University Press.

Betsey, Charles, Robison Hollister, and Mary Papageorgiou. 1985. *Youth employment and training programs: The YEDPA years.* Committee on Youth Employment Programs, Commission on Behavioral and Social Sciences and Education, National Research Council. Washington, D.C.: National Academy Press.

Brodkin, Evelyn. 1995. Administrative capacity in welfare reform. In *Looking before we leap: Social science and welfare reform*, edited by R. Kent Weaver and William T. Dickens. Washington, D.C.: The Brookings Institution, 75–90.

Bryk, Anthony, and Stephen Raudenbush. 1992. *Hierarchical linear models: Applications and data analysis methods.* Newbury Park, Calif.: Sage Publications.

Cook, Thomas, and David Campbell. 1979. *Quasi-experimentation: Design and analysis issues for field settings.* Chicago: Rand McNally.

Denison, Daniel. 1990. *Corporate culture and organizational effectiveness.* New York: John Wiley & Sons.

Feld, Barry. 1977. *Neutralizing inmate violence: Juvenile offenders in institutions.* Cambridge, Mass.: Ballinger.

Freedman, Stephen, Marissa Mitchell, and David Navarro. 1999. *The Los Angeles Jobs-First GAIN evaluation: Preliminary findings on participation patterns and impacts.* New York: Manpower Demonstration Research Corporation.

Friedlander, Daniel, and Gary Burtless. 1995. *Five years after: The long-term effects of welfare-to-work programs.* New York: Russell Sage Foundation.

Friedlander, Daniel, David Greenberg, and Philip Robins. 1997. Evaluating government training programs for the economically disadvantaged. *Journal of Economic Literature,* 35: 1809–55.

Glisson, Charles. 1992. Structure and technology in human services organizations. In *Human services as complex organizations,* edited by Yeheskel Hasenfeld. Newbury Park, Calif.: Sage Publications, pp. 184–202.

Greenberg, David, Robert Meyer, and Michael Wiseman. 1994. Multisite employment and training evaluations: A tale of three studies. *Industrial and Labor Relations Review,* 47(4): 679–91.

Greenberg, David, and Mark Shroder. 1997. *Digest of social experiments,* 2d ed. Washington, D.C.: The Urban Institute Press.

Gueron, Judith, and Edward Pauly. 1991. *From welfare to work.* New York: Russell Sage Foundation.

Hamilton, Gayle, and Thomas Brock. 1994. *The JOBS evaluation. Early lessons from seven sites.* Washington, D.C.: U.S. Department of Health and Human Services, Administration for Children and Families and Office of the Assistant Secretary for Planning and Evaluation; and U.S. Department of Education, Office of the Under Secretary and Office of Vocational and Adult Education.

Handler, Joel. 1992. Dependency and discretion. In *Human services as complex organizations,* edited by Yeheskel Hasenfeld. Newbury Park, Calif.: Sage Publications.

Hasenfeld, Yeheskel. 1983. *Human service organizations.* Englewood Cliffs, N.J.: Prentice-Hall.

Hasenfeld, Yeheskel, and Richard English (eds.). 1974. *Human service organizations: A book of readings.* Ann Arbor: University of Michigan Press.

Hasenfeld, Yeheskel, and Dale Weaver. 1996. Enforcement, compliance, and disputes in welfare-to-work programs. *Social Service Review,* 70 (2): 235–56.

Heckman, James (ed.). In press. *Performance standards in a government bureaucracy: Analytical essays on the JTPA performance standards system.* Kalamazoo, Mich.: W. E. Upjohn Institute.

Hedges, Larry, and Ingram Olkin. 1985. *Statistical methods for meta-analysis.* Boston: Academic Press, pp. 168–87.

Heinrich, Carolyn J. 1999. Do government bureaucrats make effective use of performance management information? *Journal of Public Administration Research and Theory,* 9 (3): 363–93.

Hirschman, Albert O. 1970. *Exit, voice, and loyalty: Responses to decline in firms, organizations, and states.* Cambridge, Mass.: Harvard University Press.

Katan, Yosef. 1974. The use of indigenous workers in human service organizations. In *Human service organizations: A book of readings,* edited by Yeheskel Hasenfeld and Richard A. English. Ann Arbor: University of Michigan Press, pp. 448–67.

Kemple, James, Daniel Friedlander, and Veronica Fellerath. 1995. *Florida's Project Independence: Benefits, costs, and two-year impacts of Florida's JOBS program.* New York: Manpower Demonstration Research Corporation.

Lipsky, Michael. 1980. *Street-level bureaucracy.* New York: Russell Sage Foundation.

Marcoulides, George, and Ronald Heck. 1993. Organizational culture and performance: Proposing and testing a model. *Organization Science,* 4(2): 209–25.

Mead, Lawrence. 1983. Expectations and welfare work: WIN in New York City. *Policy Studies Review,* 2(4): 648–62.

———. 1989. The logic of Workfare: The underclass and work policy. *Annals of the American Academy of Political and Social Science,* 501:156–70.

Miller, Gary. 1992. *Managerial dilemmas: The political economy of hierarchy.* Cambridge: Cambridge University Press.

Mitchell, John, Mark Chadwin, and Demetra Nightingale. 1979. *Implementing welfare-employment programs: An institutional analysis of the Work Incentive (WIN) program.* Washington, D.C.: The Urban Institute.

Nathan, Richard. 1993. *Turning promises into performance: The management challenge of implementing Workfare.* New York: Columbia University Press.

Peters, Thomas, and Robert Waterman, Jr. 1982. *In search of excellence.* New York: Harper & Row.

Pfeffer, Jeffrey. 1983. Organizational demography. *Research in organizational behavior,* Volume 5. Greenwich, Conn.: JAI Press, pp. 299–357.

———. 1997. *New directions for organization theory: Problems and prospects.* Oxford, N.Y.: Oxford University Press.

Radner, Roy. 1992. Hierarchy: The economics of managing. *Journal of Economic Literature,* 30: 1382–1415.

Riccio, James. 1984. *Treatment and custody in juvenile correctional facilities: A study of staff and resident behavior.* Ph.D. dissertation. Department of Sociology, Princeton University.

Riccio, James, Daniel Friedlander, and Stephen Freedman. 1994. *GAIN: Benefits, costs, and three-year impacts of a welfare-to-work program.* New York: Manpower Demonstration Research Corporation.

Riccio, James, and Yeheskel Hasenfeld. 1996. Enforcing a participation mandate in a welfare-to-work program. *Social Service Review,* 70 (4): 516–42.

Riccio, James, and Alan Orenstein. 1996. Understanding best practices for operating welfare-to-work programs. *Evaluation Review,* 20(1): 3–28.

Saffold, Guy, III. 1998. Culture traits, strength, and organizational performance: Moving beyond "strong" culture. *Academy of Management Review,* 13 (4): 546–58.

Scott, W. Richard. 1998. *Organizations: Rational, natural, open systems.* 4th ed. Upper Saddle River, N.J.: Prentice-Hall.

Scrivener, Susan Hamilton, Mary Farrel, Stephen Freedman, Daniel Friedlander, Marisa Mitchell, Jodi Nudelman, and Christine Schwartz. 1998. *Implementation, participation patterns, costs, and two-year impacts of the Portland (Oregon) welfare-to-work program.* Washington, D.C.: U.S. Department of Health and Human Services, Administration for Children and Families and Office of the Assistant Secretary for Planning and Evaluation; and U.S. Department of Education, Office of the Under Secretary and Office of Vocational and Adult Education.

Sherwood, Kay, and Fred Doolittle. 1999. What's behind the impacts: Doing implementation research in the context of program impact studies. Unpublished paper.

Wilson, James Q. 1989. *Bureaucracy: What government agencies do and why they do it.* New York: Basic Books.

Endnotes

*The research for this paper was funded by a grant from the Pew Charitable Trusts.

1. See Sherwood and Doolittle (1999) for a general discussion of the role of implementation research in explaining the results of impact analyses.

2. For an example of such an approach applied to a California welfare-to-work program, see Riccio, Friedlander, and Freedman (1994) and Riccio and Orenstein (1996).

3. AFDC was replaced in 1996 by the Temporary Assistance for Needy Families (TANF) program, under the Personal Responsi-

bility and Work Opportunity Reconciliation Act of 1996. However, all states continue to operate welfare-to-work programs, though now in the context of time limits for access to cash benefits. How time limits will influence the effectiveness of these programs is uncertain, but they do raise the stakes for performance. The more successful these programs are in moving recipients into jobs and off welfare, the fewer will be the number who face a termination of benefits without adequate resources to support themselves or their families.

4. Although some sample members were welfare applicants at the time they entered the study and did not become recipients, all will be referred to as recipients for ease of presentation.

5. As will become apparent, a number of the constructs used in this study can be classified under the general rubric of "organizational culture," especially in its broadest formulation. According to Denison, "The culture perspective has focused on the basic values, beliefs, and assumptions that are present in organizations, the patterns of behavior that result from these shared meanings, and the symbols that express the links between assumptions, values, and behavior to an organization's members" (1990, p.27). He asserts that "the concept had taken the business and academic world by storm" in the early 1980s (1990, p.2); however, there is little hard evidence linking culture and performance. (See also Peters and Waterman 1982; Saffold 1988; Wilson 1989; and Marcoulides and Heck 1993).

6. Although this study focuses on the direct influence of technology on performance, it is important to acknowledge that the choice of technology and its influence on performance may depend, in part, on other factors such as the organization's structure (e.g., degree of centralized decision making) and local environmental conditions. See Scott (1998) for a general review of the literature on relationships between organizational technology, structure, and environment and links to effectiveness, and Hasenfeld (1983) and Glisson (1992) for specific applications to human services.

7. One study of Work Incentive (WIN) programs in ten states using a composite measure of program performance (which combined employment and welfare outcomes) found a small, statistically significant relationship between performance and the use of the formal adjudication process in dealing with noncooperative clients. Counseling, however, was a more consistent response in the high-performing offices (Mitchell, Chadwin, and Nightingale 1979). A later study comparing welfare-to-work offices in California found a statistically significant correlation between the em-

phasis on formal enforcement of the penalty process and an office's impact on welfare payments, but not its impact on earnings (Riccio and Hasenfeld 1996).

8. In studying the employment message and related themes, the analysis also attempts to determine the influence of clients' rates of participation in job search and education and training activities on program performance. It is important to note, however, that participation patterns only partly reflect an agency's service technology. Although they may be shaped by the service options available to clients and the choices staff advocate, they also reflect decisions made by clients (including the decision whether to participate at all). Participation patterns can also be thought of as an intervening outcome between other aspects of the service technology (e.g., monitoring and enforcement) and program performance (e.g., impacts on employment and welfare outcomes).

9. The concept of organizational climate has varying meanings in the organizational literature, and in some uses it overlaps with the concepts of organizational culture and organizational structure (Denison 1990; Pfeffer 1997).

10. In a qualitative study comparing a variety of welfare-to-work programs, Bardach (1993) suggests that more effective programs were those in which staff held high expectations about client potential to succeed, and this philosophy cut across many different aspects of the program. Unfortunately, the staff surveys used in the current study did not measure staff expectations of clients per se.

11. An extensive literature on performance management in public organizations examines the ways in which performance standards and measurement provide explicit incentives for front-line staff and managers. These issues are examined, for example, in the context of the Job Training Partnership Act (JTPA) by Barnow (1992, 1999), Heckman (in press), and Heinrich 1999.

12. Mitchell, Chadwin, and Nightingale (1979) found that high performance WIN programs had managers who effectively conveyed clearly to local staff the national program's goals, provided more frequent and extensive training of staff, and had good systems for reporting job placements and grant reductions. Bardach (1993) suggests that managers of high-performing welfare-to-work programs should hold their staff to high expectations, motivate them with meaningful and fair performance standards, and provide them with support, information, and training.

13. The Job Training Partnership Act was replaced in 1998 by the Workforce Investment Act, but the latter act, too, adopts performance standards that take into account participant characteristics.

14. Mitchell, Chadwin, and Nightingale (1979) found that various measures of local socioeconomic conditions explained a high proportion of the variance in client outcomes across state and local WIN offices. A comparison of county impacts in the evaluation of GAIN shows no consistent relationship between program impacts and local labor market indicators (Riccio, Friedlander, and Freedman 1994). See also Gueron and Pauly (1991).

15. This may be a bigger challenge in organizations where staff characteristics vary substantially. For example, coalitions among staff may form based on tenure, age, gender, or other factors, and conflicts among these coalitions might affect organizational performance (Pfeffer 1983).

16. With survey responses from about 1,500 staff for seventy-two local welfare offices (or roughly twenty responses per office), enough data should be available to compute meaningful standard deviations for each office.

17. Efforts to model such threshold effects are made only if the range of variation in the office characteristics of interest is great enough. Even so, it is possible to examine threshold effects for only a small number of independent variables. A threshold effect can be specified by interacting an independent variable with a dummy variable that indicates when it exceeds a specified value. Both the variable and its interaction term are then included in the model. Because each interaction "absorbs" a degree of freedom (in our case at the office level), the procedure can only be used for a small number of independent variables.

18. Interaction terms will be specified as the product of the factors involved.

19. The high degree of statistical significance reflects the large amount of variation in estimated impacts, the large sample for each office, and the large number of offices.

20. Findings in table 6.2 were obtained for each outcome measure by sorting offices in order of the size of their estimated impact and identifying the office at each point in the resulting distribution.

21. To help assess the gains produced by using hierarchical models, their results are compared to those from two simpler approaches: (1) standard individual-level regression models (where each observation is an individual sample member) with interactions to indicate how program impacts vary with office and client characteristics, and (2) standard aggregate regression models (where each observation is a local welfare office) that specify estimated impacts by office as a function of office characteristics and mean client characteristics.

22. In addition, it may be necessary to account for how local offices
    are grouped within states and how states are grouped within the
    original three MDRC studies. If necessary, a "fixed-effect" ap-
    proach would likely be used to do so. This would involve speci-
    fying a series of dummy variables to account for the groups
    involved. It would not involve specifying additional levels in the
    hierarchical model.

23. This is a well-known property of random assignment. If covari-
    ates are not included, program impacts are estimated by the dif-
    ferences in mean outcomes for the program and control groups. If
    covariates are included, program impacts are estimated as "re-
    gression-adjusted" differences in these means. The expected val-
    ues of both types of estimators equal the true program impact.
    Hence they are both unbiased.

24. Such models are usually estimated using maximum likelihood
    procedures (Bryk and Raudenbush 1992).

Congressional Committees and Policy Change: Explaining Legislative Outcomes in Banking, Trucking, Airline, and Telecommunications Deregulation

Jack H. Knott and Thomas H. Hammond

Over the past several decades, a substantial body of literature has asserted that congressional committees play a dominant role in policymaking in the United States. The subgovernment literature, for example, makes the case for a powerful role for committees. In this view, members of Congress gain appointment to committees with jurisdiction over policy areas of interest to their constituents. If these committees come to be populated largely by members who are not representative of the rest of their chamber, these committees, in alliance with interest groups and executive agencies, are said to have the ability to dominate policy choices within their jurisdictions. Classic case studies on subgovernments in public works, transportation, tobacco, and defense demonstrate the dominant role that congressional committees can play in policymaking.

Nonetheless, there are other well-known cases, such as airline and trucking deregulation in the 1970s and 1980s, in which the preferences of congressional committees clearly did not determine policy outcomes (Hammond and Knott 1988). Instead, other parts of Congress, such as the chamber floors, as well as presidents, executive agencies, and the courts, exercised more influence over policy choice and policy change than did the committees (Dodd and Schott 1979; Smith 1988).

These conflicting studies leave the role of congressional committees in policy choice and policy change unclear. In this chapter, we
construct a formal model of legislative policymaking and use it to
explain, in part, why congressional committees can have such varying effects on policy outcomes. The model enables us to identify the
conditions under which the legislative committees will be effective
in fostering policy change, blocking policy change, and those conditions under which they will have relatively little influence over policy change. In terms of the logic of governance, we are concerned
with explaining how environmental factors influence outcomes. In
particular, we address how the strategic interaction among formal
political institutions affects legislative outcomes, and how political
institutions vary in their influence on outcomes based on their relationship to the initial legislative status quo and the policy status
quo as it develops during implementation.

We use this model of legislative procedures and policy change to
explain and interpret four cases of deregulation—in the banking,
trucking, airline, and telecommunications industries—that occurred in the 1970s and 1980s. Our model offers an explanation for
why the congressional committees had such varying effects on outcomes in these regulatory policy sectors. We demonstrate that a critical variable is how exogenous changes in the policy status quo can
determine how much influence committees should be expected to
have on legislative outcomes.

Institutional Actors and the Status Quo

To explain why legislative outcomes might change, it is necessary to
identify the conditions under which the policy status quo is in equilibrium and the conditions under which the policy status quo can
be changed. By identifying these conditions, we can understand the
relationship between the status quo and the ability of the institutional participants to block or effect policy change.

Almost every legislative bill is initially considered in a congressional committee. A committee can often defend the status quo simply
by not passing any bill; this usually prevents further action on the
floors of the House and Senate. This ability to block bills is a primary
source of power for the traditional subgovernment triangle, that is,

for the alliance of committees, interest groups, and executive agency in some issue area. If the policy status quo changes exogenously, however, through a court decision or agency action, for example, the committee must reestablish the status quo ante through legislative action. This action requires passing a bill that must not only be approved by other committees but also by the floors of both chambers and the president. This difference between defending an old policy and establishing a new one is crucial to understanding the effect of the institutional rules on the relative power of the committees.

It is sometimes suggested that exogenous changes in the policy status quo do not necessarily prevent a congressional committee from restoring the status quo ante. Even though reestablishing the status quo ante requires that the committee pass a bill on both floors of Congress and the president sign it, a generalized reciprocity norm may operate in Congress whereby congresspersons defer to the preferences and expertise of the committees with jurisdiction over particular policy issues (Ferejohn 1985). A reciprocity norm may thereby increase the chances of legislative outcomes favorable to the committees.

The norm of reciprocity never did operate perfectly, however, even in the heyday of the "textbook Congress" in the 1950s and 1960s (Shepsle 1989), and there are several reasons for believing that its influence has declined since then. First, subsequent to the 1971 Subcommittee Bill of Rights (Smith and Deering 1984; Fenno 1973; Bach and Smith 1988), for example, the power of committee chairpersons succumbed to the growing influence of party leaders through the party caucuses; partisanship as a criterion for voting on the floor increasingly conflicted with deference to the committees. Second, the growth of public interest groups, which have used the courts and the news media as weapons to further their causes, have left legislators wary of taking unpopular positions on visible public issues. Third, under the Gramm-Rudman-Hollings budget targets, the postwar practice of positive sum budgeting partially gave way to zero-sum calculations. With a more limited budgetary pie, increases for the favored programs of one committee translate into losses for the favored programs of other committees; hence the latter committee members are less likely to show deference when their own budgets may be decreased (see Wildavsky 1988, pp. 253–58). Finally, staff and legislative budgets have increased dramatically, making legislators less dependent on specialized committees for informed opinions on issues outside their own committees' jurisdictions (Shepsle 1989).

Modeling Legislative Procedures

Given that presidents were never particularly deferential to congressional committees, and if deference to legislative committee preferences is not as powerful a force on the chamber floors as it once was, then an understanding of the role of committees requires incorporating the president and the floors of both the House and Senate in our analysis. To understand variations in the impact of committees on legislative outcomes, it is useful to develop and apply a formal model of the policymaking process.

The model that we use—see Hammond and Knott (1996) for a full explication—focuses on legislative-executive policymaking procedures. It highlights the conditions under which the status quo policy is in political equilibrium and the conditions under which the status quo policy is not in equilibrium and so can be upset.

Assumptions, Terminology, and Notation

For our model, we assume that there is one issue dimension that structures all relevant aspects of the policymaking process in each regulatory arena: the actors' views on the role that economic competition should play in regulating economic activity. The more anticompetition an actor's policy preferences, the farther left on this dimension the actor's ideal policy will be. Such an actor prefers using direct government action rather than competitive forces to regulate the activities of the economic players. The more pro-competition an actor's policy preferences, the farther to the right on the spectrum the actor's ideal policy will be. Such an actor prefers allowing competitive forces to regulate the activities of the economic actors rather than direct government intervention.

Each individual actor is assumed to have an ideal point on this issue dimension. That is, each individual has a policy that is most preferred, and the farther some proposal is from the individual's ideal point, the less the individual likes it. There is a policy, called the "status quo" and labeled SQ, which is currently in effect in a regulatory arena. Whenever SQ is not located precisely at an individual's ideal point, the individual's goal is to replace SQ with some policy closer to or at his or her ideal point.

Five institutional actors are in our model: a House committee, the House floor, a Senate committee, the Senate floor, and the president. Assuming prior approval by the two committees, there are two ways that a bill can be passed into law: a bill may be approved by a majority of the House floor, a majority of the Senate floor, and by the president; or a bill may be approved by two-thirds of the House floor and two-thirds of the Senate floor (thereby overriding the president's veto).

The set of options that majority defeat SQ in one or more of these institutional bodies is the *win-set of SQ*, or $W_{...}(SQ)$, where the subscript indicates the body or bodies involved. Thus $W_{HC}(SQ)$ is the set of points a majority of the House committee prefers to SQ, $W_{HF}(SQ)$ is the set of points a majority of the House floor prefers to SQ, and $W_P(SQ)$ is the set of points the president prefers to SQ. Similarly, $W_{HS}(SQ)$ is the set of points a majority of the House floor plus a majority of the Senate floor prefer to SQ, $W_{HSP}(SQ)$ is the set of points a majority of the House floor plus a majority of the Senate floor plus the president prefer to SQ, and $W_{HS}^{2/3}(SQ)$ is the set of points that two-thirds of the House floor plus two-thirds of the Senate floor prefer to SQ. If $W_{...}(SQ)$ is empty, we use the notation $W_{...}(SQ) = \emptyset$, which means that the win-set is empty; that is, there are no policies that are preferred to SQ, given the policymaking rules in use by the body or bodies.

A *core* is a set of policies that cannot be upset, given the rules of the policymaking process. If some institutional body has a core and if SQ lies in this core, by definition there is no option that can defeat SQ in that body. Thus if SQ is in the core, $W_{...}(SQ)$ for that body must be empty. Hence, we can speak of the "House committee core," or $CORE_{HC}$ as the set of points that cannot be upset by a majority of House committee members. Similarly, the "House floor core," or $CORE_{HF}$, is the set of points that cannot be upset by a majority of the House floor; the "Senate committee core," or $CORE_{SC}$, is the set of points that cannot be upset by a majority of the Senate committee; and the "Senate floor core," or $CORE_{SF}$, is the set of points that cannot be upset by a majority of the Senate floor. Given just one issue dimension, the core for a committee or floor is located at the ideal point of the median member of the committee or floor (assuming an odd number of members).

It is also possible for policymaking among several institutions to have a core. Thus the House floor and the Senate floor might have a "bicameral core," or $CORE_{HS}$. This is the set of options that no coalition consisting of a House floor majority plus a Senate floor majority can upset. The "bicameral executive veto core," or $CORE_{HSP}$, is the set of points that no coalition consisting of a House floor majority plus a Senate floor majority plus the president can upset. Similarly, the "bicameral two-thirds core," or $CORE_{HS}^{2/3}$, is the set of points that no coalition consisting of two-thirds of the House floor plus two-thirds of the Senate floor can upset. Finally, the "bicameral veto override core" is the set of points that can be upset by neither a coalition consisting of a House floor majority plus a Senate floor majority plus the president nor by a coalition consisting of two-thirds of the House floor plus two-thirds of the Senate floor. It is labeled simply $CORE$, with no subscripts. $CORE$ is the set of points in $CORE_{HSP} \cap CORE_{HS}^{2/3}$.

Each legislative committee is assumed to be a monopoly gatekeeper for its chamber floor. If the committee sends no proposal to the floor, the floor cannot act on its own. In addition, the floor of each chamber is assumed to operate under an open rule, which means that floor amendments are allowed to committee bills. (Of course, there are many ways in which bills are considered in the Congress. For example, committees may or may not be granted monopoly gatekeeping powers, and floors may use open or closed rules—or combinations thereof—to govern floor debate. The two chambers generally use some approximation of an open rule on the floor, although House procedures are generally more restrictive than the Senate's, and the committees usually act as monopoly gatekeepers, although Senate committees are somewhat less powerful in this respect than their House counterparts. Our model thus selects what we think is an empirically sensible combination of assumptions.)

Each individual actor is assumed to have complete knowledge of the locations of the ideal points of the other actors and about the location of SQ. This knowledge is critical to committee members in deciding whether to send a bill to the floor. Finally, each committee's members are assumed to be risk-averse regarding the bills they consider sending to the floor. That is, if there is any possibility that their bill will ultimately be amended in such a way that the final product is worse for them than SQ, they will vote against sending the bill to the floor.

Propositions

Given these assumptions, what are the conditions for equilibrium and disequilibrium in our policymaking game? Our first proposition establishes the set of conditions under which policy equilibriums will exist (that is, the conditions under which SQ cannot be upset):

Proposition 1: SQ will be in equilibrium if any of the following conditions hold:

(a) $W_{HC}(SQ) = \emptyset$, that is, $SQ \in CORE_{HC}$;
(b) $W_{SC}(SQ) = \emptyset$, that is, $SQ \in CORE_{SC}$;
(c) $W_{HF}(SQ) = \emptyset$, that is, $SQ \in CORE_{HF}$;
(d) $W_{SF}(SQ) = \emptyset$, that is, $SQ \in CORE_{SF}$;
(e) $W_{HF}(SQ) \cap W_{SF}(SQ) = \emptyset$, that is, $SQ \in CORE_{HS}$;
(f) $SQ \in CORE$;
(g) $W_{HC}(SQ) \cap CORE = \emptyset$;
(h) $W_{SC}(SQ) \cap CORE = \emptyset$.

To explain: For (a) and (b), given that the House and Senate committees act as monopoly gatekeepers for legislation, if a committee's majority rule win-set over the status quo is empty, no legislation defeating the status quo will be sent to the floor for a vote. For (c) and (d), if the majority rule win-set of SQ for either the House floor or the Senate floor is empty, that chamber will reject any proposal to replace SQ with some other proposal; hence SQ cannot be changed. For (e), if there is no proposal that a majority of the House floor and a majority of the Senate floor both prefer to SQ, then SQ cannot be changed.

For (f), if SQ lies inside $CORE$, SQ cannot be replaced by any possible proposal. That is, there is no possible coalition of a House floor majority, Senate floor majority, and president, nor of two-thirds of the House floor plus two-thirds of the Senate floor that can replace SQ with some other proposal. For (g), if the set of points that the House committee prefers to SQ does not intersect the set of points $CORE$ that are in equilibrium for the House floor, Senate floor, and president, then House committee members will vote not to release a bill to the floor because the bill that would ultimately emerge would be worse for a committee majority than SQ. Similarly, for (h), if the set of points that the Senate committee prefers to SQ does not intersect the set of points CORE that are in equilibrium for the House floor, Senate floor, and president, then Senate committee members will vote not to release a bill to the floor because the bill that would ultimately emerge would be worse for a committee majority than SQ.

If these are the conditions under which SQ cannot be upset, then what are the conditions under which SQ can be upset? At the very least, one requirement for SQ to be upset is that SQ must lie outside CORE. A second requirement is that for both committees to release bills to their chamber floors, there must exist some point in *CORE* that is better than SQ for both a House committee majority and a Senate committee majority. That is, it is necessary, at the very least, that $W_{HC}(SQ) \cap W_{SC}(SQ) \cap CORE \neq \emptyset$. However, the condition that $W_{HC}(SQ) \cap W_{SC}(SQ) \cap CORE$ not be empty is not by itself sufficient to guarantee that risk-averse committee members will send a bill to the floor. The problem stems from the fact that although any bill ultimately approved will lie in CORE, the committee members may be unable to predict or control which particular bill will be chosen; the final bill may be worse than SQ for some committee majority (i.e., lie outside $W_{...}(SQ)$. Hence the committee will release a bill only if all policies that the House, Senate, and president could conceivably select are better than SQ for the committee members. That is, all points in *CORE* must fall inside the set of points that both the House committee and Senate committee consider better than SQ. Hence:

Proposition 2: SQ will be upset only if $CORE \subset \{W_{HC}(SQ) \cap W_{SC}(SQ)\}$.

These two propositions are illustrated in figures 7.1 and 7.2. Together they show the conditions under which the status quo can or cannot be upset based on the formal procedures between the Congress and the president.

Measurement and Data Issues

Our four cases of deregulation involve actors with policy preferences that ranged from strongly pro-competition to strongly anti-competition. Although other issues, such as income redistribution and national security, entered into some of the policymaking discussions, including them when applying our model to these four cases would make measurement much too complicated. Hence, our empirical application has focused on locating actors' ideal points along a single procompetition-anticompetition continuum. We did

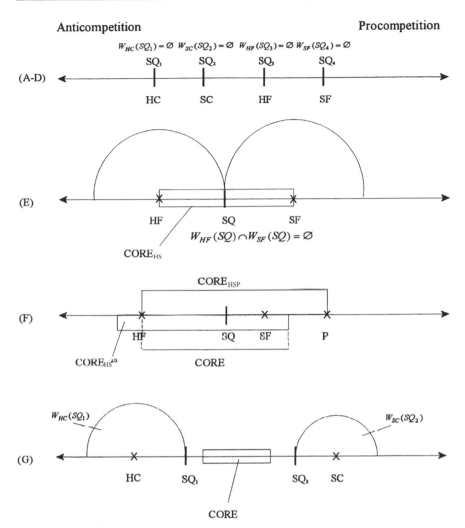

FIGURE 7.1 *Illustrations of Proposition 1*

not code participants' party identification or preferences on a liberal-conservative continuum because, in most of these deregulation cases, partisanship and broad political ideology seem not to have played a major role.

The secondary-source evidence did not allow us to locate each individual actor's ideal point on the issue dimension. However, the presence of the single dimension means that we need only know the

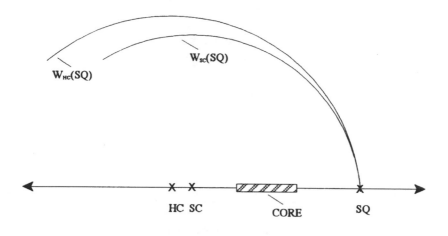

$$CORE \subset \{W_{HC}(SQ) \cup W_{SC}(SQ)\}$$

FIGURE 7.2 *When the status quo policy can be upset*

locations of the median actors' ideal points in each committee and floor relative to the locations of the median actors' ideal points in the other committee and floor. The available sources did allow us to make reasonably reliable estimates of these relative positions.

Data on the four cases were drawn from the *Congressional Quarterly Weekly Reports,* from *Congressional Quarterly Almanac,* and from other relevant published works on deregulation. Our analysis of telecommunications also relied on twelve interviews with key participants. This material was all compiled into a consolidated file for each case. Initially, one of the authors (JHK) and a graduate assistant read through the material and coded the placements of the actors' ideal points for the relevant years in each of the four cases.

To corroborate these initial placements, two other graduate assistants, acting independently and without knowledge of the initial locational placements, then coded the material as well. Each coder was given sheets of paper with one-dimensional lines for selected years and a title that indicated the particular case, whether banking, airlines, trucking, or telecommunications. Coders were also given copies of the consolidated file on each case. They were then asked to locate the relative positions of the House and Senate committees, the House and Senate floors, and the president, in terms of the actors' preferences on the pro-competition-anticompetition dimension for each case for the selected years.

The results of the placements by one of the authors (JHK) and his assistant were then compared statistically with the results of the efforts of the two coders. Two inter-coder reliability measures were used: Spearman rank-order correlations on a case-by-case basis and Kendall's Tau-B for sector-by-sector and overall comparisons. In the sector-by-sector and overall comparisons, Tau-B was used because the data are ordinal and not fully ranked. Because there were twelve issue spaces and three separate coders, thirty-six pairs of cases could have been correlated. Given missing data and some unusable codings, a total of thirty-one pairs of cases were actually correlated.

The results in tables 7.1 and 7.2 show strong agreement among the coders for three of the four cases, with much less agreement in telecommunications. Table 7.1 indicates that the average Spearman rank-order correlations for case-by-case intercoder reliability in banking, trucking, and airlines are very robust. The average rank-order correlation between coders for these three cases is 0.84. Of the twenty-five pairs of cases excluding telecommunications, 70 percent are significant at the 0.10 level. Although the Tau-B sector-by-sector correlations shown in table 7.2 are lower, with an average correlation of 0.68, they still indicate a high level of agreement. (Note that Tau-Bs generally are smaller than Spearman correlations. Tau-Bs measure the excess of agreement over disagreement as a proportion of the total. If the coders agreed half of the time, Tau-B would be equal to zero.)

TABLE 7.1

Average Spearman rank-order correlations for case-by-case comparisons

Sector	Three-Way[a]	Two-way[b]
Banking	0.93	0.93
Trucking	0.89	0.65
Airlines	0.81	0.82
Telecommunications	0.49	0.35

[a]The average correlation among the two graduate students and one of the authors.

[b]The average correlation between the two graduate students.

TABLE 7.2

Average Kendall Tau-B correlations for sector-by-sector comparisons

Sector	Three-Way[a]	Two-Way[b]
Banking	0.84	0.79
Trucking	0.58	0.47
Airlines	0.68	0.71
Telecommunications	0.42	0.27

[a]The average Tau-B correlations among the graduate students and one of the authors.
[b]The average Tau-B correlations between the two graduate students.

The telecommunications case involved special problems of measurement. During a seven-year period, only one bill reached the floor of one chamber of Congress, providing no evidence of the relative preferences of the floors in relation to the committees, especially for the later years, 1979–82. To gain a more thorough understanding of the telecommunications case, additional data were collected from several books on the subject (see especially Temin and Galambos 1987, and Coll 1986) and from a series of telephone interviews with participants in the process at the U.S. Commerce and Justice Departments and members of the relevant congressional staffs.

The following decision rules were used to settle disagreements among the coders: (a) when the two independent coders agreed on a placement on the line, but disagreed with the author, the coders' placement was used in the figure (there were only four such disagreements in thirty-six cases); (b) when there was disagreement between the coders, but one of the coder's placements agreed with the author's placement, the author's placement was used in the figure. When the coders disagreed with each other and neither agreed with the author's placement, the author made a final judgment, based on a rereading of the consolidated file. (In the thirty-six cases, only two such three-way disagreements occurred, both in telecommunications; those required reevaluation by the author.)

Finally, we also had to use our own best judgments on where the boundaries of $CORE_{HS}^{2/3}$—and thus of CORE—lay in each of our four cases; estimates of these boundary locations were not produced by the coders. Our judgments here were based on two factors. First, for many distributions of legislative preferences, $CORE_{HS}^{2/3}$ will be larger than $CORE_{HS}$ (the bicameral core) but smaller than $CORE_{HSP}$

(the bicameral executive veto core), and our locations of the boundaries of $CORE_{HS}^{2/3}$ reflect this fact. Second, for the case where veto threats played a major role (e.g., trucking deregulation), the logic of the story as portrayed by the key sources gave additional guidance as to where $CORE_{HS}^{2/3}$ (and thus CORE) probably lay. Even so, the boundaries of $CORE_{HS}^{2/3}$, and thus of CORE, often remained somewhat uncertain. For this reason, we have indicated with a "?" our guess about where a boundary of CORE lay, owing to our uncertainty about the location of its component $CORE_{HS}^{2/3}$. The uncertain boundary will always lie in the president's direction from CORE. If the president's ideal point lies between the House floor median and the Senate floor median, the boundaries of CORE will simply be coterminous with those of $CORE_{HS}$.

Deregulation in the Banking, Trucking, Airline, and Telecommunications Industries

We now use our model to interpret the four cases of deregulation in banking, trucking, airlines, and telecommunications. The banking case represents a serial and incremental approach to policy change. The committees played an important role in proposing changes, and the president did not play an important role or heavily influence legislative outcomes. The trucking and airlines cases are similar in that the committees played a defensive and "catch up" role to the administrative policy initiatives of the president, who proposed legislation, which when passed, reflected for the most part his desires. The telecommunications case was the most complicated. For most of the period under consideration, the Justice Department pursued an antitrust suit against AT&T which established the context for congressional action. The congressional committees also became embroiled in a host of related communications issues, from broadcasting to electronic publishing. Consequently, the House and Senate committees were unable to draft a bill that would succeed in deregulating telecommunications; deregulation stemmed primarily from a settlement to the antitrust suit negotiated by AT&T and the Justice Department.

There were several exogenous sources of change in the policy status quo of these four regulated industries (for a fuller discussion see Hammond and Knott 1988). These included: (1) the court system, in which judges sometimes gave procompetition interpretations to existing regulatory laws; (2) regulatory "cheaters" who operated on the edges of the regulated industry by exploiting loopholes in the regulations; (3) presidents who used their administrative powers to take unilateral actions to alter regulatory rules; (4) regulatory agencies that used independent administrative actions to alter the rules or to file lawsuits to change certain industry practices; and (e) a second congressional committee with jurisdiction overlapping that of the main committee that sent a bill to the floor or that challenged the authority of the main committee. These exogenous influences had a significant effect on outcomes in all four of the cases.

The Banking Case

Exogenous change in the policy status quo.   Beginning in the late 1960s, technological and economic developments in banking produced political pressures for changes in the statutory status quo. On the technological side, the development of electronic banking, such as Automatic Teller Machines (ATMs), made it possible for banks to evade restrictions on banking practices, and the courts tended to uphold these new practices. On the economic side, inflation during the 1970s drove interest rates for large deposits in the money markets above the rates for checking and savings accounts allowed by the Federal Reserve's "Regulation Q." Brokerage houses such as Merrill Lynch began offering money market mutual fund (MMMF) accounts for smaller deposits and eventually offered a "Cash Management Account" that included checking services on these deposits. Billions of dollars left banks for the money market funds in brokerage houses. Between 1977 and 1982, these MMMF accounts grew from $3.9 billion to $223 billion, almost half the nation's money supply at that time (Evans 1984, p. 444; Lehman 1985, p. 61; Cargill and Garcia 1982, p. 13).

By 1980 these economic pressures had risen to the point where the new MMMF accounts threatened the entire commercial banking system. In response, the regulatory agencies began "edging away from the prohibition against interest-bearing checking accounts" (*CQ Almanac* 1980a). The largest bank holding companies, however, did not believe this agency action was sufficient, and they began pressuring Congress to extend Regulation Q to the brokerage houses. This solution, however, proved unpopular with Congress and the large numbers of middle-class depositors who now benefited from the MMMF accounts. The large banks also harbored mixed feelings about Regulation Q, since they hoped that price deregulation might allow their entry into investment banking, from which they had been barred since the 1930s. Eventually, the large banks came to favor deregulation in order to compete on a "level playing field" with their new competitors.

Legislative responses. The House showed less enthusiasm for deregulation than the Senate. Under the leadership of Ferdinand St. Germain, chairman of the House Subcommittee on Financial Institutions, and Henry Reuss, chairman of the House Banking Committee, the House favored allowing interest to be paid on checking accounts (NOW accounts) and extending Federal Reserve requirements to all institutions, not just those that were members of the Federal Reserve System. Under the leadership of Senator William Proxmire, chairman of the Senate Banking Committee, the Senate wanted to abolish Regulation Q, push for Money Market Accounts for banks, and reduce the minimum deposit for a money market certificate to $1,000.

The differences between the House and Senate are explained, in part, by the reluctance of smaller banks to compete with giant brokerage houses for a share of the money market accounts, while the large New York and California banks eagerly sought such competition. If the large bank holding companies could compete successfully with the brokerage houses, the smaller banks might find themselves in a worse position. Smaller banks also feared further steps toward geographic deregulation that might open the door for large banks to operate in the states. The House tended to respond more to local banking concerns, while the Senate reflected the perspective of the large banks.

The two chambers succeeded in 1980 in passing a compromise bill, The Depository Institutions Deregulation and Monetary Control Act (DIDMCA), which established NOW accounts but also extended the Fed's reserve requirements. Meier (1985, p. 66) notes that, "Even without the act, the financial markets were substantially deregulated." He also states (p. 67) that "the net impact of the legislation was to allow the larger commercial banks to compete with nonbank financial institutions. The impact of the act, therefore, was marginal compared to the changes that had been determined by changes in technology and economics." The incremental approach of the DIDMCA did not permit banks to pay money market interest rates on checking or savings deposits because legislators worried that increases in interest rates on short-term deposits at banks would threaten savings and loan associations, which held their assets in long-term mortgages at lower interest rates.

As interest rates fell during the 1982 recession, Congress passed the Garn–St. Germain Depository Institutions Act, which took the next step of allowing Super-NOW accounts and Money Market Demand Accounts (MMDAs). It also allowed thrifts to make more commercial and real estate loans, have corporate checking accounts, and merge with other financial institutions if they faced bankruptcy. In this legislative effort, committees once again did little more than try to keep up with the technical and economic processes that were already forcing industry deregulation. The committees did not agree to geographic deregulation or complete asset-side deregulation. Under the act, banks could still not perform many of the services of brokerage houses nor could banks branch out across state boundaries. (In 1988, Congress finally passed legislation permitting securities loans by banks; see *Wall Street Journal* 1988, p. 29).

Legislative outcomes.   Figure 7.3 represents the incremental, piecemeal case of banking deregulation. The placement of the committees, floors, and president on the lines in figure 7.3 is based on a reading of the documentary evidence from the *CQ Almanac* (1976–81) and *CQ Weekly Report* (1982, pp. 2125–26). The case study evidence shows that as the economic and technical forces altered the banking and financial industry, and middle-class consumers began to benefit from MMMF accounts, the range of opinion in Congress shifted toward a more pro-competitive stance. It also shows that the Senate committee was clearly more pro-competitive than the House committee, which also tended to be less pro-competitive than either the Senate or House floors.

The House and Senate committees proposed legislation that reflected a compromise between the goals of the big banks and the worries of the smaller banks. The competition from the brokerage houses continued unabated as economic conditions improved after 1982, and the committees proposed further legislation that would move the legislative status quo even closer to the larger banks' position of open competition with the other financial institutions.

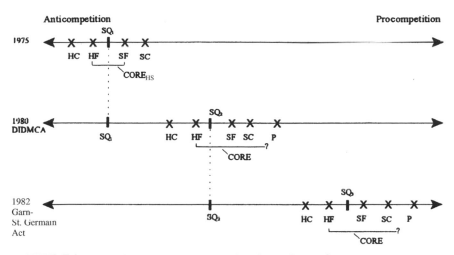

FIGURE 7.3 *Legislative outcomes in banking deregulation, 1975–1982*

The pattern of change over time represents a typical subgovernment response to threats from the outside. The subgovernment initially preferred to extend regulation to the brokerage houses. Because of strong opposition in the country and the rest of the Congress, however, the next best alternative was chosen, namely, deregulation of banks so they might compete with the regulatory "cheaters." The subgovernment succeeded in passing legislation in response to exogenous changes in the status quo because its preferences did not differ markedly from the rest of the Congress and the large middle-class constituency of the newly deregulated policy environment.

In 1982 the Garn–St. Germain Act—the new legislative status quo—was centered in *CORE*, as depicted in figure 7.4. Both the Reagan and Carter administrations had more pro-competitive preferences than what Congress ultimately approved in the 1980 and 1982 bills. In each case, though, the new legislation passed by Congress was better than the old, and so presidential vetoes would simply have restored an inferior status quo ante in each case.

The Trucking Case

Exogenous Change in the Policy Status Quo. In 1948, Congress passed the Reed-Bulwinkle Act to prevent the Department of Justice from

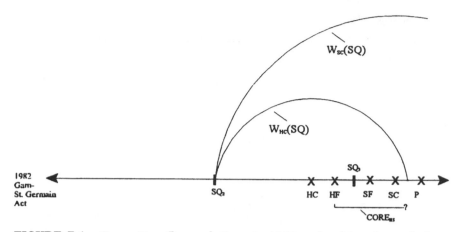

FIGURE 7.4   *Committee-floor relations in 1982 on banking deregulation*

pressing an antitrust case it had planned against the railroads; the act exempted railroads and trucks from the antitrust laws. President Truman vetoed the bill, but Congress overrode his veto with votes of 63–25 and 297–102 in the Senate and House, respectively. Transportation regulation was not a salient issue in 1948; thus, there were few political costs to overriding the president's veto (Rothenberg 1994, p. 88). The transportation subgovernment succeeded in protecting the regulatory regime in the face of presidential opposition.

Over the succeeding years, presidents continued to propose trucking deregulation. In 1962, for example, President Kennedy's Special Transportation Message called for abolishing minimum rate regulation in shipping bulk commodities, but it was "buried in Congress, opposed by the truckers, the barge operators, and the rate setters (in this case the Interstate Commerce Commission)" (Wilson 1971, p. 41, quoted in Rothenberg 1994, p. 89). In 1971 the Nixon administration prepared a comprehensive trucking deregulation bill, called the Transportation Regulatory Bill, that would have liberalized entry, allowed much greater flexibility in rates, and nullified the Reed-Bulwinkle antitrust provisions. This bill died in committee when the Nixon administration withdrew its backing to gain Teamster support in the 1972 presidential election.

In 1975 President Ford sent to Congress the Motor Carrier Reform Bill that called for drastically reducing the entry requirements into the industry. The bill never left committee. The legislature's unwillingness to reverse trucking regulation prompted President Ford to change strategy. His administration managed to alter the membership of the Interstate Commerce Commission (ICC) by adding two commissioners who were committed to deregulation. In the *Bowman Decision*, the commission subsequently approved new entrants into the common carrier market in the South. Opponents challenged the decision in the courts, but the Supreme Court ruled in 1973 that the commission's decision protected consumers, a stance that encouraged the ICC to take consumer protection into account in making decisions and also helped create a climate of opinion favorable to deregulation.

These changes in personnel and commission practice continued under President Carter, who succeeded in gaining control of the commission when several pro-regulation commissioners resigned or their terms expired, and others agreed to support deregulation in the hope that they would be reappointed when their terms expired (Rothenberg 1994, pp. 223–29). Carter rejected a legislative strategy to achieve deregulation based on his political judgment that it would fail (Rothenberg 1994, p. 224). Instead, Carter encouraged the commission to use its rule-making and juridical powers to change the status quo. As a result, between 1975 and 1979, the number of applicants for entry increased 700 percent and the number approved grew by over 800 percent. The associate director of the White House policy staff, Simon Lazarus, stated that the purpose of this administratively oriented strategy was to give deregulation opponents "a strong incentive to seek a new law themselves, defining the limits of the ICC's authority" (quoted in Rothenberg 1994, p. 224).

Legislative responses. Only after its administrative strategy had proved successful was a Carter administration bill on trucking deregulation submitted to Congress (in June 1979), cosponsored by several senators (including Ted Kennedy) whose aides had helped in its drafting. A participant in the process stated that "the ICC through its actions accelerated the passage of legislation. The ICC changes meant that the vested interests had already lost and gone home" (Rothenberg 1994, p. 237). Even the chairman of the Senate Commerce Committee, Joseph Cannon, who was a longtime supporter of the trucking industry, had become a convert to deregulation, primarily in order to "get the best deal possible given their now disadvantageous bargaining position" (Rothenberg 1994, p. 237).

To counter the Kennedy-Carter initiative, the Senate Commerce Committee and the House Public Works Committee introduced their own legislation that provided for some liberalization but mainly restricted the ICC from going any further. President Carter threatened to veto this pro-regulation bill. Because there was relatively little House or Senate support for the bill, the final legislation came to embody most of the ICC reforms. The bill passed the House 376–13 and the Senate 70–20 as the Motor Carrier Reform Act of 1980. According to Rothenberg (1994), "The statute basically preserved the new status quo, with a few concessions to placate group and congressional interests" (p. 49).

Legislative outcomes.   In the trucking case, as depicted in figure 7.5, the relevant committees in the transportation subgovernment came to support deregulation only reluctantly and as a last-ditch effort to maintain jurisdiction over transportation issues. Unfortunately for the committees and their subgovernment supporters in the industry, deregulation had become a salient political issue by 1979, and any bill *re*regulating trucking could not have withstood a presidential

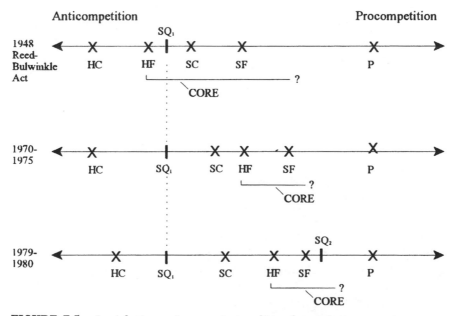

FIGURE 7.5   *Legislative outcomes in trucking deregulation, 1948–1980*

veto. As Rothenberg states, "When the executive is integrated into this process, the feasible set is whittled down to those alternatives that either a majority *and* the President can support or two-thirds will endorse despite the pressures of an executive veto" (p. 54). The committees recognized that only a pro-competition bill would surmount these procedural hurdles.

Because Ford and Carter had succeeded in exogenously changing the policy status quo through appointments and other administrative actions of the ICC, the committees had no choice but to accede to deregulatory legislation in an attempt to keep deregulation from proceeding even further (*CQ Almanac* 1980b, p. 242). The bill that passed did not go as far as President Carter preferred because it mollified the unions and regulated firms to some extent, but in the main it ratified the actions of the ICC and substantially moved the statutory status quo toward a full deregulation of trucking (*CQ Almanac* 1980b, p. 242).

The Motor Carrier Reform Act of 1980 is depicted in figure 7.6 as SQ_2. The committees proposed a bill that was less procompetitive than what the president wanted but within CORE. This bill was also more procompetitive than the majorities on the floors probably preferred. Yet given the strong procompetitive stance of the president, the floors had to accept a bill closer to his preference.

The Airlines Case

Exogenous changes in the status quo. Presidents Ford and Carter both strongly supported an airline deregulation bill (*CQ Almanac,* 1976b, p. 637). Ford successfully appointed pro-competitive members to the Civil Aeronautics Board (CAB), while Carter appointed Alfred Kahn as the chairman. Kahn was a staunch supporter of deregulation and was willing to abolish CAB to achieve this goal.

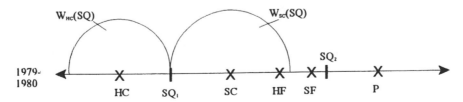

FIGURE 7.6 *Committee-floor relations in 1980 on trucking deregulation*

These appointees greatly expanded experimentation with deregulatory measures and ultimately succeeded in moving the policy status quo quite far toward complete deregulation of airlines. President Carter repeatedly stated during and after hearings on an airline deregulation bill held by the Aviation Subcommittee of the House Public Works and Transportation Committee that the bill was not as strong as he preferred. According to the *CQ Almanac* (1977c, p. 554), "loosening control over the airlines was a top priority for the Carter Administration." As outlined by the administration, President Carter sought "an automatic route entry program, a program to grant unused route authority to air carriers willing to serve those routes, price flexibility and a presumption that competition was in the public interest" (*CQ Almanac* 1978a, p. 496).

Legislative responses.   Under the leadership of Senator Ted Kennedy, a subcommittee of the Senate Judiciary Committee made airline deregulation a major priority in the 1970s and raised interest in the issue in the news media. This effort by the Judiciary Committee led to a major jurisdictional struggle over regulation of the airlines between Kennedy and Joseph Cannon, who was chairman of the Senate Aviation Subcommittee. Cannon ultimately came over to the deregulation side in large part because of his fear that his subcommittee would lose control of airline regulation to Kennedy's subcommittee (Weingast 1981). By 1977, however, even prior to major moves by CAB to independently deregulate the airlines, Cannon had reported a bill out of his committee that had several deregulatory provisions (*CQ Almanac* 1977c, p. 554).

The House supported deregulation less than the Senate (*CQ Almanac* 1978a, p. 497). A coalition of Republicans and conservative Democrats kept the deregulation bill stalled in the Public Works Aviation Subcommittee for weeks in a fight over automatic entry and unused route authority. On March 22, 1977, the subcommittee voted 13–11 to favor the Levitas Substitute, which basically gutted the deregulatory features of the bill. The full committee then forwarded the amended bill to the floor by a vote of 13–3. In conference, according to *CQ Almanac,* the House conferees "gave in to the Senate's stronger provisions on a number of key deregulation provisions" (1977b, p. 504).

Both chambers overwhelmingly approved the legislation once the bill reached the floors. The Senate passed its deregulation bill 83–9 in April, and the House passed its bill September 21 by a vote of 363–8 (*CQ Almanac*, 1977b, p. 496). According to the analysis in the *CQ Almanac* (1978a, p. 496), this act "gave President Carter all he wanted in a deregulation bill" by clearing the way for eventual abolition of the CAB. The Air Transportation Regulatory Reform Act passed in 1978 despite the opposition of the airline industry. Only three airlines under CAB authority supported the Senate version of the bill: United, Frontier, and Air West. Other airlines, according to *CQ Almanac* (1977c, p. 555), warned that the bill would "lead to chaos, drive some airlines out of business and thus create less competition." Nonetheless, they lost.

Legislative outcomes. Through the administrative actions of the CAB, the president was able to move the policy status quo significantly toward a pro-competition stance by early 1978 (see figure 7.7). Documents show that the members of Congress had moved in a pro-competition direction, which forced the committees to move their position closer to that of President Carter in order to keep any control over airline policy. The Airline Deregulation Act of 1978, depicted in figure 7.8 by SQ_2, corresponded directly to the policy status quo established by President Carter. This particular option was passed by the legislature and signed by Carter.

Because CAB, with the president's support, had moved the policy status quo into CORE, this policy could not be upset by a majority in the Congress, even though a majority likely favored legislation that

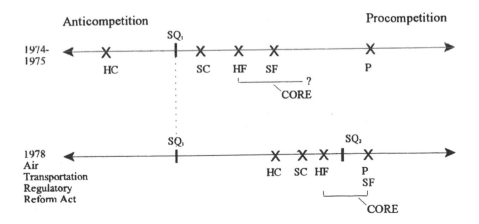

FIGURE 7.7 *Legislative outcomes in airline dereguation, 1974–1978*

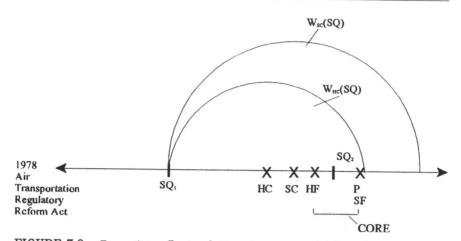

FIGURE 7.8   *Committee-floor relations in 1978 on airline deregulation*

was somewhat less procompetition; President Carter would have vetoed any bill that attempted to reregulate the industry. In other words, the president's ability to move *SQ* unilaterally, via administrative action by his appointees on CAB, ultimately permitted him to get something close to his ideal point.

The Telecommunications Case

In contrast to banking, trucking, and airlines, Congress succeeded in passing a legislative bill deregulating telecommunications only many years later than the era (the 1970s and the 1980s) under consideration here. The reasons for the congressional failure are complex, making the interpretation of this case difficult. Three circumstances distinguish telecommunications from the other regulatory sectors: the antitrust suit against AT&T provided an alternative avenue for policy change; AT&T held a dominant monopoly position in the industry; and the connections between telecommunications and a variety of other communications issues greatly complicated the political decision-making process.

Exogenous changes in the status quo.   The initial pressures for deregulatory relief for AT&T came from decisions in court cases initiated in the 1960s over other firms' rights to connect to and provide equipment for the AT&T telephone network. The Federal Communications Commission (FCC) and court efforts to deal with these equipment and interconnect issues resulted mainly in pro-competition decisions. The culmination of this trend toward court- and agency-mandated competition came with the FCC's major proposals, the Competitive Carrier Proceedings and the Computer II Rules, announced in 1980, to allow other firms to compete with AT&T for telephone equipment.

Starting in 1975, Congress began considering several bills to deregulate telecommunications. At roughly the same time, the Justice Department began pursuing an antitrust suit against AT&T, which was initially filed in 1974. The suit eventually came to trial in the District of Columbia under federal district court of Judge Harold Greene. The case raised issues of AT&T's liability for illegal antitrust activities against competitors and also raised the possibility of a deregulatory relief program that included a restructuring of the company. Over time, the suit affected AT&T's stance toward legislation as well as the positions of the White House and the U.S. Departments of Commerce, Justice, and Defense. It also gave the Judiciary Committees of the House and Senate an opening to claim jurisdiction over the legislation. But perhaps most important, the suit offered an alternative avenue for interest groups and legislators to seek change in the status quo.

In January 1982, the Justice Department and AT&T reached an agreement to divest the operating companies from the parent company, AT&T. The divestiture decision (as subsequently modified by Judge Greene to restrict AT&T from certain practices) plus the increasingly pro-competition FCC rulings served as the basis for subsequent telecommunications policy. The FCC retained regulatory authority over telecommunications, although it chose not to exercise that authority in telephone equipment and interconnect services. The local telephone companies were still subject to state-level public utility commission rate regulation, and AT&T was still subject to long-distance rate regulation as the dominant carrier (although its competitors in long distance were not subject to the same regulation). In addition, AT&T no longer had to operate under the 1956 consent degree that barred it from entering other communications markets, such as computers and data processing.

The legislative responses. From the beginning, Lionel Van Deerlin, chairman of the Subcommittee on Communications of the House

Commerce Committee, took the position that the regulatory difficulties with telecommunications offered an opportunity for a comprehensive rewrite of the 1934 Communications Act. Not only would telephone and data processing issues come under review but numerous other issues governing broadcasting, national defense, the news media, alarm systems, electronic publishing, and cable television would come under review as well. Sorting out these contrary political interests, many of which cut across liberal-conservative lines, proved too much for the committees. No alternative bill to the status quo could be crafted that could gain the support of a majority on the communications subcommittees until 1981, and no bill (with one exception) that passed the House and Senate subcommittees ever succeeded in gaining a majority on either chamber's floor.

Despite the congressional failure to pass legislation deregulating telecommunications, the Communications Subcommittee chairmen in the House—Torbert McDonald, Lionel Van Deerlin, and Timothy Wirth—had supported deregulation since 1975, published staff reports, and held hearings on the subject throughout the 1970s and early 1980s. These staff reports attacked the FCC for anticompetitive restrictions on cable television and other restrictions (Derthick and Quirk 1985, p. 67). Similarly, Ernest Hollings, chairman of the Senate Subcommittee on Communications, and Robert Packwood, chairman of the Senate Commerce Committee, supported pro-competition telecommunications legislation throughout this period.

Several issues prevented Congress from building a consensus on telecommunications deregulation. First, the bills considered from 1976 to 1979 attempted a comprehensive rewrite of the 1934 Communications Act that governed television, broadcasting, and publishing. This approach raised too many cross-industry conflicts to succeed. In 1980 both subcommittees shifted to a focus on just common carrier legislation.

Second, the dominant position of AT&T created an intense debate over safeguards against private monopoly. One participant made the analogy to airline deregulation, in which a firm might own and operate 90 percent of all gates and airports. Hollings and Wirth strongly favored competition, but they wanted to protect AT&T's competitors during a regulatory transition period, which meant that they did not favor complete deregulation immediately. Third, the judiciary committees took seriously the charges of antitrust violations against AT&T and opposed congressional legislation because it might interfere in the prosecution of the Justice Department's antitrust case.

Furthermore, the House and Senate subcommittees shifted positions relative to each other from the late 1970s to the 1980s (see figure 7.9). Under President Carter, the Senate subcommittee chaired by Hollings tended to be more pro-competition than the House subcommittee chaired by Van Deerlin. When the Republicans took over the Senate in 1981, the Commerce Committee leadership shifted to Robert Packwood, who actively worked with the Reagan administration to pass a deregulation bill. Meanwhile, leadership of the House subcommittee passed into the hands of Wirth, who took a procompetition, anti-AT&T stance. The Republicans tended to favor

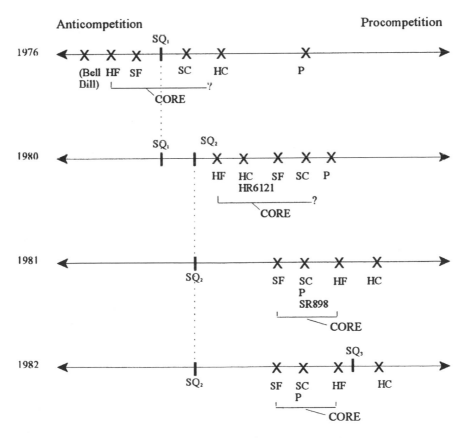

FIGURE 7.9 *Legislative outcomes in telecommunications, 1976–1982*

smaller changes in the Bell system, while the Democrats supported larger system changes and protection for competitors against predatory actions by a deregulated AT&T.

Several bills were considered by these two committees between 1975 and 1982, but with the exception of the 1980–81 bills in the House and the Packwood bill in the Senate in 1981, none of the bills ever gained majority support on the subcommittees. The bills included the following:

- Consumer Communications Reform Act (HR 12373 and HR 8, 1976–77): These are the two versions of the so-called "Bell Bill" that were introduced into Congress and debated in 1976–77. The bills proposed to legalize AT&T as a national monopoly, prevent competition in long-distance lines, and allow AT&T to cut prices to drive "inefficient" smaller producers of telephone equipment out of business (*CQ Weekly Report* 1976, pp. 2615–21.) The bills never left subcommittee.
- Bills considered in 1978–79 (S 611, HR 3333, HR 13015) were comprehensive efforts to rewrite the 1934 Communications Act. They would have required AT&T to divest itself from Western Electric, something that AT&T sharply opposed at the time. According to *Congressional Quarterly* (1979, p. 2148), "These bills were put on hold because of objections from different interests within the industry." The bills never left the subcommittees.
- The Van Deerlin Bill (HR 6121, 1980): This House bill was the first narrowly focused effort at common carrier deregulation. It would have imposed restrictions on AT&T so as to give smaller firms a better chance to compete (*CQ Almanac* 1981, p. 555). It was reported out of the Commerce Committee in August 1980 but was challenged in the mark-up process by the Judiciary Committee, which wanted time to consider its effects on the pending antitrust suit against AT&T. The Judiciary Committee reported the bill out adversely, and the bill never reached the floor of the House.
- The Packwood Bill (S 898, 1981): This bill, which was based on the Van Deerlin bill and originally numbered S 2827, would have created separate subsidiary companies in AT&T to compete in unregulated markets. The bill kept the AT&T system intact and left AT&T with a monopoly over telephone service (*CQ*

Almanac 1981, p. 555; Temin and Galambos 1987). The S-898 bill was opposed by Hollings, who believed it did not provide sufficient safeguards against AT&T dominance. Nonetheless, it passed the Commerce Committee in July 1981 by a 16–1 vote and the Senate in October 1981 by a 90–4 vote.

- The Wirth Bill (HR 5158, 1981–82): Just prior to the divestiture agreement, in December 1981, Chairman Wirth succeeded in passing a deregulation bill out of the House Communications Subcommittee that imposed more restrictions on AT&T than the Senate bill. After the divestiture, Wirth rewrote his bill to address what he considered some of the weaknesses of the agreement, especially provisions that gave AT&T more market power than Wirth and the subcommittee believed were safe. The bill passed the committee by a unanimous vote; however, with vigorous opposition from AT&T, the bill was withdrawn from consideration on the floor in July 1982.

The presidents played a relatively minor role in telecommunications deregulation. President Ford gave no support to the Bell Bill, but neither did he take any actions or come out in favor of deregulation. President Carter spoke strongly in favor of a deregulated industry in his 1980 State of the Union address and supported Van Deerlin's bill, HR-6121. President Reagan, in his initial comments in 1981, favored keeping Bell as a national monopoly and opposed the antitrust suit. Secretary of Defense Casper Weinberger also opposed the suit on the grounds that a breakup of AT&T's integrated communications network would threaten national security (Temin and Galambos 1987). On the other hand, the U.S. Justice Department, through the efforts of Assistant Attorney General William Baxter, strongly supported the antitrust case and favored divestiture. When the Senate passed the 1981 Deregulation Bill, the administration endorsed it (*CQ Almanac* 1981, p. 557). Yet even this bill would have preserved Bell's national monopoly over telephone service. These shifts in presidential position are shown in figure 7.9.

Legislative outcomes. Interpreting the telecommunication case in terms of our model, the years 1976–77 and 1978–79 are relatively straightforward. The legislative status quo is represented by the 1934 Communications Act. The Bell Bill would have proved even more anticompetitive than the 1934 act because it would have disallowed the FCC's procompetition rulings and antitrust judicial decisions. The floors of the House and Senate stood either slightly to the anticompetition side of the 1934 act (because there was some sentiment for the Bell Bill) or at least they were less procompetition than the subcommittees and reluctant to move away from the 1934 act. As one participant put it, "The floors felt that if the system ain't broke, why fix it?" (*CQ Almanac* 1977b, p. 706). Consequently, the House committee was wary of reporting out the Bell Bill at all because some version of it might have achieved success on the floors—a result clearly unacceptable not only to the House committee but also to Senate committee. The committees therefore stalled on bringing the bill out of committee and held hearings to raise interest and support for procompetition positions. In our notation, following Proposition 1, SQ (the 1934 act) was in CORE and so could not be upset: the House and Senate floors might have supported the leftward (anticompetition) movement in policy toward the Bell Bill, while the president, as well as the House and Senate committees, wanted to move policy rightward (in the procompetition direction).

The situation became more complicated in 1980–82. The 1981 Senate bill, S-898, which was based on HR-6121, was developed and guided through the Senate by Packwood, chair of the Commerce Committee, over the opposition of Hollings, chair of the Communications Subcommittee. In the 1980 election, however, Van Deerlin, who led the drafting of HR-6121, was defeated for reelection. His successor, Wirth, had little sympathy for Van Deerlin's approach and favored stricter controls on potential monopoly abuses by AT&T. Our interpretation, therefore, is that the House committee was more procompetition than the Senate committee in the sense of wanting more protections for AT&T's competitors (see figure 7.10 for our diagram of the situation in 1982). (This interpretation rests on the assumption that restrictions on AT&T's potential for monopoly abuses indicate a pro-competition stance.)

FIGURE 7.10 *Committee-floor relations in 1982 on telecommunications*

Some of the participants interviewed indicated that the subcommittee chairmen, Senator Hollings and Representative Wirth, really did not want to pursue legislation because of the "conflicting industry interests" on any chosen bill. They used the subcommittee hearings and committee bills to signal congressional preferences to Judge Greene and the Justice Department, and in 1983 to the FCC, concerning what Congress considered to be a proper deregulatory solution (Ferejohn and Shipan 1990). Indeed, after divestiture, Wirth wrote Judge Greene in detail about the additional provisions he would like to see incorporated into the divestiture agreement. Greene agreed to make many of these provisions preconditions of the final settlement.

The placement of the floors in this later period relative to the House committee and Senate committee is the most difficult measurement problem. The empirical evidence and our interviews with participants suggest that the floors, while much more pro-competition than earlier, were still not inclined to accept the breakup of AT&T or to accept further restrictions on AT&T's operations to guarantee competitive markets. Consequently, we have placed the floors in 1981 in line with the S-898 bill that favored deregulation but that did not dismember AT&T (see figure 7.9). Most participants interviewed also believed that the floors gave deference to the committee version of the Senate bill, once it passed the committee.

The most dramatic policy change occurred in 1982 with the settlement between the Justice Department and AT&T to break up the AT&T monopoly and create several smaller, regional Bell operating companies. The settlement left the AT&T parent company with long-distance telecommunications, Western Electric, and Bell Laboratories but broke up the telephone monopoly. This solution proved to be even more pro-competition than any of the bills proposed or passed by either chamber of Congress.

The new settlement produced a policy status quo that lay outside and to the right of *CORE*. Why then did the Congress not propose a bill that would pull the new *SQ* back into *CORE*? The answer to this question hinges on the conflict between Representative Wirth and his subcommittee, on the one hand, and the House floor, Senate floor, and Senate Commerce Committee, on the other. To Wirth and his subcommittee allies, the concern was over maintaining competition in the long run, and they feared that an unfettered AT&T would crush those who tried to compete with it. A regulatory transition period, which imposed restrictions on what AT&T could do and which gave competitors time to establish themselves in the telecommunications market, was considered necessary. Wirth and his allies thus saw themselves as more pro-competition than their opponents and wanted to move policy even further rightward, in the pro-competition direction, from the new *SQ.* Their fear was that any bill passed by Congress to upset this *SQ* would risk allowing AT&T to reestablish its monopoly; that is, policy would move leftward toward *CORE,* in an anticompetition direction. To Wirth, then, it made sense to withdraw his bill from consideration by the full Commerce Committee. It was for this reason that Congress did not pass any bill ratifying what had been exogenously imposed by other actors (the courts and the Justice Department). In our notation, the court-imposed *SQ* remained in equilibrium owing to Proposition 1(g): $W_{HC}(SQ) \cap CORE = \emptyset$.

Another factor was the disinclination of Congress to become embroiled in any further efforts to legislate change in communications. Such efforts invoked opposition from AT&T's competitors, AT&T itself, electronic publishers, security companies, and others. Congress and the administration adopted a wait-and-see attitude that, as one participant put it, indicated that the government "wanted to let the dust settle" before taking any legislative action.

Generalizations: When Are Congressional Committees Powerful?

Our analysis of these four cases of deregulation permits some generalizations about the conditions under which committees are effective in blocking or promoting policy change. These conditions are illustrated in figure 7.11.

The first condition involves situations in which the committees are on one side of *CORE* and *SQ* is on the other side of *CORE:*

> **Condition 1:** If the committees lie in or to the right (left) of *CORE* and if *SQ* lies to the left (right) of *CORE,* the committees can propose bills that they prefer to the *SQ,* which could be approved by some combination of the House, Senate, and president.

Figure 7.11 calls this the "policy change position." It is a favorable position for the committees, as any bill that they favor will also pass the House and Senate and be signed by the president. Condition 1 is applicable to the banking case in 1980 and 1982, in which the committees were in *CORE,* while the legislative status quo lay to the left of *CORE.* Consequently, the committees proposed new legislation, sent it to the floors, and saw it readily passed by the floors and signed by the president. When the committees' ideal points actually lie inside *CORE,* the primary concern for risk-averse committee members is to ensure that the ultimate bill produced by the House, Senate, and president lies inside the committees' win-sets of *SQ.*

In our next two conditions, *SQ* and at least one committee ideal point are on the same side of *CORE:*

> **Condition 2**: If *SQ* lies between at least one committee and *CORE,* then the committee will be able to block any policy change but will also be unable to move the status quo toward itself.

Figure 7.11 refers to this proposition as the "blocking position." Even though the president and the floors would prefer an *SQ* more to the right, the committee would oppose releasing any bill that reflects floor preferences. For example, despite the efforts of Presidents Nixon and Ford to get trucking deregulation legislation passed, the committees never released any of these bills to the floors.

> **Condition 3**: If a committee lies between the *SQ* and *CORE,* but the committee's win-set, $W_{HC}(SQ)$ or $W_{SC}(SQ)$, does not intersect *CORE,* then there is no bill the committee can propose that it prefers to *SQ* and that will be approved by some combination of the House, Senate, and president.

Figure 7.11 refers to this situation as the "alternate blocking position."

These circumstances seem to have prevented Congress from passing any legislation in the breakup of AT&T in 1982. The court decision had moved the policy status quo to the right of the House and Senate committees, which themselves were to the right of the floor majorities and the president. Consequently, the committees (and the House committee, in particular) favored the new policy status quo to any legislation that might come out of the legislative process.

In our next pair of conditions, the committee is in a position in which it must make a potentially profitable but potentially hazard-

Condition 1: The Policy
Change Position

(A)

(B)

Condition 2: The
Blocking Position

Condition 3: Alternate
Blocking Position

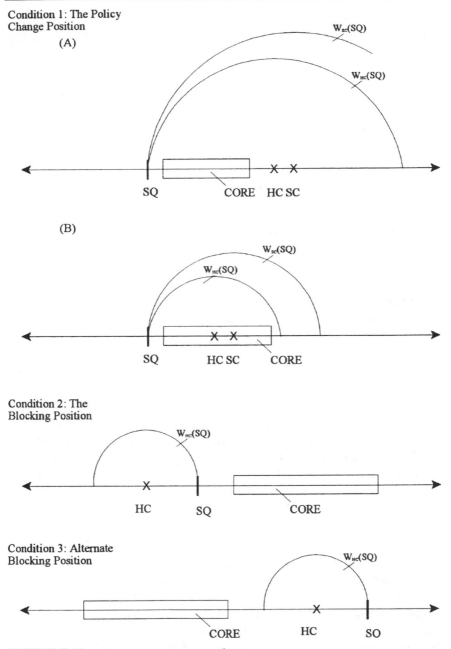

FIGURE 7.11   *Figure continues on facing page.*

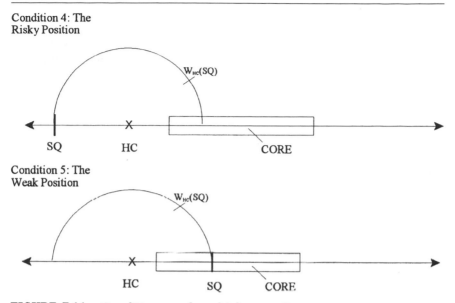

FIGURE 7.11 *Conditions under which committees are or are not powerful*

ous guess about what the floors and the president would do if a piece of legislation were released to them:

> **Condition 4a:** If the House committee lies between the *SQ* and *CORE*, and $W_{HC}(SQ) \cap CORE \neq \emptyset$, then the House committee members face a risky choice over whether to send a bill to the floor.

> **Condition 4b:** If the Senate committee lies between the *SQ* and *CORE*, and $W_{SC}(SQ) \cap CORE \neq \emptyset$, then the Senate committee members face a risky choice over whether to send a bill to the floor.

In figure 7.11, we refer to this as the "risky position." If the committee members guess that the ultimate bill passed by Congress and signed by the president would lie in $W_{HC}(SQ) \cap CORE$, then the committee would send the bill to the floor. However, as shown in figure 7.11, not all of *CORE* lies inside $W_{HC}(SQ)$, which means that there is a probability that the ultimate bill would lie outside $W_{HC}(SQ)$ though still in *CORE*. Only if the House committee members can secure a guarantee from floor members that the final bill will be better for them than *SQ* would they likely feel safe in sending the bill to the floor (this guarantee might take the form of a promise from the Rules Committee that a closed rule would be granted for floor debate plus assurance from the leadership that the committee members would represent the House in any conference committee with the Senate).

The final condition involves a situation in which *SQ* is inside *CORE:*

Condition 5: If *SQ* lies inside *CORE,* then the committees cannot change the status quo.

In this last condition, the committees find themselves in a weak position. By the definition of *CORE,* no point inside it can be defeated by any other point. Consequently, if *SQ* lies inside *CORE,* no other policy can defeat it, which means that the committees are in no position to change the status quo. In both the trucking and airline deregulation cases, for example, President Carter was able to move the policy status quo to this location via his appointments and other activities with the ICC and CAB. For the airline and trucking industries, the passage of legislation could not possibly restore the status quo ante (because President Carter vowed to veto any such bills), but it at least could prevent further deregulation. Hence the legislation that passed gave President Carter most of what he wanted rather than reflecting the preferences of the committees.

These five conditions characterize the full range of influence that the congressional committees might have. Note that the degree of influence for the committees depends on an interaction between the locations of the actors' ideal points and the location of the status quo policy. Holding constant the actors' ideal points, changes in the location of *SQ* can be expected to change the relative power of the various actors. This general theoretical point is essential to understanding committee power, yet it has not been a central element of textbook treatments of Congress nor has it been an element of well-known typologies of regulation and the policy process (e.g., Lowi 1972; Wilson 1971).

It is also essential to note the critical role that the president plays in any adequate understanding of committee power and the legislative process. Short of a veto override, the president is the one actor whose support is essential for a committee to change the status quo.

In addition, presidents also have considerable discretion over appointments and can often unilaterally change the status quo (see Moe and Howell 1999), thereby potentially altering the committees' ability to protect their preferred policies.

Finally, it must be recognized that legislative procedures directly affect the conditions under which legislative committees are powerful. Although committees may be able to protect a static status quo, exogenous forces (or the president) may lead to a status quo that the committees want to change, and on occasion subgovernments may even become internally divided. To change policy, however, they have to contend with the many other actors and procedures in the policy process; the coalition necessary to change the status quo is far larger than the one required to protect it. To the extent that the general norm of reciprocity is weakening, and the capacity of legislators to deal with a broad range of issues is growing, then these legislative procedures are critical to understanding the role of the committees in the policymaking process.

References

Bach, Stanley, and Steven S. Smith. 1988. *Managing uncertainty in the House of Representatives.* Washington, D.C.: Brookings Institution Press, 12, 23–27.

Cargill, Thomas, and Gillian Garcia. 1982. *Financial deregulation and monetary control: Historical perspective and impact of the 1980 act.* Stanford: Hoover Institution Press.

Coll, Steve. 1986. *The deal of the century: The breakup of AT&T.* New York: Atheneum.

CQ Almanac. Vol. 32, 1976a. Bell Telephone presses case for monopoly. September 25, pp. 2615–21.

CQ Almanac. Vol. 32, 1976b. Transportation and communications, pp. 637–38.

CQ Almanac. Vol. 33, 1977a. House panel considers major overhaul of 1934 Communications Act. June 4, pp. 563–66.

CQ Almanac. , Vol. 33, 1977b. Prospects for AT&T anti-competition bill dim but lobbying continues. April 16, p. 706.

CQ Almanac. Vol. 33,1977c. Airline deregulation, pp. 554–56.

CQ Almanac. Vol. 35, 1978a. Congress clears airline deregulation bill, pp. 496–504.

CQ Almanac. Vol. 35, 1978b. Airline deregulation, p. 471.

CQ Almanac. Vol. 36, 1979. Banking deregulation, pp. 321–24.

CQ Almanac. Vol. 37, 1980a. Broad banking deregulation bill approved, pp. 275–77.

CQ Almanac. Vol. 37, 1980b. Congress clears trucking deregulation bill, pp. 242–48.

CQ Almanac. Vol. 38, 1981. Telecommunications pace interrupted, pp. 555–60.

CQ Almanac. Vol. 38, 1982. AT&T bill dropped, killing rewrite efforts, pp. 331–32.

CQ Weekly Report. 1976. Bell Telephone presses case for monopoly. September 25, pp. 2615–21.

CQ Weekly Report. 1977. Prospects for AT&T anti-competition bill dim but lobbying continues. April 16, p. 706.

CQ Weekly Report. 1982. Limited banking reform bill awaits floor action in Senate. August 28, p. 2125–26.

Derthick, Martha, and Paul Quirk. 1985. *The politics of deregulation.* Washington, D.C.: Brookings Institution.

Dodd, Lawrence, and Richard Schott. 1979. *Congress and the administrative state.* New York: John Wiley & Sons.

Evans, Gary. 1984. The evolution of financial institutions and the ineffectiveness of monetary policy. *Journal of Economic Issues,* 18: 439–48.

Fenno, Richard. 1973. *Congressmen in committee.* Boston, Mass.: Little, Brown.

Ferejohn, John. 1985. Logrolling in an institutional context: A case study of Food Stamps legislation. Working Papers in Political Science, no. P85–5. Stanford: The Hoover Institution.

Ferejohn, John, and Charles Shipan. 1990. Congressional influence on bureaucracy. *Journal of Law, Economics, and Organization,* 6: 1–27.

Hammond Thomas, and Jack Knott. 1988. The deregulatory snowball: Explaining deregulation in the financial industry. *Journal of Politics,* 50: 3–30.

———. 1996. Who controls the bureaucracy? Presidential power, congressional dominance, legal constraints, and bureaucratic autonomy in a model of multi-institutional policy-making. *Journal of Law, Economics, and Organization,* 12: 121–68.

Lehman, Nicholas. 1985. Change in the banks. *The Atlantic Monthly,* 256: 60–68.

Lowi, Theodore. 1972. Four systems of policy, politics, and choice. *Public Administration Review,* 32: 298–310.

Meier, Kenneth. 1985. *Regulation: Politics, bureaucracy and economics.* New York: St. Martin's Press.

Moe, Terry, and William Howell. 1999. The presidential power of unilateral action. *Journal of Law, Economics, & Organization,* 15: 132–79.

Rothenberg, Lawrence. 1994. *Regulation, organizations, and politics: Motor freight policy at the Interstate Commerce Commission.* Ann Arbor: University of Michigan Press.

Shepsle, Kenneth. 1989. Congressional institutions and behavior: The changing textbook Congress. In *Can the government govern,* edited by John E. Chubb and Paul Peterson. Washington, D.C.: Brookings Institution.

Smith, Steven. 1988. An essay on sequence, position, goals, and committee power. *Legislative Studies Quarterly,* 13: 151–76.

Smith, Steven S., and Christopher J. Deering. 1984. *Committees in Congress.* Washington, D.C.: CQ Press.

Temin, Peter, and Louis Galambos. 1987. *The fall of the Bell system: A study in prices and politics.* New York: Cambridge University Press.

Wall Street Journal. 1988. Draft bill giving banks securities role is to be unveiled today by St. Germain, p. 29.

Weingast, Barry. 1981. Regulation, reregulation, and deregulation: The political economy of agency clientele relationships. *Law and Contemporary Problems,* 44: 147–77.

Wilson, James Q. 1971. The dead hand of regulation. *The Public Interest,* 7: 39–58.

Wildavsky, Aaron. 1988. *The new politics of the budgetary process.* Glenview, Ill.: Scott-Foresman.

CHAPTER 8

How Networks Are Governed

H. Brinton Milward and Keith G. Provan

Command and control mechanisms associated with bureaucracy are giving way to much more complicated relationships for the delivery of health and human services. Nonprofit organizations, private firms, and governments all play a role in the new world of devolved public policy. The unit of analysis in this world is the network. Networks, while less stable overall than private firms or governments, have stable features whose contours are shaped by law, funding structures, and norms and values shared by members of the network.

This chapter examines various approaches to governing networks among public agencies, nonprofit organizations, and private firms that deliver taxpayer-funded services. The governance problem is how to design institutions that can be effective in a world where few organizations have the power to accomplish their missions alone (Bryson and Crosby 1992, pp. 3–21). In health, mental health, children's services, drug and alcohol prevention, and welfare, responsibility for policy design has devolved to state governments, and policy implementation now occurs in a decentralized network of local government agencies, nonprofit organizations, and private firms. In "The Maker," Jorge Luis Borges wrote of a bureau of cartography in a fictional South American country whose sole task was to construct a map as big as the country. As in this story, the danger of network analysis is creating a network as complex as the reality it is supposed to represent. This is a danger we do our best to avoid.

Over the past eight years, we have conducted research on networks consisting mainly of nonprofit organizations that jointly produce mental health services in communities across the United States. These services are produced either under contract with public agencies or once removed from government with private, nonprofit "authorities" who operate under a master contract with the state. In the course of research assessing the performance of these networks, we became convinced that questions of governance were just as important as questions of management.

Governance

In common usage, "government" refers to the formal institutions of the state—the executive branch, legislature, and the courts—and their monopoly of legitimate, coercive power. Governance is a more inclusive term concerned with creating the conditions for ordered rule and collective action, often including agents in the private and nonprofit sectors, as well as within the public sector. The essence of governance is its focus on governing mechanisms (grants, contracts, agreements) that do not rest solely on the authority and sanctions of government (Stoker 1998, p. 17). These mechanisms, or tools, are used to connect networks of actors, who operate in various domains of public policy such as welfare, health, or transportation. A critical empirical question is the degree to which they operate autonomously or are steered by the state.

Modern governments by their scale and scope are complex and highly differentiated. Complexity has been compounded by the trend toward establishing principal-agent relations with private firms and voluntary agencies as a result of purchaser-provider relationships. At the same time, the central government has become "hollowed out" as power has devolved to state and local governments (Stoker 1998, p. 19). Thus a variety of government agencies have chosen to share their authority for collective action with nonprofit agencies and private firms in a network of mutual dependence.

For many reasons—political, economic, and organizational—governments around the world have chosen networks of providers—some governmental, some nonprofit, and some private firms—to deliver taxpayer funded services. Osborne and Gaebler (1992) describe governance as supplying collective services to citizens through various tools, government provision being only one of them. Thus tools such as contracts, quasi markets, and franchises allow the government to "steer rather than row," as Osborne and Gaebler put it.

What is so astonishing about this worldwide movement away from government provision and toward government procurement is that there is little evidence that central governments know very much about how to govern or manage networks. U. S. General Accounting Office reports, headlines in newspapers, and television specials on "fleecing the taxpayer" regularly report failures of federal and state government agencies to monitor and control their contractors. In Arizona, the Department of Environmental Quality ceased to monitor its privatized vehicle emissions inspection program because of budget cuts mandated by the state legislature. This occurred after the program was rocked by charges that inspectors for the private firm were soliciting bribes from motorists whose cars had failed the test (*Arizona Daily Star*, September 22, 1999).

At the same time, there is little evidence that we know much more about how to manage decentralized programs at the community level. There is very little empirical evidence that integrating human services, community policing, urban enterprise zones, public-private partnerships, or community coalitions to build social capital have a consistently positive effect on community-level outcomes. Good things do happen at the community level; it is unlikely, however, that they can be traced to any particular approach to solving community problems. What happens on the ground is very complex, and it is not always possible to determine why, for example, the crime rate fell. It may fall in an area with community policing and also in an area with no community policing. Also, evaluation is time-consuming, expensive, and often bears bad tidings. The Treaty of Westphalia, which ended the Thirty Years' War in 1648, outlawed killing the messenger for the message. Unfortunately, this convention is often honored in the breach. As James Q. Wilson points out, foundations—and we would add governments—prefer to fund causes, not research.[1] This is why so many new program initiatives or "best practices" are based on one or two success stories.

The Hollow State

We have referred to the current fashion of contracting out government services to networks of largely nonprofit organizations (with some private firms included) as the "hollow state." The hollow state is a metaphor to describe the increasing reliance of the public sector on contracting with nonprofit agencies and for-profit firms to deliver taxpayer-funded goods and services (Milward 1994, 1996; Milward and Provan 1993).[2] It would be very useful to know the size of the hollow state. Statistics on networks are rarely kept, and multilevel data sources are difficult to find. Although most observers believe that governments are more often contracting for services than they have in the past, there are no data sets that would allow us to answer the question of just how hollow the hollow state is.

By the hollow state, we mean that there's a degree of separation between a government and the services it funds. For instance, in the Arizona behavioral health system, four layers separate the federal substance abuse and mental health block grant from the client, with no services provided until the third or fourth layer. Determining eligibility, contracting, monitoring, and providing clinical services are all carried out by nonprofit organizations or private firms.

In a general sense, the hollow state then refers to any situation in which a government agency relies on others (private firms, nonprofit organizations, or other government agencies) to work together to deliver public services. Carried to its extreme, it refers to a government that, as a matter of public policy, has chosen to contract out all of its production capability to third parties. There is obviously a great deal of territory between these two extremes, but although hollowness varies from case to case, the central task of the hollow state does not vary: it arranges networks rather than manages hierarchies, the traditional task of government. Public managers find themselves arranging networks that enable them to gain the advantages of scope and scale without the negatives associated with bureaucracy (i.e., redundancy and rising costs).

The fact that a hollow state relies on networks is a weakness as well as a strength. Because of hierarchy, bureaucracies are more predictable and stable over time. Networks—the mainstay of the hollow state—are inherently weaker forms of social action. Because they must coordinate production jointly, networks are inherently unstable over time. Managers are continually faced with problems that can lead to instability, such as negotiating, coordinating, monitoring, holding third parties accountable, and writing and enforcing contracts—all for organizations that are relatively independent of the funder. Governing a set of contractual relationships demands specification, negotiation, monitoring, and perhaps litigation as well as a group of public managers with the necessary skills. In agency theory terms, problems also arise because of the asymmetry of information between the principal (government) and the agent (the firm or nonprofit organization). The separation of ownership and management can create costs. Principals can incur significant costs associated with contracting, such as monitoring for compliance and ensuring that the agent produces services of reasonable quality (Jensen and Meckling 1976). The third-party agents may also organize themselves politically to pressure elected representatives to intervene in disputes between the government agency and its network of nonprofit organizations and firms.[3]

Although unrecognized in the literature on principal-agent theory, delegating authority to nongovernment agents can potentially lead to a loss of legitimacy for government action accomplished at arm's length. "Political principals can transfer power to their agents, within limits set by law, but they cannot transfer legitimacy in the same way" (Majone 1997, p. 13). The State of Arizona recently contracted with Value Options, the second-largest, for-profit managed mental health company in the country, to run the mental health system of Phoenix, the nation's sixth-largest city. Texas, although temporarily unable to obtain a federal waiver from the Clinton Administration, is planning to turn over the Texas welfare system to a company such as Lockheed Martin or EDS. Depending on one's values, this may be innovative or reckless. Whatever one's values, it is well to remember that privatization may change the venue, but government is still responsible for the results. In paying someone else to do the work, government still has to police the contractor. The more reach contractors have under a privatized system, the less capacity government is likely to retain, however. The claim of hopeless government incompetence may become a convenient self-fulfilling prophecy (Kuttner 1989).

The hollow state does not arise from conditions at the local level, where governments are fragmented and authority widely diffused. Rather, it flows from the central problem of governance in the United States—its separation of powers and wide diffusion of authority. Allen Schick captured the implications of our institutional design for the problem of governance:

> Consider the implications for the conduct of government of the fact
> that three-quarters of the federal budget is transferred to outsiders.

This country has functioned for almost two hundred years with the notion that as chief executive the president presides over an executive establishment that constitutes the U.S. government. But the president is not chief executive of the fifty states and thousands of local governments that obtain $100 billion in federal grants, or of the 36 million Americans who receive Social Security checks each month. . . .

Until we comprehend what is involved in governing a government of political networks rather than a government of administrative compartments, we will not know how to manage (Schick 1985, p. 125).

Network Governance

Why does the hollow state rely on networks more than when services are funded directly by the state? In a general sense, this is an empirical question that may vary by policy area. Simply because trash hauling has been privatized does not mean that a network of garbage firms will have to pick up the trash. Ten different firms may have contracts with a city to pick up garbage in ten different areas of the city. Each firm has a contract with the city, but each needs no connection with the other to do the job. Two elements, however, are key to our definition of the hollow state: joint production and having several degrees of separation between the source and the user of government funds. Both elements combine to ensure that hierarchies and markets will not work and that networks are the only alternative for collective action. If several different levels of government fund a service, there is no command and control relationship in our constitutional scheme, and hierarchy is not an option. If ten different agencies must each deliver a unique service to a client, and collectively these services allow a client to overcome his or her dependence on welfare and enter the world of work, a competitive market is not applicable. Education, day care, health care, housing, food assistance, job coaching, and vocational training may be needed to move a client from welfare to work. Unless there is some level of coordination and collaboration between these individual agencies, it is unlikely that the client will be able to negotiate with each agency to make the transition from welfare to work. In thin markets, such as social services, where there are limited providers for any one service, it is difficult to imagine enough agencies to allow for competitive contracting for each individual service.

Although there may be competitive bidding among nonprofit agencies and private firms to provide social services, the competition is usually for the right to organize the network of services. Rarely is there competitive bidding for each element of service that makes up a network of services. Network governance is concerned with how control is maintained over the set of contracts that govern the provision of a set of services.

The Literature on Network Governance

This chapter and this book evolved from a shared attempt among scholars of public management to study governance empirically. Recent efforts to codify and evaluate what we know about governance have great potential (Lynn, Heinrich, and Hill 1999). This review of the literature on governance of networks shares the same objective. As noted in a recent survey of interorganizational coordination, the literature on network governance dates back to the early 1960s when Litwak and Meyer (1966, pp. 39–42) spoke of "mechanisms of coordination" in a study of social service organizations. Since then, references in the organizational literature to network governance and coordination have been few and far between (Alexander 1995, p. 47).

The mechanisms of coordination were a very important issue in public administration during the 1970s, when policymakers and planners were attempting to derive order from the numerous programs created by the War on Poverty. The subtext of the extensive literature on service integration is how either to force or to encourage cooperation among independent agencies, many of which are separately funded (Kagan with Neville 1993). Very little of the work on taming the programs of the Great Society was based in organization theory. It is policy-oriented in its desire to control programs that created a plethora of agencies that either duplicated services or allowed clients to fall through the cracks of an uncoordinated service delivery system. The work is very much concerned, however, with governance among a network of agencies. Although there are numerous case studies and "lessons learned," none is empirical in the sense that it tests whether coordinated services perform better than uncoordinated services (Yessian 1991).

Current efforts to create alliances, joint ventures, and partnerships require some type of interorganizational approach to governance. Much of this work assumes that coordination results from perceived mutual benefit among participants or from the efforts of a strategic actor in the network (Faerman, McCaffrey, and Van Slyke 1999). Although we are concerned with how to create partnerships and alliances, and how governance emerges from these coordination efforts, governments are still forcing, or strongly encouraging, networks of organizations to adopt particular governance mechanisms. Whether it is states such as Ohio requiring an alcohol, drug, and mental health board to oversee state funding in every town in the state, or whether it is the federal government requiring a single state agency to administer state highway funds, these institutional structures require organizations to be governed similarly.

These are examples of "coercive isomorphism" as described in the institutional theory of organizations (DiMaggio and Powell 1983). In the real world, coercion is infrequently used alone. Even those who have authority sometimes choose not to use it. Kentucky used incentives and moral suasion in attempting to get county governments to take responsibility for garbage collection in rural areas, where trash was a blight on the landscape and on the environment (O'Connell 1999). State environmental officials believed that voluntary compliance would be far more effective than heavy-handed coercion, and much less likely to cause county governments to use their power in the legislature to thwart the environmental regulations. "Thus," O'Connell says, "consensus building is part of the process of state-local relations even when one level of government has the ability to impose sanctions upon another. In many, perhaps most instances, power is exercised gingerly and the lower level has much to say in the implementation process" (p. 2).

Although not formally an interorganizational study, the findings on what O'Connell calls "indirect accountability" are clearly applicable to network governance. He finds that the reluctance to compel local officials directly to comply with the law stems from a web of relationships between state and local appointed officials and their ties to elected officials. The first efforts at compliance attempt negotiation rather than force. If negotiation fails, then state officials will more closely monitor how local officials spend the money rather than just monitoring the results. Just as state officials believe that coercion is not a winning long-term strategy with local officials, they also believe that coercion is not a winning strategy for local officials to use with their constituents who also vote. Thus even if failure occurs, the state will still try to negotiate. This approach seems to have worked in one instance: garbage collection in Kentucky increased substantially, and there was no backlash from the voters.

O'Connell's study shows that governance in multitiered networks is far from a simple principal-agent relationship. In a discussion of mandated coordination structures, Alexander (1995, pp. 59–66) shows how network relationships vary by differences in structural levels, just as policymaking differs between levels of the federal system. What holds all levels together is their interdependence and the fact that none of the organizations can accomplish their objectives alone. Alexander offers a compelling example: "The social services agencies participating in the coordinating committee are doing so because they need each other's referrals for clients, and their cases require the other programs' complementary services. They could ignore this, but at their own risk, because their interdependence has been asserted by the federal agency that is their common source of funds" (p. 68).

Alter and Hage refer to this type of coordination as a performance objective or a program goal (1993, p. 82). It is the end sought by generations of program planners and advocates. It is the justification for the push for service integration in almost every field of domestic public policy (Kagan with Neville 1993). Alter and Hage develop a very complex theory of network governance that rests on coordination. At its heart is the assertion that "interorganizational coordination is *a method or a process*—not an outcome—that must occur at all hierarchical levels and that utilizes a wide range of methods" (1993, p. 90, italics in original). Their levels are those of the federal system and their methods include *policymaking coordination* methods such as interagency commissions; *administrative coordination,* which might include joint programs; and *operational coordination* methods such as case management. In this regard, their methods of coordination are like our administrative links that were divided between administrative links and service links (Provan and Milward 1995).

Although we use them to develop the linkage structure of our networks, Alter and Hage use them to drive their theory. The theory Alter and Hage (1993) develop is quite useful for understanding what drives various types of coordination in interorganizational networks in the public and nonprofit sectors. Like that proposed by Alexander (1995), it is also a great resource for reviewing the interorganizational research over the past forty years. For evaluating what type of governance mechanism works better than another and why, however, their theory is of little help because it intentionally does not focus on outcomes.

A paper by Jones, Hesterly, and Borgatti attempts to develop a general theory of network governance. The authors note that although governance is frequently mentioned in network studies as providing important benefits, organizational scholars are quite vague on how and when governance will occur and on the role that it plays in helping organizations in the network resolve problems of adapting, coordinating, and safeguarding exchanges (1997, p. 912). Their definition of network governance "involves a select, persistent, and structured set of autonomous firms (as well as nonprofit agencies) engaged in creating products or services based on implicit and open-ended contracts to adapt to environmental contingencies and to coordinate and safeguard exchanges" (p. 914). The paper is an impressive attempt to explain how network governance emerges.

Jones, Hesterly, and Borgatti's argument is that exchange attributes of the network members lead to the development of a social structure, and through the social structure, control mechanisms develop that allow for the efficient governance of the network. Using both transactions cost economics (Williamson 1975, 1985) and structural embeddedness of networks (Granovetter 1985), Jones, Hesterly, and Borgatti develop a theory of network governance that goes far beyond the metaphorical use of the term. The theory, however, is subject to limits when applied to networks of organizations funded largely by a central source. In a clarification of this point, Candace Jones stated, "If for example, agencies fundamentally define or alter exchange attributes but do not oversee the exchanges between providers and do not engage in sanctions, then their role alters our theory by providing an institutional precursor to our model" (Jones 1999). The "institutional precursor" is the funding agency. To the extent that it sanctions and oversees exchanges in the network, the institutional precursor limits the ability of the network members to create their own governance structure. In theories of network governance as an emergent phenomenon, "formal contracts may exist between some pairs of members, but these do not define the relationships among all of the parties" (Jones, Hesterly, and Borgatti 1997, p. 916). A vocational training agency and a psychiatric hospital may have contracts with a mental health authority, but the contracts do not specify the relationship between the vocational training agency and the hospital. "To enhance cooperation on shared tasks, the network form of governance relies more heavily on social coordination and control, such as occupational socialization, collective sanctions, and reputations, than on authority or legal recourse" (Jones, Hesterly, and Borgatti 1997, p. 916).

The theory, however, fits certain types of nonprofit networks that develop self-governing mechanisms. A community coalition of human service agencies (much like the community decision organizations in Warren, Rose, and Bergunder 1974), which develops governing mechanisms in a field such as mental health, would fit the theory quite well. Although we previously stated that the danger of network analysis is creating a map as big as the country, this type of self-organized governing mechanisms is related to policy networks at the national level in functional areas like health and human services (Milward 1982).

The relationship between organized and self-organized governance is explored in an extremely rich case study of the Derivatives Policy Group, which developed a governing structure for buying and selling financial derivatives, largely unregulated at the time (Faerman, McCaffrey, and Van Slyke 1999). From 1994 to 1998 six large financial firms worked in cooperation with the U.S. Securities and Exchange Commission (SEC) and the Commodity Futures Trading Commission to develop a structure for buying and selling financial derivatives. The study stands in contrast to the other work reviewed in this chapter in that it deals with how governance emerges from the behavioral interaction of individuals representing a number of different organizations as they face a set of incentives.

Faerman, McCaffrey, and Van Slyke derive four factors that influence cooperation and lead to agreement on a policy to bind a group of major financial firms and the government. First, members' initial disposition toward cooperation was important to securing agreement. Second, the incentives in play were very important in pushing the parties toward agreement. Both the firms and the government agency were afraid of action by Congress to regulate the sale of derivatives, an option that neither the firms nor the government agencies wanted because of the difficulty in predicting the outcome. These incentives operated much as the incentives on parties to a lawsuit who decide to settle because of the unpredictability of a jury trial. Third, leadership was critical. Several highly respected individuals in the group understood both the government's concerns and the firms' concerns. Having an honest broker was very important in reaching agreement. Fourth, the number and variety of organizations involved in this case were quite small. There were six firms and one government agency. The study found that small size and limited variety were important in achieving agreement. This finding stands in contrast to the current practice of ensuring that decision-making groups are diverse and broadly representative.

Network governance is the result of many different factors. In the case of derivatives, it emerged as a result of both behavioral and environmental factors. In our work, we have tried to make a clear distinction between network governance structures based on contractual ties and interorganizational networks held together by historical patterns of collaboration, personal relationships, and trust. Our work is similar to that of Uzzi (1997) who found that both forms could co-exist. We believe that networks of public and nonprofit agencies must have both to be effective. In mental health, as in other areas of health and human services, contractual ties compose an important, but limited piece of network relationships. Thus while the principal-agent model appears to fit the hollow-state contracting relationship, it seems less useful for explaining more informal, trust-based ties that typically hold a network together over time. Clear principal-agent relationships and ties based on trust facilitate network governance. Strong ties between actors in networks can help to clarify agency problems by helping both parties to act in their long-term mutual interest (Granovetter 1992). In the empirical part of our research, we have chosen to focus more on contractual ties.

In our 1995 study of community mental health networks (Provan and Milward 1995), one of the mental health networks, Providence, Rhode Island, was dominated by a powerful organization, the Providence Center, that functioned like a monopoly and had much higher levels of client and family satisfaction than the other networks. The structure of the Providence mental health network—its dominant organization and the state funding agency—conformed closely to principal-agent theory, with the state Department of Mental Health as the principal and the Providence Center as the agent. It also was a network that was characterized by "centralized integration" among the providers. Thus a clear principal-agent relationship existed at the community level between the Providence Center and the other providers in the network as well as between the state department of mental health and the Providence Center. As Miller (1992) describes the theory, "agents are perceived as having distinct tastes (such as the desire to limit risk taking or costly effort), which they pursue as rational maximizing individuals. The principal's job is to anticipate the rational responses of agents and to design a set of incentives such that the agents find it in their own interests (given the incentive system) to take the best possible set of actions (from the principal's perspective)" (p. 2).

Although this theory has wide acceptance in economics, it is at variance with almost all of the best-practice literature in community mental health and human services generally. The findings reported in Provan and Milward (1995) run counter to much of the conventional wisdom on public-sector service delivery that stresses service integration through public authorities that concentrate local funding in one set of hands and arrange for the provision of community-based services by a network of providers (Kagan with Neville 1993; Shore and Cohen 1994). We believe that the reason for this disjuncture between principal-agent theory and integrating services is because of the different perspective each maintains. Principal-agent theory looks at the world from the taxpayer's perspective. Those pressing for service integration often do so from the perspective of clients in distress.

One could go crazy trying to figure out all of the potential principal-agent relations in a human service system that spans levels of government, branches of government, and multiple contractual relationships with nonprofit organizations and private firms. Some relationships, however, are more important than others. It is important who the principal's principal happens to be, what power and authority the principal's principal possesses, and whether he or she is subject to influence (Lynn 1996). Nonprofit agencies that have a contract to organize a system of services for a government agency are particularly vulnerable. They exist at the sufferance of government and often receive most of their funding from there as well. Most have a multiyear contract from a state government to organize a system of services in a local community or multicounty area. The legitimacy they have is delegated by the government agency that tendered the contract they hold. Their legitimacy is limited. Because of pressure to engage in competitive contracting, the state will often rebid the contract every few years.[4]

Rebidding contracts frequently has several negative effects on co-operation among the set of providers who hold contracts with the mental health authority. First, because the authority's legitimacy is conditional, it encourages end runs to the state legislature to try to loosen the bonds that the authority exerts over the providers. The legislators, who are popular candidates for a provider's board of di-rectors and who always need local support in their electoral efforts, will sometimes intercede with the state agency (the principal's prin-cipal) to pressure the nonprofit authority to demand less in terms of performance or more in terms of the money that flows to the pro-vider under the contract. Second, because the nonprofit authority must compete for the contract when it is rebid, the providers may fail to cooperate because they fancy themselves winning the con-tract in a new round of bidding. Even if they do cooperate, another bidder may win the contract, and long-term investment in coopera-tive endeavors and infrastructure may be wasted under what Smith and Lipsky (1993) call a different "contracting regime."

Stability and Network Governance

Stability is not a virtue that most economists would recommend as a universal solvent promoting performance. Their nostrum in recent years has been competitive tendering. Putting providers at risk, ac-cording to economic theory, should put them on their toes and make them more efficient and innovative in designing and delivering their services.[5] In some sense, economists are right. A system can be too stable, too inward focused. If resources are not constrained, a stable system is subject to redundant and rising costs. There is, however, a key difference between the work of a mental health pro-vider and a private garbage hauler operating under a competitively tendered contract. The garbage hauler is responsible for picking up trash in a defined area of a town. The firm's success does not de-pend on thirty different trash haulers doing their job correctly for the town government to be pleased. What is to be produced can be clearly defined, and responsibility for adequate service can be fixed and measured. Trash hauling has a single production function.

With mental health, or with most other human services, in con-trast, one provider specializes in mental health treatment using therapy and drugs. A second provider specializes in day treatment, providing a place for seriously mentally ill individuals to congregate during the day and engage in hobbies and group therapy. A third provides group housing for the mentally ill. A fourth provides an inpatient psychiatric facility where a client who becomes psychotic can be treated. A fifth runs a suicide prevention hotline. A sixth runs a vocational training program. A seventh runs the crisis facility where the client is stabilized, a psychiatric evaluation is performed, and if eligible, the client is enrolled in the network and gains access to its services. All of these separate providers must do their jobs reasonably well and must refer their clients to the other providers for needed services if the network is to perform well. In other words, community mental health networks, unlike trash haulers, have a joint production function. This need to produce services jointly is characteristic of all types of health and human services delivered in a community setting. As mentioned earlier, the need to produce services jointly is one of the defining characteristics of the hollow state.

A system in flux will be unable to coordinate referrals or develop a stable system of services that clients need in a deinstitutionalized community setting. A stable system, even one that is poorly designed or inadequately funded, allows the individuals and agencies working in it the time to work out problems and agree on a division of labor. It also allows the principal time to learn how to govern. Learning to govern is a process of trial and error. If the right to deliver services is competitive and a new organization wins the bid, it is almost certain that performance will decline in the short run. New infrastructure must be developed. The new authority must learn which agencies produce quality services at a reasonable cost and which can be trusted to cooperate with other agencies. Costs can expand quickly unless effective controls are in place to monitor and evaluate services. New and costly drugs may quickly increase costs far beyond projections. Public-interest lawsuits and new laws and regulations can quickly expand the client population with rights to services. Capitated services are a particularly difficult problem. All of these problems must be reduced to tolerable levels if a new system is to be reasonably stable.

Stability in certain types of relationships may be more important than others. Stable funding relationships may be critical, for example. If the receipt or level of funding is highly uncertain, it may be impossible for a network to do a decent job. On the other hand, there are many relationships in networks other than funding. In our

minds, stability of funding does not mean that all other types of network relationships are stable as well. The number of clients served,
or the carrying capacity of the network, is a critical variable. Is the
client population reasonably stable or is it growing at an exponen-
tial rate? Is the carrying capacity of the network in reasonable balance with the resources the network receives? Leadership and the
ability of a network to resolve conflict and seize new opportunities
will likely vary as well. Thus a key question is: How can networks
be governed to take advantage of their flexibility at the service level
in the face of either stability or instability of their funding and oversight by their principals?

One of our key findings (Provan and Milward 1995) is that human service systems that are stable are more likely to perform well
than are systems in a state of flux. Both of our highest performing
community mental health networks were quite stable. Both of our
lowest performing community mental health networks were unstable. By stability we mean that the network has not been recently
changed in any of its key structural components or that the master
contract with the state has not been rebid. Thus stability, up to some
point, promotes effective performance. On the other hand, one of
the key assertions about the strength of networks is that they are
flexible and adaptive. How can both of these statements be true?
The answer lies in the evolution of networks over time. We assert
that at some point, an unstable network becomes stable enough to
perform reasonably well while still remaining flexible and adaptive.
Later the same network becomes rigid and inflexible, rendering it
unable to adapt to changing conditions. Therefore, hypotheses
about networks are likely to be confirmed or rejected based on the
state of development of the network. The difficulty of giving management advice on network governance is exacerbated by the fact
that what is true at one point may not be true at another point
(Knoke 1998). In a recent study, Hoffman (1999) traces the institutional evolution and change of the U.S. chemical industry as a network that forms around and in opposition to the environmental
movement. In this case, what holds as a finding on network governance is dependent on the point in time the network is studied.

The key is finding a balance between innovation and rigidity.
Systems need to be changed and reinvigorated. In the public and
nonprofit sectors, however, change is often adopted for its own sake
rather than to solve problems. New political leadership wants to

throw out the old regime. Advocates are constantly demanding that more money be spent and the latest methods adopted. Contractors often believe they will get a better deal in a new system. Public interest lawyers go to court to uphold their view of clients' rights. What we do know is that no system can be changed every few years and produce quality service. Continual change increases the rewards for noncooperation in an existing system, creating the impetus for yet more change. If we must change a system, we must do it infrequently and, if possible, incrementally.

Interaction Effects between Institutional Design and Stability

The monopoly model that Providence employed is not the only institutional design that is likely to promote stability, development of common purpose, and relative effectiveness (Provan and Milward 1995). Many new mental health systems shift some or all of the risk to the providers and from the authority that holds the contract with the state. If this agency gives the money to the providers in a risk-bearing contract, a major source of conflict has been eliminated. The providers, along with the authority, are at risk if the system fails and thus share the same incentive to make the network function effectively. This type of model is now being employed in Tucson (Provan, Milward, and Roussin 1998).

Theoretically, this model should dampen political infighting between providers and the authority. The mental health authority has a contract with the state to arrange for the flow of funds to a provider network. The authority bids out part of its authority to provider networks with a strong lead agency that will take an at-risk contract based on a per-member, per-month case rate. Because the lead providers develop their own networks of providers, unhappy providers can complain only about the lead agencies, and the pressure on the mental health authority is diverted to other targets. The lead agency, like the mental health authority, is both a principal and an agent. The lead provider is in a relationship with the providers in its network exactly like the Providence Center was with its providers. The lead agency produces services and knows many of the costs of production, which allows it to contract with those agencies that produce good quality services at a reasonable cost. According to Miles and Snow (1992), in the private sector, an organization that contracts too much out "runs the risk of becoming a 'hollow' corporation, a firm without a clearly defined essential contribution to make to its product or service value chain. Firms need to occupy a wide enough segment of the value chain to be able to test and protect the value of their contribution" (p. 67).

Governance and Outcomes

Given the paucity of empirical literature on the relationship between governance structure and outcomes, does it make any difference which type of structure is chosen? This is a critical question for future research and is related to the more general question of what constitutes relevant outcomes for networks. Stakeholders in taxpayer-funded systems, whether the organizations involved are public, private, or nonprofit, want to know whether the systems they fund or are served by are effective. Assessing effectiveness is, therefore, critical for developing a meaningful theory of networks. Yet whose perspective should be adopted when making this determination? Choice of outcomes appears to be critical for understanding which governance structures are most effective. We address this question in our forthcoming book, but let it suffice it to say here that there are at least four different perspectives on effectiveness for network evaluation.

- Individual clients and advocacy groups believe effectiveness flows from governance structures that allow flexibility at the provider level (which likely includes promoting services integration) and responsiveness to individual client needs.
- Agency managers and network administrators believe effectiveness results from governance structures that encourage stability, agency and network growth, and resource acquisition.
- Local officials and community leaders consider structures that result in efficient operations, cost reduction, and containing and limiting the visibility of social problems to the larger community as most effective.
- Funders and regulators promote structures that foster control and monitoring to ensure that they cannot be blamed for bad outcomes.

These four perspectives are separated to highlight differences among them. Funders and regulators are clearly concerned with efficiency and cost reduction as well as control and monitoring. Likewise, agency managers who deal with vulnerable populations such as the seriously mentally ill are very concerned with avoiding blame for poor outcomes, as are funders and regulators. No one involved in running a system of services wants a client to commit suicide outside her office after leaving a note saying he is ending it all because he cannot get the services he needs from the agency.

Conclusion

This chapter has examined the dimensions of various approaches to governing networks of public agencies, nonprofit organizations, and private firms that deliver taxpayer-funded services.

The essence of governance is its focus on governing mechanisms—grants, contracts, and agreements—that do not rest solely on the authority and sanctions of government. We noted that in contrast with the great enthusiasm for reinventing government and contracting out many of its functions, there is little evidence that central governments know very much about how to govern or manage networks. The same thing appeared true at the community level, where there is little evidence that local governments know much more about how to manage decentralized programs in their community effectively.

We have developed a metaphor and a model to describe this situation—the hollow state. The hollow state refers to any joint production situation in which a governmental agency relies on others (firms, nonprofit organizations, or other government agencies) to deliver public services jointly. Networks, the mainstay of the hollow state, are inherently weaker forms of social action. Because of the need to coordinate joint production, networks are unstable over time. Because of hierarchy, bureaucracies are more predictable and stable over time. The hollow state flows from the central problem of governance in the United States—its separation of powers and wide diffusion of authority.

Much of the work on network governance assumes that coordination results from the perception of mutual benefit on the part of the participants. Although we are concerned with how to create partnerships and alliances, and how governance emerges from these coordination efforts, network governance in the hollow state often consists of governments forcing or strongly encouraging networks of organizations to adopt particular governance mechanisms. Although the governance mechanism may be forced on the network, coercion is infrequently used alone. Even those who have authority sometimes choose not to use it. In networks funded with taxpayer dollars, clients are also voters.

Much of the literature on network governance focuses on what drives various types of coordination in interorganizational networks in the public and nonprofit sectors, and this literature is a great resource for understanding why and under what conditions cooperation occurs. However, from the perspective of evaluating what type of governance mechanism works better than another and why, these theories of cooperation are of little help given that they intentionally do not focus on outcomes.

Jones, Hesterly, and Borgatti (1997) develop an impressive theory to explain how network governance emerges in decentralized networks. Although their theory of governance does not directly apply to networks mandated or funded by a central source, it is nonetheless extremely helpful in understanding how governance emerges in networks and the role that both contracts and informal features of networks (such as reputation and trust) play and the ways they serve to strengthen ties among firms. The authors conclude that network governance relies more heavily on social coordination and control, such as occupational socialization, collective sanctions, and reputations, than on authority or legal recourse.

The relationship between organized and self-organized governance is explored in a case study of the Derivatives Policy Group (Faerman, McCaffrey, and Van Slyke 1999), which deals with how governance emerges from the behavioral interaction of individuals representing a number of different organizations facing a set of incentives. Four factors are advanced to explain why the group was successful. First, initial dispositions toward cooperation on the part of all members of the group were important in allowing agreement to be reached. Second, the incentives in play were very important in pushing the parties toward agreement. Third, leadership was critical; several highly respected individuals in the group understood both the government's concerns and the firms'. Fourth, the group's small size and limited variety were quite important in achieving agreement.

In our work (Provan and Milward 1995; Milward and Provan 1998), we have tried to make a clear distinction between network governance structures based on contractual ties and interorganizational networks held together by historical patterns of collaboration, personal relationships, and trust. Our emphasis on stability as a key variable stems from these informal ties. We believe that networks of public and nonprofit agencies must have both to be effective. Thus while the principal-agent model appears to fit the hollow-state contracting relationship, it seems less useful for explaining more informal, trust-based ties that typically hold a network together over time. Clear principal-agent relationships and trust-based ties facilitate network governance. Strong ties between actors in networks help to clarify agency problems by encouraging all parties to act in their long-term mutual interest.

We believe that if a system must be changed, it must be done infrequently and, if possible, incrementally. When a reasonable level of funding is combined with an institutional design that creates incentives for agents to perform as promised and the system is stable, reasonable outcomes are likely to result. Networks aligned in this fashion are more likely to solve collective action problems than ones that are not, especially if the state encourages cooperation by allowing enough time for networks to stabilize. Stability would increase the probability that, over time, cooperation would replace conflict, and network governance could focus on managing efficiently and effectively. When questions of governance have been resolved, the concerns of management can be more effectively addressed.

References

Alexander, Ernest. 1995. *How organizations act together: Interorganizational coordination in theory and practice.* Amsterdam: Gordon and Breach Publishers.

Alter, Catherine, and Jerald Hage. 1993. *Organizations working together.* Sage Library of Social Research 191. Newbury Park, Calif.: Sage Publications.

Arizona Daily Star. September 22, 1999. Cuts curtail oversight of emission testing. Metro Section, 1–2B.

Borges, Jorge Luis. 1998. *Collected fictions.* New York: Penguin Books, 325.

Bryson, John, and Barbara Crosby. 1992. *Leadership for the common good.* San Francisco: Jossey-Bass.

DiMaggio, Paul, and Walter Powell. 1983. The iron cage revisited: Institutional isomorphism and collective rationality in organizational fields. *American Sociological Review* 48: 147–60.

Faerman, Sue, David McCaffrey, and David Van Slyke. 1999. Understanding interorganizational cooperation: Public-private collaboration in regulating financial market innovation. Paper presented at the Academy of Management Annual Meeting, Chicago, Ill., August.

Ferris, James, and Elizabeth Graddy. 1997. New public management theory: Lessons from institutional economics and government contracting. In *Advances in international comparative management.* Supplement 3. *International perspectives on the new public management,* edited by Lawrence R. Jones, Kuno Schedler, and Stephen W. Wade. Greenwich, Conn.: JAI Press, pp. 89–104.

Granovetter, Mark. 1985. Economic action and social structure: The problem of embeddedness. *American Journal of Sociology* 91: 481–510.

———. 1992. Problems of explanation in economic sociology. In *Networks and organizations: Structure, form, and action,* edited by N. Nohria and R. Eccles. Boston: Harvard Business School Press.

Hoffman, Andrew. 1999. Institutional evolution and change: Environmentalism and the U.S. chemical industry. *Academy of Management Journal* 42: 351–71.

ICMA. December 1998. Draft core beliefs. Washington, D.C.: International City Management Association.

Jensen, M. and W. Meckling. 1976. Theory of the firm: Managerial behavior, agency costs and ownership structure. *Journal of Financial Economics* 3: 303–60.

Jones, Candace. 1999. Personal communication.

Jones, Candace, William Hesterly, and Stephen Borgatti. 1997. A general theory of network governance: Exchange conditions and social mechanisms. *Academy of Management Review* 22: 911–45.

Kagan, Sharon, with Peter Neville. 1993. *Integrating services for children and families.* New Haven, Conn.: Yale University Press.

Kettl, Donald. 1988. *Government by proxy: (Mis)managing federal programs.* Washington: Congressional Quarterly Press.

Knoke, David. 1998. Personal communication.

Kuttner, Robert. 1989. False profit. *The New Republic.* February 6.

LeGrand, Julian, and Will Bartlett (eds.). 1993. *Quasi-markets and social policy.* London: MacMillan.

Litwack, Eugene, and Henry Meyer. 1966. A balance theory of coordination between bureaucratic organizations and community primary groups. *Administrative Science Quarterly* 11: 31–58.

Lynn, Laurence, Jr. 1996. Assume a network: Reforming mental health services in Illinois. *Journal of Public Administration Research and Theory* 6: 297–314.

Lynn, Laurence, Jr., Carolyn Heinrich, and Carolyn Hill. 1999. The empirical study of governance: Theories, models and methods. Paper presented at the workshop on "Models and Methods for the Empirical Study of Governance," University of Arizona, April 29–May 1, 1999.

Majone, Giandomenico. 1997. The agency model: The growth of regulation and regulatory institutions in the European Union. EIPASCOPE *European Institute of Public Administration* 3: 9–14.

Miles, Raymond and Charles Snow. 1992. Causes of failure in network organizations. *California Management Review* 34: 53–72.

Miller, Gary. 1992. *Managerial dilemmas.* Cambridge: Cambridge University Press.

Milward, H. Brinton. 1982. Interorganizational policy systems and research on public organizations. *Administration and Society* 13: 457–78.

———. 1994. Nonprofit contracting and the hollow state. *Public Administration Review* 54:73–77.

———. 1996. Symposium on the hollow state: Capacity, control and performance in interorganizational settings. *Journal of Public Administration Research and Theory.* 6:193–95.

Milward, H. Brinton, and Keith Provan. 1993. The hollow state: Private provision of public services. In *Public policy for democracy,* edited by Helen Ingram and Steven Rathgeb Smith. Washington: Brookings Institution, pp. 222–37.

———. 1998. Principles for controlling agents: The political economy of network structure. *Journal of Public Administration Research and Theory* 8: 203–21.

Mosher, Frederick. 1981. The changing responsibilities and tactics of the federal government. *Public Administration Review* 40: 541–48.

O'Connell, Lenahan. 1999. Indirect accountability in state local relations: The example of solid waste policy in Kentucky. Paper presented at the Academy of Management Annual Meeting, Chicago, August.

Osborne, David, and Ted Gaebler. 1992. *Reinventing government.* Reading, Mass.: Addison-Wesley.

Provan, Keith G., and H. Brinton Milward. 2000. Do networks really work? A framework for evaluating public-sector organizational networks. *Public Administration Review* 6: in press.

Provan, Keith G., H. Brinton Milward, and Kimberly Roussin. 1998. Network evolution to a system of managed care for adults with severe mental illness: A case study of the Tucson experiment. In *Research in community mental health,* edited by Joseph Morrissey. Greenwich: Conn.: JAI Press, pp. 89–113.

Provan, Keith, and H. Brinton Milward. 1995. A preliminary theory of network effectiveness: A comparative study of four community mental health systems. *Administrative Science Quarterly* 40: 1–33.

Salamon, Lester. 1981. Rethinking public management: Third-party government and the changing forms of government action. *Public Policy* 29: 255–75.

Schick, Allen. 1985. The budget as an instrument of presidential policy. In *The Reagan presidency and the governing of America,* edited by Lester H. Salamon and Michael S. Lund. Washington, D.C.: Urban Institute Press, pp. 91–125.

Shore, Miles, and Martin Cohen. 1994. Introduction: Special issue on providing treatment to people with mental illness. *The Milbank Quarterly* 72: 31–35.

Smith, Steven Rathgeb, and Lipsky, Michael. 1993. *Nonprofits for hire: The welfare state in the age of contracting.* Cambridge, Mass.: Harvard University Press.

Stoker, Gary. 1998. Governance as theory: Five propositions. *International Social Science Journal* 155: 17–28.

Thompson, Fred. 1993. Matching responsibilities with tactics: Administrative controls and modern government. *Public Administration Review* 53: 303–18.

Uzzi, Brian. 1997. Social structure and competition in interfirm networks: The paradox of embeddedness. *Administrative Science Quarterly* 42: 35–67.

Warren, Roland, Stephen Rose, and Ann Bergunder. 1974. *The structure of urban reform.* Lexington, Mass.: Lexington Books.

Williamson, Oliver. 1975 *Markets and hierarchies: Analysis and antitrust implications.* New York: Free Press.

———. 1985. *The economic institutions of capitalism: Firms, markets, and relational contracting.* New York: Free Press.

Yessian, Mark. 1991. *Services integration: A twenty-year retrospective.* Washington, D.C.: Office of the Inspector General, Department of Health and Human Services.

Endnotes

1. Wilson made this remark at a 1996 Washington meeting of university grantees.
2. Mosher (1981) and Salamon (1981) first identified the scope and scale of federal government contracting. It has been called

"third-party government" (Salamon 1981) and "government by proxy" (Kettl 1988). As it applies to government and nonprofit contracting, we have called it "the hollow state" and Smith and Lipsky (1993) have called it "the contracting regime." The key point in all of these formulations is that governance occurs whether or not a government agency is directly involved.

3. For a discussion of principal-agent problems in networks, see Milward and Provan (1998). Ferris and Graddy (1997) discuss principal-agent problems related to public management.

4. Advocates of privatization often miss a key distinction in their schemes for competitive contracting. What they say they want is competitive contracting for government services; competition, they say, will bring down the price for contracted services. What often happens instead is that the competition is *for* the market, not *within* the market. One party is awarded a government-granted property right to be the sole purchaser of tax-payer-funded services (Thompson 1993). This process results in the government creating one authorized buyer. Because of the once-removed principal-agent relationship between the government and the agencies providing the services, prices are unlikely to drop unless the government diligently monitors and evaluates the cost of the services provided. There is no hidden hand to push the parties toward efficient outcomes.

5. For a critical and interesting view of the role of governments creating quasi markets on both sides of the Atlantic, see LeGrand and Bartlett (1993).

Networks, Hierarchies, and Public Management: Modeling the Nonlinearities

Laurence J. O'Toole, Jr., and Kenneth J. Meier

Much remains to be learned regarding the link between public management and performance.[1] Lynn, Heinrich, and Hill (in this volume) provide an extensive review of both theory and applications to distill some of the core elements of the public management literature. In the process, they identify key variables or sets of variables that should be considered in efforts to model or test empirically the relationship between management and program performance. Although written independently of Lynn, Heinrich, and Hill, this chapter can be viewed as an extension of their work. They identified the key variables; our objective is to specify the relationships among some of these variables.

Our objective is to understand the ways that managers shape the outputs and outcomes of public policy. We do this within an important management context—the rise of networks as common public management structures. This chapter constitutes a first step on the road to modeling the performance of public management—in particular, how one might conceive of the relationship between public management and other important variables, vis-à-vis performance.[2]

Models of Public-Managerial Impact: A Rationale for Two Steps Forward

Our review of the literature reveals few efforts to specify a model for what might be called public-managerial influence on performance.

Before this volume, the core journals in recent years have shown not a single explicit modeling effort, let alone careful testing.

The closest example is the research of Wolf (especially 1993), who tests several competing explanations for public agency effectiveness and devotes attention to agency "leadership," a concept related but not identical to our use of management. His units of analysis are agencies (actually, distinct effectiveness evaluations of agencies) rather than programs (or their distinct performance assessments), which are the focus of our analysis.[3] Important, nonetheless, Wolf finds that agency leadership matters in explaining effectiveness.

Two aspects of Wolf's work limit its applicability for present purposes and suggest reasons to undertake our modeling effort. First, his approach assumes linearity (1993, p. 169); exploration of alternative specifications was beyond Wolf's purview but is central to our interest. Second, as he notes, the analysis identifies but does not address endogeneity (p. 176). In particular, we think, management may be in part determined by other elements considered as part of the explanation, such as structure. We argue in this chapter that these kinds of interactions, which we treat ultimately as reciprocal, also must be considered in modeling the impact of public management.

We seek, therefore, to move our understanding of public management forward in two ways. First, we treat the need to consider nonlinear relationships seriously because we believe such specifications are more accurate representations of the ideas and observations of researchers. Second, we consider the notion that management matters not only in terms of its direct impact on performance—alone and in combination with other variables—but also in different ways for different structural contexts. This second step requires us to consider structure as a variable, and we do by representing how hierarchies and networks contribute to performance. For this reason in particular, we model not "agency" performance but program performance.

As documented in considerable detail in the literature on program implementation, many, and perhaps an increasing portion of, public programs operate through multiorganizational networks of linked agencies and other units (see Provan and Milward 1995; O'Toole 1997; Hall and O'Toole 2000; on the intergovernmental aspects, see Agranoff and McGuire 1998). Reasons are multiple, including governments' propensity to address "wicked" problems, reliance on cross-cutting mandates, popularity of public-private and other forms of partnerships, growing prominence of third-sector agencies as participants in program delivery, political and economic incentives to engage in complex contracting arrangements (Kettl 1993), as well as political and technical inducements to add participants during implementation to increase service delivery capacity and co-opt influential actors into the coalition. Milward, Provan, and Else (1993) depict the results of such trends as a "hollow state," with a core of public management surrounded by an array of cross-institutional, primarily extragovernmental, ties. Despite the importance of these developments, their manifestations have varied considerably across governments, policy sectors, and programs. Accordingly, substantial variety remains in the institutional settings for public programs. For many programs, in fact, single agencies, or what Hjern and Porter (1981) call "lonely organizations," remain the relevant contexts (Montjoy and O'Toole 1979).

The point about nonlinear relationships above can also be explained briefly. Nonlinear functions and interactive relationships involving public management seem implicitly to be at the heart of what many scholars assert or observe in assessing performance. A persuasive literature documents excellence in public management as well as some of the special requisites of quality public management in more complex, networked settings (see, for example, Ban 1995; Behn 1991; Cohen and Eimicke 1995; Doig and Hargrove 1987; Holzer and Callahan 1998; Ricucci 1995; Thompson and Jones 1994; Gage and Mandell 1990; Klijn 1996; O'Toole 2000).

Much of the logic used in this literature regarding the importance of management involves, in effect, claims about nonlinear causality and interactive influence. Consider, for instance, the typical observation that skillful public managers make the most of resources available toward added value in performance. If this claim is to be tested carefully, an appropriate specification would require the use of an interaction term to represent the claim that neither resource levels alone, nor management independently, nor their summed effects explain what these variables plus their interrelation can explain.

Some Concepts and Initial Assumptions

Although our model is inductive and based on the prior work of empirical researchers as reflected in the published literature (rather than axiomatic and deductive from a few central assumptions), specifying our assumptions and defining core concerns is still valuable. Three core concepts form the base of our modeling effort: hierarchy, network, and management.

Hierarchies and networks are structural notions. The key dimension distinguishing them is formal authority to compel. A hierarchy is a stable set of relations with positions arrayed in a pattern of formal superior-subordinate authority links. Although functioning hierarchies vary greatly in structure, and although formal structure tells only part of the story, we simplify by treating hierarchy as a stabilizing or buffering arrangement. Formal authority to compel is related to stability, but stability can be considered a product of hierarchy, not a part of the formal authority's definition. Hierarchy, that is, can provide institutional support for the current bundle of routines, information systems, values, and other elements that influence production—thus crystallizing a stable cooperative effort, the operational status quo. In so doing, formal organization makes it possible to coordinate efforts toward a common purpose without overwhelming the capacities of individual decision makers (Simon 1976). Still, stability may or may not be related to performance. Sometimes stability in the face of a performance-driven need to adapt or a need to be flexible can hinder effectiveness. Either way, government agencies constitute structures composed more or less around the hierarchical principle.

By considering hierarchy as a common form, we can focus on an additional structural dimension: the extent to which public programs are located fully within a single (hierarchical) agency or spread across parts of two or more organizations—within a single government, located across governments (such as intergovernmental grant programs), or encompassing links between public agencies and businesses or nonprofit organizations. Such patterns of two or more units, in which all the major components are not encompassed in a single hierarchical array, are designated here as networks. Hierarchies, then, or parts of hierarchies, can be embedded in larger networked arrays. The nodes of networks can be occupied by individuals, organizations (including hierarchies), or parts of organizations.

Networks themselves, of course, can vary greatly in structural complexity. One aspect of complexity is the sheer number of units connected in the multiorganizational array. O'Toole and Meier

(1999) use the number of units to explain how, and perhaps in what functional form, networks offer a more complex public-managerial environment than do hierarchies. Complexity, in this view, increases geometrically, not arithmetically, with the number of units.

Our interest is in networks of a frequently occurring type: those that are not well-established but instead are in formation or flux; they are in flux or formation owing either to the establishment of a relatively new program or to a shift or perturbation in the environment of an existing program.[4] Networks like these, quite common for public programs, represent a considerable degree of structural fluidity and, therefore, contain substantial uncertainty regarding relations, commitments, understandings, power, and information. Although hierarchies frequently offer stability, these networks introduce instability and uncertainty, along with additional resources and capacity to act.

Networks of this type are quite common, but the literature contains evidence of highly stable networks as well (O'Toole 1996; Hall and O'Toole 2000). Two instances are "iron triangles" of agency, interest groups, and legislative committee(s)—the very metaphor conveying anything but fluidity—and the interdependent patterns evident in corporatist political systems, where business, labor, and government, in particular, meet and bargain as coequals to reach common understandings, which they are then obligated to execute during implementation.

The first example (iron triangles) is largely irrelevant for our purposes given that it refers to a kind of policymaking coalition, rather than a network responsible for delivering program performance.[5] The second example is more significant. It points to a contingent aspect of the assumption we make about networks and uncertainty. With the limited concertation mechanisms and lack of consensus-building and enforcing institutions in the United States, we expect policy networks in this country to be structurally more open, shifting, and uncertain during implementation than comparable programs in less pluralistic regimes.

Of course, these interpretations of hierarchy and network are extreme. Therefore, we use in our models a dimension of structural variation: from complete stability (designated hierarchy) to total structural fluidity and consequent uncertainty (network). Actual structural settings range somewhere between these two poles. In treating pure hierarchies and networks as poles on a continuum, we ignore "markets" as institutional options. Although markets can also be used to implement public policy, we are interested in the management function in hierarchies and networks. Pure markets by definition are not directly and overtly managed by anybody.[6] We are particularly interested in how hierarchies and networks differ in their abilities to provide stable program operations. Our interest in program performance and public management's role in it directs our attention to the hierarchy-network dimension.

And what of public management? Management refers to conscious efforts to concert actors and resources to carry out established collective purposes (O'Toole 2000). The management function includes, then, the tasks of motivating and coordinating actors toward performance consistent with established intent, among other things. Considering this function broadly requires us to represent both the stabilizing and the more opportunistic elements that can contribute to performance. Among these latter possibilities are management's efforts to leverage other inputs to performance, to take advantage of environmental "disturbances" that can provide chances for performance improvements, and to reshape the structural setting for both management and operations. By "public" management, we mean the performance of these functions for public programs—programs established authoritatively by governments.

Considering the management function in both hierarchies and networks reminds one that the task itself does not presume a particular structural arrangement, that is, hierarchies and the accompanying formal authority managers possess in such settings. In more networked contexts, managers may need to concert people and resources toward public purposes, with these elements distributed across different agencies, governments, or sectors. To some analysts, the very term "management" may seem misleading. A cluster of terms has been introduced with the aim of conveying the more multilateral aspects of this function in interorganizational settings, terms such as "fixing," "multilateral brokerage," and "facilitation" (Bardach 1977; Mandell 1984; O'Toole 1983). Here, we use the term "management" to encompass the entire set of tasks related to this function, whether operating in hierarchies or networks. The key difference between management in these two settings is that in networks management, challenges also arise from the uncertainties and complexities of the structurally ambiguous setting itself.

One additional point about public management bears mention: the function can be shared by actors occupying multiple positions rather than a single locus in the institutional setting. In hierarchies, of course, those attempting management are linked via an authority arrangement, and, therefore, coordinating managerial moves from the top is possible in principle. In networks, however, efforts to "manage" the network—including in the interest of different and potentially competing conceptions of purpose—can come from a number of directions or actors, with only limited potential to render these consistent. As one manager tries to shape the setting and its performance along one course of action, others, at other nodes in the system, can be pressing or concerting people and resources in another direction.

In the model below, we simplify by treating "management" as an implicitly unitary set of efforts. In other words, we model the overall network management. We do develop some distinct elements to the managerial function and consider them separately, but the models developed do not address directly the possibility of independent and uncoordinated—even potentially contradictory, or strategically opposed—management efforts. We do not consider explicitly how this feature of management in networks complicates the management function itself, but we would argue that the point is related to the nature of the games that managers must play. Other managers in a network can force a given manager to play a given game by their initiating a move. In effect, then, management as represented in our models can be considered as a more simplified vector sum of the full set of management efforts. The moves composing the vector eventually need to be categorized and analyzed by both direction and heterogeneity (consistency). This complication could be the subject of later modeling efforts.

Building the Model

Our objective in modeling management in both hierarchies and networks is to generate some precise predictions that can be tested empirically if adequate data can be found. We start with some simple concepts and then gradually add complexity. As suggested earlier, the model should not be considered deductive from a few axioms but rather reflective of current theory and research on management, networks, and hierarchies.

Relationship to the Reduced Form Model of Lynn, Heinrich, and Hill

For comparability, we use terms and symbols similar to Lynn, Heinrich, and Hill in chapter 1 of this volume. Their reduced form model links program outputs to five other factors:

$$O = f(E, C, T, S, M),$$

where O = program outputs; E = environmental factors; C = clientele characteristics; T = treatments (or program technologies, etc.); S = structures; and M = management.

When we use terms that are similar to Lynn, Heinrich, and Hill's, we employ the same symbols. When our meaning differs or when we wish to distinguish our arguments from theirs, we use a different symbol. After presenting our model, we will return to the Lynn, Heinrich, and Hill model to document specific similarities and differences.

The Basic System

Organizations, programs, and delivery systems can be characterized as inertial.[7] Such institutional arrangements offer significant advantages, from the point of view of performance, as analysts at least since Max Weber have noted. Current outputs will be greatly influenced by past outputs. If one defines outputs as O, then the basic model of any organization can best be represented with an autoregressive equation:

$$O_t = \beta_0 O_{t-1} + \varepsilon_t \tag{1}$$

where current performance (O_t) is the result of past performance (O_{t-1}) discounted by a rate of stability (β_0) and a series of shocks to the system (ε).[8] We leave unexamined in this effort the nature of O: what outputs the program produces, how they are measured, and whether multiple dimensions should be considered.[9]

The rate of stability (which can be thought of as $[1-\delta]$ where δ is the rate of change) is generally constrained to a value between 0 and 1. As values approach 1, the system becomes highly stable; as values approach zero, the system moves quickly toward entropy.[10] If values exceed 1.0, the system will increase without limit, that is, it will explode.[11]

Shocks to the system (ε) can come from a variety of environmental forces. Legislatures or executives can change program priorities, increase or decrease program funding or scope; organizational rivals or coalition members can make decisions that directly or indirectly affect the organization; or the economic or social environment can change. All these shocks are exogenous, but there may also be endogenous shifts in the dominant coalition, as well as deliberate, planned shocks. Efforts at "organization development" are familiar instances of the latter. In the sections below, we specify some of the exogenous elements of ε and incorporate them into our model.

Networks and Hierarchies

As already noted, networks and hierarchies can be viewed as two poles of a continuum with hierarchies characterized by authority relationships allowing individuals to demand compliance by others.[12] Networks, in contrast, typically lack authoritative links between nodes, and collective action requires negotiation and cooperation. Viewed in this way, a network can be oversimplified and considered as the absence of hierarchy.

Networks and hierarchies generate predictable impacts on the inertial system, once one notes that formal authority is linked to stability. If we think for a moment of the ideal-typical hierarchy *(H)* and the ideal-typical fluid network *(N)*, then in a hierarchy the rate of stability approaches 1.0.

$$\text{if } H, \text{ then } \beta_0 \to 1.0 \tag{2}$$

Because hierarchies are by nature stable, we would not expect the stability coefficient to be much below 1.0. For a flexible network, the rate of stability often moves away from 1.0 to some lesser value and in extreme cases to 0.

$$\text{if } N, \text{ then } \beta_0 \to 0 \tag{3}$$

Hierarchies in this logic are more stable systems. Once set on a path, they will generally continue along their trajectory with little deviation barring a major shock to the system. Networks, in contrast, are loosely coupled; indeed, they are often characterized by a lack of institutionalization. Members (often themselves portions of hierarchical organizations) may be only imperfectly aware of their own interdependence, links between nodes may be imperfectly formed and in flux, uncertainty is likely to be high, and influences from outside the system are likely to penetrate more readily. Networks lose a great deal of energy simply in their day-to-day operation (or, alternatively, require a great deal of energy to maintain). Even without shocks to a network, the network will eventually run down unless additional efforts are made to maintain and revitalize it. Networks, in short, need management.[13]

Defining networks and hierarchies as poles of a continuum permits us to conceptualize a network as the absence of hierarchy, and hierarchy as the epitome of institutionalized action. If we had a good measure of hierarchy (H) and normalized it to approach 1.0 at the highest levels of hierarchy and to approach 0 at the "pure" network level, then equations (2) and (3) can be combined with equation (1) for a more general view of organizational inertia. Because the rate of stability is, in part, a function of the hierarchy of the system

$$\beta_0 = f\,(H), \tag{4}$$

we can partition the rate of stability into hierarchy (H) and other factors (β_1), including the functional adjustment to hierarchy, thus producing the more general equation:

$$O_t = \beta_1 H O_{t-1} + \varepsilon_t \tag{5}$$

This equation shows that an increase in hierarchy results in a more inertial or stable program structure. In a pure hierarchy with $H = 1$, we would expect $\beta_1 H$ to be very close to 1.0. The bulk of the variation in $\beta_1 H$, therefore, must be contained in the hierarchy term unless we permit β_1 to have values substantially less than 1.

Shocks and Reaction to Shocks

A major difference between networks and hierarchies is in how they are affected by external shocks from the environment.[14] The literature on innovation and change in organizations suggests that hierarchical systems do not respond quickly to environmental changes

(Zaltman, Duncan, and Holbek 1973). Hierarchical systems, however, tend to buffer shocks with a fair degree of effectiveness. Networks, in contrast, are more open so that buffering is less effective.

Shocks that penetrate the organization's buffering mechanism, however, have different effects on hierarchies and networks. Although shocks are less likely to pass through the hierarchy's buffering, when they do reach the organization, they can have a dramatic impact.

Returning to equation (1) for a hierarchy (and thus $\beta_0 \to 1$):

$$O_t = \beta_0 O_{t-1} + \varepsilon_t \tag{1}$$

we divide the ε_t into some shock X_t that gets through the organization's buffering system with an initial impact of β_2 and a random component ε_t

$$O_t = \beta_0 O_{t-1} + \beta_2 X_t + \varepsilon_t \tag{6}$$

In this case, a one-unit change in X_t results in a β_2 change in O_t, all other things being equal. However, this is the effect of X_t on O for time t only. Because X_t has increased the value of O_t, in year $t + 1$, this larger value of O_t also influences the size of O_{t+1}. Because O_t is β_2 larger as the result of X_t, then O_{t+1} will be $\beta_2\beta_0$ larger as the result of the impact of X_t the previous year. Such impacts reverberate through the system in future years, gradually getting smaller in size (forming distributed lag—see Hamilton 1994) but still cumulating into a relatively large impact.

The overall impact (I) of a one-unit change in X can be determined by the following formula, where the terms are defined as above:

$$I = \beta_2/(1-\beta_0) \tag{7}$$

A small shock that penetrates an organization's buffering system, as a result, can have a major long-term influence on the organization, depending on the size of the coefficient of stability. To illustrate, suppose the initial year impact (β_2) had a value of 1. If the coefficient of stability is 0.99 (quite feasible in a strongly hierarchical organization), then the total impact is 100 or (100=1/(1 − 0.99). If the coefficient of stability is only 0.7, the total impact of X falls to 3.33. Because networks are generally less stable, shocks that breach the organization's defenses will have less impact in networks. Shocks can have a variety of functional forms and both short- and long-run impact; with adequate data, all these impacts can be estimated.[15] The important point in our discussion, however, is that relatively small changes in a system can have major long-run implications simply because program structures are inertial.

Buffering

Organizations establish units or processes to buffer environmental shocks. In a network, the boundary between the network and its environment blurs. Buffering in networks is more difficult to accomplish simply because networks create more interdependencies that cannot be isolated from the technical core of the system. (For a game-theory explication of this point, see Scharpf 1997.)

We think that the most appropriate way to model the buffering process is simply to use the reciprocal of hierarchy as the factor that discounts any environmental shocks:

$$O_t = \beta_1 HO_{t-1} + \beta_2 X_t(1/H) + \varepsilon_t \tag{8}$$

In this way, an increase in hierarchy limits the impact of an exogenous shock on the organization. Any shock that gets through the buffering process of hierarchy, however, can have a substantial long-run impact on the organization. For a network, in contrast, buffering is weaker, and therefore, shocks easily reach the organization. The impact of these shocks, however, is far less—simply because the networks are more loosely coupled.

Management: A Tangent and a Reformulation

What we shall call the normal theory of management is simply that it is one additional factor that affects program performance.[16] The normal theory would require modifying equation (6) to have management (M) combine with other factors in a direct, linear manner:

$$O_t = \beta_0 O_{t-1} + \beta_2 X_t + \beta_3 M + \varepsilon_t \tag{9}$$

If X_t stands for a matrix of all other factors that affect the system, such as resources, constraints, external demands, and so forth, then the test for whether management matters in a program structure is whether the coefficient for management (β_3) is significantly different from zero. Management can have a substantial impact either with a large coefficient or by operating through a large coefficient of stability over a long period of time.

A more elaborate theory of management would relax the linear aspect and permit management to interact with each of the other terms in the equation, as in equation (10), which represents an interactive model of management:

$$O_t = \beta_0 O_{t-1} + \beta_2 X_t + \beta_3 M + \beta_4 MO_{t-1} + \beta_5 MX_t + \varepsilon_t \tag{10}$$

In this case, the test of whether management had a nonlinear impact would be a joint test (either f-test or log-likelihood ratio test) that both β_4 and β_5 are equal to zero. Equation (9) can be viewed as the same as equation (10) if β_4 and β_5 are restricted to equal zero.[17]

Equation (10) is clearly a nonlinear specification of the role of management. An alternate view of nonlinear relationships would be simply to estimate the entire equation as a set of nonlinear relationships, as in equation (11)

$$O_t = \beta_0 O_{t-1}{}^{\beta 1} X_t{}^{\beta 2} M^{\beta 3} + \varepsilon_t \tag{11}$$

Although this equation creates some difficulties depending on the assumptions made about the error term, it can be estimated by either taking the log of both sides of the equation and then estimating via ordinary least squares or by using nonlinear regression to estimate the equation.

The difficulty with each of these conceptualizations of management is that they do not consider the structure in which the program operates. O'Toole (2000; see also 1996) argues that management becomes more important in a network situation than in a hierarchy. In a network, not only must managers spend more time on maintenance within the structure (because the network is less inertial), but they also must spend more time interacting with the environment because the structure is more open to environmental influences. None of the above specifications incorporates the greater importance of management in networks as compared with hierarchies.

A crucial task of management is to maintain structure: to frame goals, set incentives, and negotiate contributions from members and

relevant others (Barnard 1938; Simon 1976).[18] This system maintenance aspect of management can best be modeled as in equation
(12), where management *(M)* supplements hierarchy *(H)* in the inertial (read *structural*) portion of the model:

$$O_t = \beta_1(H+M)O_{t-1} + \beta_2X_t + \varepsilon_t \tag{12}$$

In this equation, as hierarchy increases, the role of management
becomes less necessary because hierarchy by itself generates a relatively stable system. As hierarchy declines, however, this system
tends toward entropy unless management increases its impact on
maintaining the structure.

Creating and maintaining structures is only one function of management; let us term this function M_1.[19] An equally important function is guiding how the system interacts with its environment—in
modeling terms, how it deals with the shocks to the system. We designate this second aspect of management as M_2. Different subscripts
imply that these functions can vary independently yet still have
something in common that we consider management.

M_2 can be modeled, but only if the management strategy of the
system is known relative to the environment. Management can
adopt a strategy of either buffering the environment or actively seeking to exploit the environment for the benefit of the program system.[20] If the decision is to buffer the system from the environment,
this management strategy can be modeled as follows, where management interacts with hierarchy in the buffering processes:

$$O_t = \beta_1(H+M_1)O_{t-1} + \beta_2X_t(1/HM_2) + \varepsilon_t \tag{13}$$

In this equation, management dampens the impact of environmental shocks and works with hierarchy in this process.

Management that seeks to exploit the environment will not try to
buffer environmental shocks but rather will attempt to magnify
some of them so that they have a major impact on the program structure (and quite likely other systems that interact with the program).
Exploiting the environment means operating in opposition to the
dampening effect of hierarchy, as follows:

$$O_t = \beta_1(H+M_1)O_{t-1} + \beta_2X_t(M_2/H) + \varepsilon_t \tag{14}$$

Equations (13) and (14) can be combined into a more general model of the system's action by defining a new variable, M_3, as the portion of environmental management that will be devoted to exploiting the environment and by assuming that environmental actions that do not attempt to exploit the environment will be used to buffer that environment (designated as M_4). Equation (15), then, combines buffering and exploiting the environment in the same model:

$$O_t = \beta_1(H+M_1)O_{t-1} + \beta_2 X_t(M_3/HM_4) + \varepsilon_t \tag{15}$$

Rearranging the terms of equation [15], we get

$$O_t = \beta_1(H+M_1)O_{t-1} + \beta_2(X_t/H)(M_3/M_4) + \varepsilon_t \tag{16}$$

Equation (16), representing a general model of public management, is useful because the ratio of M_3 to M_4 describes how risk-seeking management is. As the amount of effort devoted to exploiting the environment increases, this ratio increases. As the system devotes greater efforts to buffering, the structure becomes more risk averse, and the size of this ratio decreases.[21]

With regard to equation (16), it might also be useful to think of the three forms of management summing to some constant value. Organizations must decide how to allocate their managerial resources (M) to three tasks: M_1 or stabilizing the internal operations of the system; M_3 or exploiting shocks in the environment; and M_4 or buffering the organization from environmental shocks. Because hierarchies are more stable and have greater buffering capacities, they can operate with fewer managerial resources than a network and still maintain an equal level of performance. At equal levels of managerial resources, a hierarchy can devote more of those resources to dealing with the environment than can the network.

Comparisons with the Lynn, Heinrich, and Hill Model

The different versions of the model in the preceding section constitute the basic account. Our effort is an extension of Lynn, Heinrich, and Hill in that we take several variables that they discuss and sketch the functional forms they are likely to take in affecting program outputs. This section of the chapter specifies how we envision other parts of the Lynn, Heinrich, and Hill model being incorporated into our basic approach to public management.

In both the Lynn, Heinrich, and Hill model in this volume, $O = f(E, C, T, S, M)$, and our base model in equation (16), $O_t = \beta_1(H+M_1)O_{t-1} + \beta_2(X_t/H)(M_3/M_4) + \varepsilon_t$, outputs *(O)* are defined in similar terms. We divide the environment thus far into X (a series of shocks) and ε (a random component) and use the subscript L to designate the Lynn, Heinrich, and Hill model:

$$E_L = f(X, \varepsilon) \tag{17}$$

Both X and ε in our model are matrices of forces rather than a single influence or variable. (Lynn, Heinrich, and Hill also treat their E as an array of forces, including such elements as external monitoring, economic performance, and technology.)

We define S_L as the structural part of our model or

$$S_L = \beta_1(H+M_1)O_{t-1} \tag{18}$$

In this manner, we stress the contributions of structure to program and organizational stability. Program outputs in our approach are modeled as an autoregressive process that permits us to incorporate several interesting organizational processes, such as path dependence, entropy, and small changes producing large, long-term impact. We specifically define hierarchy as part of the model, given that we are interested in the contrast with networks. Management, in our view, has a role to play in the "structural" aspect of the model. Management can contribute to stability by being a substitute for hierarchy, with the precise hypothesis that hierarchy and management are to some extent interchangeable and could be a factor in some type of long-run equilibrium.[22]

This point can be pursued. Managers operate within the constraints of structure while also crafting those constraints over the longer haul so as to shape the possibilities for future performance (see O'Toole 2000; Simon 1976). Although managerial tasks such as shaping structures and building cultures are frequently discussed in the literature of public management,[23] how to deal with such tasks in systematic empirical investigations is a topic that is sometimes noted (as in Wolf 1993; Ingraham and Kneedler 2000) but has thus far eluded formal treatment.

Our general theory treats hierarchy and management as substitutes for each other in terms of both organizational stability and buffering. Over time, management can invest in creating greater structure, that is, in increasing the hierarchy of the organization. Thus even though an absence of hierarchy creates a need for greater management, effective management can build a "capital stock" of hierarchy that reduces the need for management in the future.[24] The relationship between hierarchy and management, therefore, is dynamic over time:

$$H_t \rightarrow M_t \rightarrow H_{t+1} \tag{19}$$

Our models have not explicitly addressed two items in the Lynn, Heinrich, and Hill model: client characteristics and treatments. In lieu of the term "client characteristics" (a human service organization term), we prefer the term "target (population) characteristics." Many programs do not view the individuals with whom they interact as clientele but rather targets for behavior modification. Especially when government programs are involved, the notion of clients is misleading because what distinguishes government from nongovernment actors is not the ability to serve clientele but the ability to coerce target populations and coerce them legitimately.[25]

Target populations constitute at least one node in the program's network. An interesting policy question is how that target node is defined; the social construction of a target population reflects a set of policy biases that permeate policy design (Schneider and Ingram 1997). Targets can be defined as a legitimate node in a policy network (for most policies that rely on voluntary compliance) with rights of participation. Other policies can have active targets that might even be major forces in the establishment of public policy. In family planning policy, for example, Planned Parenthood not only implements federal family planning policy as a grantee in some states but is also an active player in shaping public policy at the national level (Critchlow 1996). Similar points could be made about the heavy influence target groups have on policy and its execution in corporatist political systems. In the United States, still other policies (such as child support collection or criminal justice) define targets not as a network node but as a target to be shaped and altered—even if it remains important to recognize that targets themselves are strategic actors.

Although target populations vary, and this variation goes well beyond social constructions to actual characteristics that affect implementation, in our base model we have clearly relegated target populations to the environment. Hence equation (17) should be modified to:

$$E_L = f(X, \varepsilon), \text{where } X = f(Y, C_L) \tag{20}$$

and C_L represents characteristics of the target population, including their social construction, and Y represents the nontarget population portion of the environment.

Equation [20] is probably not fully specified. Other environmental forces, especially in networks (though beyond the network units involved in program operations themselves), include additional government organizations, private-sector service providers (such as competitors), citizen advocacy groups who are neither clientele nor targets, and media outlets. In addition, all policy environments include a set of actors who might be termed "sovereigns," or principals—those organizations with the formal right to define goals and assign resources. Sovereigns are usually elements of government, but any organization with the ability to fund a program (e.g., a foundation) or define goals should be considered a sovereign. A relaxation of the government-as-sovereign requirement might also permit our model to be applied to private-sector situations. We leave the further unpacking of the environment and its nuances for future research.

One aspect of the environment, however, is relevant to our distinction between networks and hierarchies. Networks and hierarchies clearly differ in the size of the environmental matrices that they have,[26] with the network environment having more elements, as shown in (21), where the subscripts designate elements in the environment of (n)etworks and (h)ierarchies:

$$\Sigma E_n > \Sigma E_h \tag{21}$$

This generates a far more complex environment for the network than for the hierarchy.

One element of the Lynn, Heinrich, and Hill model we have not discussed is treatments *(T)*. Treatments, we believe, should be divided into two parts. One portion is imposed on the program by its environment, often by the sovereigns in binding statutes or other authoritative pronouncements. These exogenous aspects of treatments (T_e) should be considered part of the program's environment or

$$E_L = f(X, \varepsilon), \text{ where } X = f(Y, C_L, T_e). \tag{22}$$

Other aspects of treatments, including specific procedures, operational goals, incentive systems, and so forth are clearly endogenous to the program and within the purview of management. We would argue that these managerially relevant aspects of T should be considered part of the "structural" component of the model (equation (18) above, or the first (structural) term in our base model, equation (16). As such, this portion of T should be incorporated into M_1.

We divide management into three parts: contributing to structural features (equation [18], now understood as including parts of S, M, and T from the reduced form model of Lynn, Heinrich, and Hill), buffering the environment, and exploiting the environment. Although we specifically discuss these three functions of management, we do not believe that they constitute the sum total of program or organization management.

We believe our version of management as strategic action is essentially compatible with the framework of Lynn, Heinrich, and Hill. In an examination of Reagan administration appointees, Lynn (1984) argued that management strategy, management talent, and the fit of the strategy to the problem are three separate elements in determining managerial effectiveness. We see management strategy as the choices among crafting structures, buffering the environment, and exploiting the environment. In the latter category, management strategy entails establishing cooperative games with other management nodes (including those within the network, if relevant) and structuring those games such that desired outcomes are produced.

By no means, then, does our perspective turn management into a rote or routine task. Indeed, the model clearly shows the range of managerial challenges and expected options. In any management decision, problems can develop. First, the manager might lack the talent to accomplish the desired tasks. Second, the manager may possess the talent but select the wrong strategy to deal with the issue. This includes such possibilities as assuming trust relative to another node and ending up in a "prisoner's dilemma" as a result, creating hierarchical structures when more fluid organizational forms would be more effective, cutting budgets when program redirection is needed, and countless other management blunders.[27] Clarifying the place of management in program performance, then, in the Lynn, Heinrich, and Hill formulation or in our more specific version, suggests no diminishment in the importance of managerial strategy. Rather, it clarifies the crucial albeit contingent significance of strategic choice by skillful public managers.

The Measurement Question

Modeling is one thing, testing the accuracy of models yet another. A key challenge facing our modeling effort is measuring management. We think that eliminating ambiguity in measuring management can be accomplished in the same way as eliminating the ambiguity in management's relationships with other factors—by precisely defining key terms and differentiating the component parts of management. One aspect of management in our theory is the nature of strategic choices. Management opts to invest time in building structure broadly defined (as explained in the preceding section) or in dealing with environmental relationships. Time spent on each of these tasks and the strategies used could provide reasonable indicators of management choices in this regard.

The importance of the M_3/M_4 ratio in equation (16) is that it simplifies another measurement issue. This ratio reflects management's risk orientation; as it increases, management focuses more on exploiting the environment and less on buffering. The advantage of the ratio is that it can be measured directly without having to measure either M_3 or M_4. A good measure of risk-taking, for example, might be program aggressiveness in budgeting cycles.

Lynn's (1984) discussion of Reagan appointees suggests two other aspects of management in need of measures—management skill and the fit of the strategy with the problem. Although scholars have not measured management skill frequently, Wolf's (1993) use of expert judgments illustrates that it is possible. Although direct measures of management skill are obviously preferable, an alternative is via certain assumptions relative to performance, given that good management should lead to positive organizational performance.[28] If a fully specified production function for a program is modeled, then the difference between predicted and actual performance would be those factors omitted from the model, including management. If these increments are stable when management is stable and change when management changes, we have a reasonable indirect measure of management. The complexity of public programs and the difficulty in generating a fully specified production function for most programs, however, mean we need to work out the problems in this approach while investigating subjects less complex than public management.[29]

The fit between managerial strategies and managerial problems is, of course, the situational aspect of management. At times, stability is good for an organization and its performance. At other times, with a turbulent environment, one needs adaptive and flexible management. In networks, some leverage on management strategies can be gained by examining the games that network managers try to establish, both within the network (for instance, with other managers at other nodes) and between the network and parts of its broader environment. The preference for some types of games over others and the methods of establishing trust could provide a great deal of insight into management strategy. Investigations of linked or connected games could also provide helpful insight (for instance, Tsebelis 1990).

Other measurement issues are raised by our model, but these pale in comparison to those involved with measuring management. We freely admit we have not solved all the measurement problems, but we have a strategy for addressing them using an approach similar to our modeling approach. We plan to distinguish management's principal component parts, show how those are related, and then measure the individual elements. Part of that process is accomplished in this chapter, the rest is on our agenda.

Implications

Our effort at modeling the management dimension of programs has several implications for the study of public management. First, it is possible to go beyond ambiguous prescriptions and provide precise specifications that are consistent with the observations of public management scholars. The models presented here, however, should be viewed as hypotheses. We could well be wrong, but we care less about being correct in the details than we care about becoming a catalyst for work along these lines. Progress can be expected only through precise and ultimately falsifiable predictions about managing public programs. Only then can the empirical research interact with theory to provide a cumulative body of knowledge.

Management, in our view, is crucial but also contingent. We emphasized how management is influenced by structure (networks versus hierarchies); future work is likely to specify other contingencies. We also argue that structural contingencies are shaped by prior management activities. Management in our models has several functions—buffering, exploiting the environment, maintaining a stable system, establishing structural forms, and so forth. The model is the first step in a more explicit unpacking of the sometimes ephemeral management notion.

Management is a dynamic process, and dynamic processes must be studied in a way that directly incorporates change and stability. Our autoregressive approach is consistent with the real world of public management and can take advantage of a set of powerful and flexible statistical methods. We see this as a major advantage over other theories that lack this dynamic component.

The model also offers a concrete rationale for why network settings are less buffered. By presenting management in its structural context, we introduce a way of understanding why many networks are more complicated environments for performance and management. Management is not the whole story, however, in shaping network stabilization. Shared values (Meier, Wrinkle, and Polinard 1999b), common routines, and standardized learning are other methods of network stabilization (O'Toole and Meier 1999). Some of these sources of stability result from strategic management choice; others evolve from repeated interactions among network participants.

Our analysis sets the environment to the "game-playing" parts of public management. We do not and cannot offer specific predictions about managerial moves, behavior, or choices. In fact, our analysis simplifies on a critical point by assuming that management is a function performed via a single actor or office. There is good reason to question this assumption; multiple managers may be working at cross-purposes in a network. Although these can be conceptualized as a vector sum for modeling purposes, the complication creates a possibly inherent measurement problem. The theoretical argument here is that management is more important in more networked settings, but the possibility of multiple points of management means we may be unable to demonstrate the point empirically (O'Toole 2000). To be more precise, demonstrating it would require identifying the managerial points and offices of leverage, developing sensible measures of the differing emphases on the different forms of management (the different types of M) sketched in the modeling effort, and then compiling a vector sum in time series for testing.

Finally, a major issue should be noted. In this modeling effort, we have not placed much stress on the importance of an appropriate data set(s) to test the ideas. Data demands, in fact, might seem unrealistic. Although perfect data would be ideal, our more realistic hope is that the model can be segmented and approached in parts for testing. We view this chapter as the initiation of a research agenda rather than the sketch of a one-shot research design.

References

Agranoff, Robert, and Michael McGuire. 1998. Multinetwork management. *Journal of Public Administration Research and Theory,* 8 (1) (January): 67–91.

Ban, Carolyn. 1995. *How do public managers manage?* San Francisco: Jossey-Bass.

Bardach, Eugene. 1977. *The implementation game.* Cambridge, Mass.: MIT Press.

Barnard, Chester. 1938. *The functions of the executive.* Cambridge, Mass.: Harvard University Press.

Behn, Robert. 1991. *Leadership counts.* Cambridge, Mass.: Harvard University Press.

Cohen, Steven, and William Eimicke. 1995. *The new effective public manager.* San Francisco: Jossey-Bass.

Critchlow, Donald. 1996. *The politics of abortion and birth control in historical perspective.* University Park, Pa.: Pennsylvania State University Press.

Doig, Jameson, and Erwin Hargrove, eds. 1987. *Leadership and innovation: A biographical perspective on entrepreneurs in government.* Baltimore: Johns Hopkins University Press.

Frederickson, H. George. 1999. The repositioning of American public administration. *PS* 32, 4 (December): 701–11.

Gage, Robert, and Myrna Mandell, eds. 1990. *Strategies for managing intergovernmental policies and networks.* New York: Praeger.

Hall, Thad, and Laurence O'Toole, Jr. 2000. Structures for policy implementation: An analysis of national legislation, 1965–66 and 1993–94. *Administration and Society* 31:6 (January): 667–86.

Hamilton, James. 1994. *Time series analysis.* Princeton, N.J.: Princeton University Press.

Hjern, Benny, and David Porter. 1981. Implementation structures: A new unit of administrative analysis. *Organization Studies,* 2 (3): 211–37.

Holzer, Mark, and Callahan, K. 1998. *Government at work: Best practices and model programs.* Thousand Oaks, Calif.: Sage.

Ingraham, Patricia, and Amy Kneedler. 2000. Dissecting the black box: Toward a model and measures of government management performance. In *Advancing public management: New developments in theory, methods, and practice,* edited by Jeffrey Brudney, Laurence J. O'Toole, Jr., and Hal Rainey. Washington, D.C.: Georgetown University Press.

Joyce, Philip G., and Patricia Ingraham. 1998. Government management: Defining and assessing performance. Unpublished manuscript.

Kettl, Donald F. 1993. *Sharing power: Public governance and private markets.* Washington, D.C.: Brookings Institution.

Kickert, W. J. M., E. H. Klijn, and J. F. M. Koppenjan, eds. 1997. *Managing complex networks: Strategies for the public sector.* London: Sage.

Klijn, Erik-Hans. 1996. *Regels en sturing in netwerken: De invloed van netwerkregels op de herstructurering van naoorlogse wijken* [Rules and Steering in Networks: The Influence of Network Rules on the Reconstruction of Post-war Neighborhoods]. Delft, The Netherlands: Eburon.

Krause, George A. 1998. Agency budget requests and risk bearing behavior in bureaucratic organizations. Paper presented at the annual meeting of the Midwest Political Science Association, 23–25 April 1998.

Lynn, Laurence E., Jr. 1984. The Reagan administration and the renitent bureaucracy. In *The Reagan presidency and the governing of America,* edited by Lester M. Salamon. Washington, D.C.: The Urban Institute, pp. 339–70.

Mandell, Myrna. 1984. Application of network analysis to the implementation of a complex project. *Human Relations,* 37: 659–79.

Meier, Kenneth, Robert Wrinkle, and J. Polinard. 1999a. Equity versus excellence in organizations. *American Review of Public Administration,* 29 (1) (March): 5–18.

———. 1999b. Politics, bureaucracy, and farm credit. *Public Administration Review* 59 (July–August): 292–302.

Milward, H. Brinton, Keith Provan, and Barbara Else. 1993. What does the "hollow state" look like? In *Public management: The state of the art,* edited by Barry Bozeman. San Francisco: Jossey-Bass, pp. 309–22.

Montjoy, Robert, and Laurence O'Toole, Jr. 1979. Toward a theory of policy implementation: An organizational perspective. *Public Administration Review* 39 (5) (September–October): 465–76.

Moore, Mark. 1995. *Creating public value: Strategic management in government.* Cambridge, Mass.: Harvard University Press.

O'Toole, Laurence J., Jr. 1983. Inter-organizational cooperation and the implementation of active labour market training policies: Sweden and the Federal Republic of Germany. *Organization Studies,* 4 (2) (April): 129–50.

————. 1996. Rational choice and the public management of interorganizational networks. In *The state of public management,* edited by Donald F. Kettl and H. Brinton Milward. Baltimore: Johns Hopkins University Press, pp. 241–63.

————. 1997. Treating networks seriously. *Public Administration Review,* 57 (1): 45–52.

————. 2000. Different public managements? Implications of structural context in hierarchies and networks. In *Advancing public management: New developments in theory, methods, and practice,* edited by Jeffrey L. Brudney, Laurence O'Toole, and Hal G. Rainey. Washington, D.C.: Georgetown University Press, pp. 19–32.

O'Toole, Laurence J., Jr., and Kenneth Meier. 1999. Modeling the impact of public management: Implications of structural context. *Journal of Public Administration Research and Theory,* 9 (October): 505–26.

Ostrom, Elinor. 1990. *Governing the commons: The evolution of institutions for collective action.* Cambridge: Cambridge University Press.

Poveda, Tony. 1990. *The FBI in transition.* Pacific Grove, Calif.: Brooks/Cole.

Provan, Keith G., and H. Brinton Milward. 1995. A preliminary theory of interorganizational network effectiveness. *Administrative Science Quarterly,* 40 (1): 1–33.

Rainey, Hal G., and Paula Steinbauer. 1999. Galloping elephants: Developing elements of a theory of effective government organizations. *Journal of Public Administration Research and Theory* 9, (1): 1–32.

Ricucci, Norma. 1995. *Unsung heroes: Federal executives making a difference.* Washington, D.C.: Georgetown University Press.

Sabatier, Paul, and Hank Jenkins-Smith, eds. 1993. *Policy change and learning: An advocacy coalition approach.* Boulder, Colo.: Westview Press.

Scharpf, Fritz W. 1997. *Games real actors play.* Boulder, Colo.: Westview Press.

Schneider, Anne, and Helen Ingram. 1997. *Policy design for democracy.* Lawrence, Kansas: University Press of Kansas.

Selznick, Philip. 1949. *TVA and the grass roots.* Berkeley: University of California Press.

Simon, Herbert A. 1976. *Administrative behavior,* 3d ed. New York: Free Press.

Thompson, Fred, and Lawrence R. Jones. 1994. *Reinventing the Pentagon.* San Francisco: Jossey-Bass.

Tsebelis, George. 1990. *Nested games.* Berkeley: University of California Press.

Wolf, Patrick. 1993. A case survey of bureaucratic effectiveness in U.S. cabinet agencies. *Journal of Public Administration Research and Theory,* 3 (2): 161–81.

Wood, B. Dan, and Richard Waterman. 1994. *Bureaucratic dynamics: The role of bureaucracy in a democracy.* Boulder, Colo.: Westview Press.

Zaltman, Gerald, Robert Duncan, and Jonny Holbek. 1973. *Innovations and organizations.* New York: Wiley Interscience.

Endnotes

1. We acknowledge with thanks the helpful comments of George Frederickson, Amy Kneedler Donahue, Laurence E. Lynn, Jr., Hal G. Rainey, and Janet Weiss on earlier drafts of this chapter.

2. Hypothesizing the details of the internal production function of public management is not a task explicitly addressed here. For an intriguing effort along these lines, see the Government Performance Project (Ingraham and Kneedler 2000; Joyce and Ingraham 1998; Ingraham and Donahue, this volume). Another approach is offered by Rainey and Steinbauer (1999), who sketch elements of a theory of "effective government organizations" (our units of analysis are government programs). They consider features of "leadership" and other elements of public management (such as "development of human resources") but do not model the relationship among any of these elements, nor between them and other variables. Still, they seek a theoretical explanation of effectiveness and draw from empirical evidence to sketch propositions for testing. Rainey and Steinbauer contend that "such theories as we have need much more articulation" (p. 2, note 2) and argue that not all relationships should be expected to be linear. And, like us, they attend to the "accounts of the most influential and innovative agency leaders" which "emphasize their ability to turn into opportunities the constraints that supposedly impede many executives, and otherwise to cope with the pressures and complexities of their roles" (p. 20). The present effort seeks, among other things, an ex-

plicit representation of this opportunities-*cum*-constraints core of the public management function. We argue that public management encompasses significantly more than the POSDCORB notions of yesteryear, and we use our sketch of some of public management's requisites to develop what we regard as a plausible model for its impact on performance.

3. We emphasize programs as units of analysis because we direct attention to public management in and through networks. In principle, the question of the unit of analysis is flexible. The appropriate unit depends on the research question being explored. The modeling agenda sketched below should be applicable for organizations as well, including the task of exploring the impact of differing degrees of structural stability on performance across public organizations.

4. Although we do not address how networks are formed, a number of possibilities can be proffered. A network can be imposed from authoritative parts of the environment, for instance via statutes or regulations (see Hall and O'Toole 2000). An alternative possibility is for individual administrators to create a network in order to reduce the uncertainty that they face (see Frederickson 1999). Self-organizing among clusters of units, perhaps through a variety of motives across the relevant actors, represents yet a third (see Ostrom 1990). For studies of some aspects of public management in different complex networks, see Kickert, Klijn, and Koppenjan 1997.

5. Sabatier and Jenkins-Smith, among others, have explored clusters of multiple actors operating *through* phases of the policy process (see, for instance, 1993). The attention in such investigations, nonetheless, tends to be devoted to issues beyond program performance.

6. Markets in practice are often structured beyond the simple elements suggested by neoclassical economics and thus may come to resemble networks. How structure and rules affect markets is an important question of policy design, but one we will not discuss in this chapter.

7. We use the term "organization" or "program structure" as a general notion, not a synonym for hierarchy. The actual type of structure in a given case is an empirical question. Management itself can also be considered an inertial system (a topic for future research and modeling).

8. By shocks we mean changes that affect the program either positively or negatively. This definition is from the modeling literature and should be distinguished from the ordinary-language

meaning of the term. The latter often connotes a completely un-expected event or a disruptive force; neither of these senses is necessarily implied in our characterization.

9. All these issues can be handled through appropriate conceptual-ization and methods (for a treatment of multiple goals, see Meier, Wrinkle, and Polinard 1999a).

10. By limiting the value of β_0, we are essentially setting up a servo-mechanism with negative feedback. When β_0 is larger than 1.0, positive feedback occurs.

11. When positive feedback exists and program structures "explode" is an interesting question, but one that will not concern us here. Programs can die in two distinctly different ways, with a bang (that is, through positive feedback) or with a whimper (running down to entropy).

12. Compliance is, of course, a matter of degree. The Barnard (1938)-Simon (1976) view of authority is such that compliance can never be assumed.

13. Strictly speaking, stability can be a product of additional influ-ences beyond either hierarchy or network management. See O'Toole and Meier (1999).

14. Our definition of environment is more encompassing than Lynn, Heinrich, and Hill. It includes both the environmental forces they note and also the clientele factors.

15. The techniques of ARIMA modeling or combining ARIMA mod-eling with traditional time series can do this. For an illustration, see Wood and Waterman (1994).

16. Normal not in the sense that this perspective matches the typical observations of scholars and practitioners, but normal signifying the basic approach under the simplest assumption possible: that management is just another input to production.

17. In the language of modeling, equation (10) is the unrestricted equation because all coefficients are allowed to take on any value, and equation (9) is the restricted equation because some coefficients must be equal to zero.

18. Note that this function is both structural and similar to what Lynn, Heinrich, and Hill refer to as treatments.

19. This approach, involving a partitioning of public management into distinct components, may seem reminiscent of Moore's fa-miliar notion of managing upward, downward, and outward (1995). The two conceptualizations are similar, but the sets of functions/directions are not.

20. Buffering is perhaps more common, but there are public and pri-vate sector cases where top management seeks to exploit the en-

vironment to either influence policy or generate long-run support. Selznick's (1949) study of the TVA is one example; another is J. Edgar Hoover's use of publicity and federal focus on specific crimes to enhance the FBI (Poveda 1990).

21. An illustration of the use of organizations' preferences for risk in the budgeting process can be found in Krause (1998).

22. We discuss the long-run equilibrium relationship between management and hierarchy in O'Toole and Meier (1999).

23. Consider, for instance, the long line of classic cases such as Hoover at the FBI, Lilienthal with the TVA, Moses, Triborough, and Webb at the helm of NASA.

24. As discussed in O'Toole and Meier (1999), system stability can be enhanced via means other than management. These include shared goals, norms, and metaprocesses used in decision making.

25. Advocacy and service, on the one hand, and legitimate coercion, on the other hand, represent poles of a broad set of possible relationships. These include inducing cooperation through incentives (mixed-motive relationships built around exchange) and coproduction (government and nongovernmental actors jointly producing results).

26. Again, the environmental matrices discussed here do not refer to the structure handling program operations but to the constellation beyond this structure—in the broader environment. Networks are complex internally and can be expected to have more environmental elements.

27. In O'Toole and Meier (1999), we discuss six extensions of the theoretical model. These are (1) documenting the greater environmental complexity in networks, (2) using hierarchy to limit the number of possible relationships in a network, (3) testing the interrelationship between hierarchy and management (also discussed here), (4) exploring the greater variance in networks and modeling that variance, (5) emphasizing the key element of trust that is required to operate management networks, and (6) sketching other sources of system stability aside from hierarchy.

28. The work of the Government Performance Project is relevant here. See the chapter by Ingraham and Donahue in this volume.

29. Two potential areas come to mind to test this approach—the impact of coaches in athletic team performance and the role of private sector management on growth and profits.

Dissecting the Black Box Revisited: Characterizing Government Management Capacity

Patricia W. Ingraham and
Amy Kneedler Donahue

This chapter presents the conceptual framework and introduces the analytical approach for an ongoing empirical research project seeking to answer three questions for public management researchers, government practitioners, and the citizen-consumers of public goods and services. The questions are: (1) How well do public entities perform? (2) How does management influence performance? and (3) How can management be assessed? The ultimate goal is to develop a comprehensive and valid evaluation of government management that at once supports fruitful academic study, effectively communicates to citizens the nature and results of government management systems, and assists public managers in understanding and learning about successful management practices. To this end, our work aims to create and apply measures of the ability of public entities to acquire, sustain, maintain, and deploy an administrative infrastructure that supports the professional management of programs and effective implementation of policies. In particular, we seek to characterize a key intervening variable in the classic performance equation that relates resources to results: government management.

Understanding the "black box" that traditionally has been used to depict government management necessitates separating management into its constituent components and identifying the dominant relationships between essential elements—a process we have referred to in earlier work as "dissecting the black box." In 1997 we initiated this process by proposing a preliminary model of government management performance.[1]

In this chapter, we further develop this early model into a conceptual framework that can support analysis. We demonstrate how this framework allows us to hypothesize about the influence that each of the components of a government's professional administrative infrastructure has on its level of capacity, and about how this may affect government performance. We also propose that government management may be evaluated in the context of this framework via a criteria-based assessment approach.

Management Capacity and Why It Is Important to Measure

Before describing our theoretical framework, it is first necessary to define the concept of "management capacity," a notion central to our view of government management, and to explain why understanding, operationalizing, and measuring management capacity is ultimately vital to understanding government performance.

In our view, government management can be divided into two components for analytical purposes. That is, in very simplified terms, governments are composed of two complementary sets of organizational structures, procedures, and technology: those related to administrative functions and those related to policy implementation. The former are a precursor to the latter. The administrative functions and their associated infrastructure involve generic staff activities such as financial management, human resources management, capital management, and information technology management. These activities support all of the other managerial work of government more directly related to running programs (functions typically referred to as policy implementation).

We realize that by making this distinction we might appear to be reviving the long-discarded politics-administration dichotomy. This is not our aim. We recognize that, in reality, what we identify as distinct dimensions of government management—administrative support and policy implementation—operate simultaneously and interact in highly complex ways to influence a government's performance, all immersed in a context rich in political exigencies. Our argument, however, is that the staff functions and program-policy functions also have independent effects on government performance, and thus should be distinguished in order to develop a richer understanding of government management. That is, we would like to know what independent effect the quality of a government's generic staff functions has on a government's ability to accomplish its policy implementation goals. Our interest and research efforts focus on this by examining what we term government's "management capacity."

By capacity we mean government's intrinsic ability to marshal, develop, direct, and control its human, physical, and information capital to support the discharge of its policy directions. That is, management capacity concerns the extent to which a government has the right resources in the right place at the right time. To borrow an analogy from physics, we are focusing on a government's administrative potential energy (which refers to the available power an entity has for activity as a result of the arrangement of its systemic components), as distinct from its kinetic energy (which is the power an entity exerts when it is actively functioning). A government's management capacity typically resides in what we refer to as "management subsystems": administrative substructures created to address a government's financial, human resources, capital, and information technology needs.

Our notion of capacity is also intertemporal; that is, it depends on the extent to which a government can maintain a reliable and appropriately configured resource base over time, success at which necessitates functions such as strategic planning, performance measurement, and performance monitoring. In addition, our notion of capacity encompasses both a public entity's intrinsic administrative ability (i.e., its innate potential to perform), and its ability to carry out its administrative functions under existing environmental conditions, such as resource constraints and political imperatives. Finally, our definition is not simply structural; rather, it seeks to explore the quality of a government's management systems and the extent to which they are mutually enabling in support of meeting the government's overall administrative needs.

Our use of the concept of capacity both varies from and overlaps with uses of the term elsewhere in public administration and political science scholarship. As many authors have pointed out, a wide range of definitions of capacity appear in the literature, but there is some agreement that capacity is a dimensional concept and with important common elements (Malysa 1996; Gargan 1968; Honadle

1981). Malysa (1996), in fact, provides a useful summary of these definitions and dimensions in the context of state wetlands management. In this research, however, we focus on capacity as it applies narrowly in the context of public management of those functions common across governments. This builds on the work of Meier (1988), which relates bureaucratic capacity to government performance and develops a theoretical argument that bureaucratic capacity is necessary for good public policy (Meier 1994).

As governments move toward greater emphasis on results, they and their constituents have sought to improve government performance, as evidenced by the nature of modern reform efforts. At the same time, many critical environmental influences on performance, such as elections; economic, social, and physical conditions; the media; and social perception of the scope and scale of policy problems, are beyond the control of public organizations and their managers. In contrast, the systems created within and across governments to manage resources and to translate them into public services are substantially influenced by public organizations. We recognize the limits of this statement; legislative mandates and design are frequently responsible for duplicative and overlapping financial management systems, for example. Nonetheless, to understand how to improve public performance, the nature of performance itself and the quality of public management must receive prime consideration.

Ultimately, our long-term research agenda pursues characterization of the relationship between management capacity and policy performance; that is, how does the quality of a government's administrative infrastructure affect policy outcomes? At this stage, however, we are concerned with modeling and measuring management capacity itself: What are the dimensions and determinants of the quality of government's administrative functions? In effect, we focus on evaluating a key intervening element in the traditional policy performance equation that relates resources and results: the so-called black box, as shown in figure 10.1.

FIGURE 10.1 *The classical policy/performance equation.*

The key justification for this approach is the intuitively logical assumption that if the middle of this equation (public management) operates poorly, then the link between resources and results is attenuated, and policy ends cannot be met as effectively as they could be if the public management systems functioned well. In short, we assert that governments with more management capacity have the ability to perform better than governments with less management capacity, all else being equal. Whether governments with more capacity actually perform better than governments with less capacity (in other words, whether their ability to perform is translated into the desired results) depends on the influence of other determinants, such as the political environment or economic conditions. Because specifying this intervening variable ultimately allows us to understand the potential to achieve policy outcomes that is created by the configuration and operation of a government's management systems, it gets at the heart of government effectiveness; public organizational structures and managerial behavior are drivers of policy outcomes that public administrators control to a large extent.

Several sets of stakeholders are concerned with government effectiveness, and therefore, sound measures of government management capacity may simultaneously serve multiple purposes. Academic researchers and other policy analysts, for example, would like to be able to incorporate reliable, valid, and accurate measures of public bureaucracies into models of policy systems in order to account for the role of public management in policy implementation. Citizens, on the other hand, seek clear, understandable explanations of what their governments do and how well they work. At the same time, elected officials demand information about how effectively and efficiently public resources are employed in providing public goods and services. Discussions about the nature of performance and reform efforts are integral to contemporary debates about the continuing role of government in society. Thus rigorous analysis of and prescriptions to improve government performance must also consider the thorny issue of how to assess and improve government management. In addition, the diversity of interests suggests the need for a model that is at once general and parsimonious. That is, to be able to accommodate the multitude of purposes to which it is likely to be put, a model of government management must elegantly capture a complex web of relationships, but must also permit variation to be identified along specific, meaningful dimensions. This is the challenge addressed by this discussion.

Assumptions

Our research framework and approach proceed from a foundation of assumptions that are widely accepted, but relatively untested and somewhat controversial.[2] As we have already implied, the base assumption is that management capacity has an important influence on the overall performance of government; in other words, effective management is positively related to effective performance. A multitude of prescriptions for performance enhancement in both the private and public sectors depends on this assumption. For example, "total quality management," "benchmarking," and "reinventing government" seek to increase productivity and profits by refining management (Kettl 1995; Ingraham, Thompson, and Sanders 1997). Similarly, public administration and public management have attempted to base disciplines on this assumption (witness the multitude of managerial techniques designed to facilitate the choice of maximally efficient and effective policy alternatives promulgated by the field of policy analysis in the 1960s and 1970s). In the public administration literature, however, there has been little development of formal and empirical links between management capacity and government performance, although a great deal of research has sought to examine performance (for recent examples, see ICMA's Comparative Performance Measurement Data Report 1998; Hatry et al. 1999; Schick 1999; Rainey and Steinbauer 1999; and Kettl 1995). The association between capacity and performance, largely overlooked by earlier empirical research, can be ignored no longer.

A second assumption is that effective management is fundamentally concerned with the extent to which the various functions of management are performed within and contribute to a holistic management system, a concept we refer to as "the degree of integration." We explain below that management is composed of distinct component systems that have typically been considered as separate functions, a legacy that has flowed from early twentieth century public administration prescription. As the following discussions illustrate, we argue that good management depends not only on the good performance of each of these systems independently, but particularly on the extent to which these management subsystems operate according to consistent objectives, are mutually supporting, and are well coordinated. Management systems in combination, not isolation, create the yet unmeasured concept of effective management capacity. These management systems government-wide, not the behavior of individual managers, are therefore our units of analysis.

Finally, we assume that sound leadership has a positive influence on effective management and thus on overall government performance. We argue that leadership contributes to management capacity in two significant ways: it influences each management subsystem independently by emphasizing specific activities, and it marshals these systems to operate within a coherent and cohesive administrative framework. Here the notion of "vision" commonly identified in the leadership literature (Abramson 1989; Behn 1991; Lynn 1987; Ricucci 1995) is important because it frames the mission and the consequent goals and objectives, together with organizational and societal values, in a broader purpose. To sharpen the link between leadership and performance, it is necessary to examine how leadership translates into more formal, performance-based activities. Creating systemic operational support for mission and vision is one key factor leading to effective performance. It is that manifestation of leadership that is represented in the model presented here.

What about Politics?

It is important not to discount the roles that politics and the political environment play in policy content, management effectiveness, and policy performance. The effort to separate politics from management is an old problem for public administration and public management. The politics-administration dichotomy is an obvious, and perhaps the most enduring, example. Yet we continue to need frequent reminders that the politics and processes of public management are core manifestations of the democratic setting in which public management and performance occur. The political environment plays a crucial role in determining how effective performance will be defined. The clarity—or lack thereof—of public goals and objectives is directly connected to the politics of organizational mission and support. The capacity of the organization to marshal resources to attain its goals and objectives is directly related to levels of external political support and understanding.

The point, then, is not that politics is either a good or a bad influence on policy processes and on the performance equation that we examine. That issue has been extensively, if not decisively, argued elsewhere (e.g., Wilson 1887; Goodnow 1900; Lowi 1979; Waldo 1980; Schick 1995; Wildavsky and Caiden 1997). Our point is that politics and the political environment are necessary parts of any discussion of efficiency, productivity, or performance in the public sector. Management activities and systems do not exist as ends in themselves, but as one part of the complex performance equation for public organizations. At the same time, we argue that management matters in ways that are central to public performance. All else being equal, if public organizations have good managers and good management systems, they are more likely to be effective performers. We also assert, however, that it is important not to construe such management capacity as demonstrated performance. It is, rather, a platform for performance—a measure of positive or negative potential. Similarly, it is a mistake to consider performance—and measurement of performance—in a context that does not include real ability and capacity to perform and to meet public expectations.

The Government Performance Framework

We now propose a framework that seeks to specify the key relationships inherent in the government management and policy performance system. Our conceptualization is portrayed in figure 10.2.

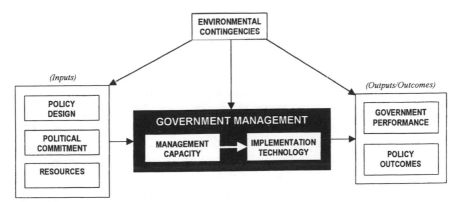

FIGURE 10.2   *The black box dissected: A revised version of the classical policy/performance equation.*

This model elaborates on the classical view (figure 10.1) in which resources and policy are transformed by public administrative institutions into results in the form of policy outcomes (Easton 1965). It incorporates our notion of management capacity, discussed above, and the idea that capacity supports implementation.

Environmental Factors

It should be noted that a variety of environmental factors affect government performance and policy outcomes. These factors are considered exogenous to this framework, as shown in figure 10.2. They embody a broad array of influences and contingencies, including both properties of the larger context within which government operates and properties of the government's jurisdiction. Examples of environmental factors likely to be significant include characteristics of the constituent populations and socioeconomic conditions. Most of the implementation literature, for example, recognizes the dramatic effect that local environmental conditions can have on the character of programs and their outcomes and, thus, on policy performance (Pressman and Wildavsky 1984; Mazmanian and Sabatier 1989; Linder and Peters 1987). It is likely that environmental factors affect public management subsystems as well. Human resources management processes, for example, are likely to be affected by demographic characteristics such as the size and qualifications of the available labor pool. Capital management, in turn, would more likely be affected by other environmental conditions, such as the weather.

A Closer Look at Management Capacity

Within this framework, the character of the four broad, core management subsystems we mentioned above (financial management, human resources management, information technology management, and capital management) drives management capacity. For most governments and for most policy areas, we assert that these subsystems are likely to be present and are essential to the quality of management, and ultimately to the ability to pursue and support public policy goals successfully. Management capacity fundamentally depends on the configuration, tasks, procedures, and work processes of government's management subsystems. The characteristics of the management subsystems are discussed in earlier work (Ingraham and Kneedler 2000) and summarized in appendix A.

Management capacity also rests on the ways in which these management subsystems are interrelated. Within the context of government management, the relationships among the management subsystems and their contribution to management effectiveness vary along two crucial dimensions. The first is the extent to which the management subsystems are orchestrated as part of a unified, cohesive whole with shared values, common goals, aligned objectives, and mutually supporting tasks; that is, the extent to which they are integrated. The second is the extent to which a formalized system of managing for results is present. Our view of the components of management capacity is shown in figure 10.3.

Integration in Management Capacity

Integration concerns the extent to which the management subsystems are orchestrated as part of a unified, cohesive whole with shared values, common goals, aligned objectives, and mutually sup-

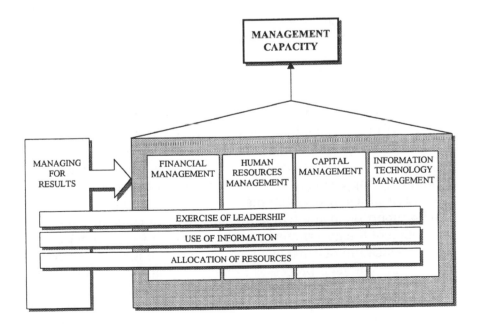

FIGURE 10.3   *A schematic of government management capacity*

porting tasks. We suggest that integration is primarily accomplished through three key activities: the exercise of leadership, which has other effects and was discussed above; the use of information; and the strategic allocation of resources.

Leadership.   Leadership essentially refers to the ability of senior executives and appointed and career officials to make decisions; to provide guidance and direction; to develop the institution's mission, vision, and values and communicate them to all its members; and to coordinate the behavior of all organizational components and subsystems to behave in a manner consistent with the institutional and broader public values in order to achieve the stated mission and ultimately to realize policymakers' intent.

Use of Information.   The freedom, consistency, and speed with which managers cause information to flow throughout a government, the attention that managers give data, and the willingness of managers to share knowledge converge to facilitate or thwart the overall integration of the management subsystems. Although the information technology management subsystem, a mechanism concerned with the collection and availability of timely and accurate data, supports the transmission and use of information, it is the interaction of government managers with information that can enable the management subsystems to operate in concert.

Allocation of Resources.   The decisions managers make about how resources will be garnered and distributed across a government and the activities that facilitate this decision-making process influence the extent to which the management subsystems are configured to be mutually supporting. The classic example of such an activity is the budget process, whereby managers negotiate over how money will be apportioned and which fundamentally affects the collective perception of the government's goals and priorities. Another example is the location of capable human capital throughout the government. Although such processes as recruiting and hiring personnel are the purview of the human resources management system, the presence, behavior, and attitudes of people at key points of intersection among the management subsystems affect the degree of harmony in the system as a whole.

A Results Focus in Management Capacity

Another factor that affects how the management subsystems influence management capacity is the degree to which a formalized system of managing for results is present and in use by the government. This system is itself formally developed as a management subsystem by some governments and can have an important impact on the quality of the other subsystems. We view managing for results as the dominant mechanism by which leaders identify, collect, and use the information necessary to evaluate the institution's performance in pursuit of key objectives to make decisions and direct institutional actions. Managing for results comprises a set of tools through which organizational learning processes are formalized. It is thus an important management subsystem and a key tool for leaders seeking to improve the ability of the other subsystems to support the overall institutional management capacity and to contribute to successful policy outcomes.

By our definition, governments that are managed for results focus continually on discovering the most effective ways of achieving their objectives, employing these techniques across all management subsystems, and monitoring agency activity in light of these objectives. Such a results orientation rests on two vital components. The first is the ability to identify clear objectives. The second is a means to assess progress toward those objectives according to accepted criteria or standards, a mechanism often referred to as "performance measurement." Thus management capacity is not only driven by the characteristics and degree of integration of the management subsystems, but also by broader mechanisms for tracking activities and performance relative to overall objectives.

Hypothesizing about Capacity and Performance Levels

Thus far, we have identified three fundamental components to management capacity. The first is the set of management subsystems, presumed common to almost all government settings, that embody the intrinsic administrative activities of governments. The second is the set of integrating factors that facilitate the orchestration of these management subsystems in a coherent totality. The third is the existence of a formal managing-for-results system that lends a substantial framework to organizational learning processes. In an effort to assess a government's ability to manage, we can hypothesize about the relationships among these dimensions. Presuming that the administrative structures and technologies may be more or less coherent across governments, that leaders may be more or less effectual, and that the degree to which integration and a managing-for-results focus exist in any given government may also vary, it is possible to imagine a variety of regimes across which a government's ability to manage can be expected to vary in complex ways.

To illustrate, we describe some contingencies. It is, for example, conceivable that a government has the fundamental management systems in place but lacks (or at least fails to communicate) an overarching structure of goals and objectives to unify these systems. Integrative activities such as exercise of leadership focused on the "big picture," sharing and using pertinent information about the system as a whole, and distributing resources to support the larger system rather than each individual subsystem are absent. The result is a classic "stove-piped" arrangement in which each management subsystem operates in isolation—and perhaps competition—and has an independent effect on management capacity.

Similarly, in a given government, it might be the case that a formalized results orientation is missing, and thus the government has no institutional mechanism for ensuring that the activities of each of the management subsystems are informed by their effects on performance outcomes. Absent a coherent managing-for-results system, cohesion may exist in a government, but it will not be driven or enlightened by a perspective of effects, results, and outcomes.

We can guess at the implications such contingencies may have for management capacity. For example, in the case in which a government is both integrated and supported by an operational managing-for-results system, the management subsystems collectively influence the quality of management, and there is an interactive relationship between the management subsystems and the managing-for-results system. The vehicle for this interaction is the same set of forces that serve to integrate the management subsystems. In other words, the exercise of leadership, the use of information, and the allocation of resources all serve to bind the tools of performance management to administrative functions.

In high-performing government entities, the management subsystems that we identify will most likely contribute powerfully and positively to overall management effectiveness through the intrinsic ability of each to link to and integrate with the others. Moreover, each management subsystem, separately and as part of a collective management system, acts primarily in response to the potential for success created by a managing-for-results perspective and system, which powerfully enhances their overall management capacity. The managing-for-results system, too, is not an isolated function, but one that substantively interacts with the management subsystems via activities surrounding leadership, information, and resources. Some of the interorganizational network literature hints at these kinds of effects (see, e.g., O'Toole and Montjoy 1984; Gage and Mandell 1990).

On the other hand, it may be that those governments in which the management subsystems operate in isolation from one another and in which performance information is not part of the management process will typically perform relatively poorly. Some likely constraints on performance are management subsystems working at cross-purposes, inconsistent success because it is based on happenstance rather than systematic feedback, repeated failures because there is no mechanism to recognize or institutionalize learning from errors, and organizations becoming rule-bound and inflexible in the face of the uncertainty owing to limited information, narrowly focused leadership, and competition for resources.

Why might we hypothesize that the combination of integration and managing for results has such positive effects on the quality of management not seen in their absence? We believe the key is that these two characteristics acting in concert lend the government two valuable attributes. The first is the ability to gain and sustain momentum, or the impetus to improve over time. That is, these governments are particularly good at understanding their progress. They can learn from both success and failure by managing for results, and they can incorporate appropriate support or changes government-wide through integrative mechanisms. The second attribute is the ability to strike crucial balances. For example, these governments are able to support centralized goals by unifying integrative activities and simultaneously promoting flexibility and innovation through performance-based feedback.

It could also be that either integrative activities or managing for results, but not both, are in place in a government. Our suspicion is that these governments are likely to underperform because they gain neither the power of one of the two factors nor the synergistic effect of both factors together. Thus if they seek to achieve good performance, these governments are likely to expend significant energy to overcome their handicap and may develop sophisticated compensation mechanisms that may be recognizable. For example, excessive regulations could compensate for the uncertainty that arises in the absence of performance data, or rigid hierarchies may compensate for poor communication across management subsystems. Nonetheless, these governments are likely to derive some positive benefit in terms of performance from the dimension that is operating (either integration or managing for results) despite the constraint posed by the absence of the other.

Scholarly literature to bolster these hypotheses is scant. Moreover, governments are not, in reality, ideal types and thus will not fit neatly with any one of these hypothesized configurations. Nonetheless, this exercise demonstrates that our proposed framework can help develop and test hypotheses about a government's potential for performance. It is our expectation that we can generally evaluate a government's management capacity by assessing it according to the three dimensions we identify: the management subsystems, the degree of integration, and the character of results-based management. To facilitate this assessment, it is necessary to specify a system of indicators that permits us to characterize each government along these dimensions. The next section discusses considerations in developing and applying such a system.

A Criteria-Based Assessment Approach to Measuring Capacity

One of our goals is to be able to evaluate a given government's management capacity. In a sense, we would like to treat capacity as our dependent variable. Unfortunately, no direct measures of capacity exist, so we have chosen to get at capacity via a system of criteria-based assessment—in effect treating capacity as latent. We assert that the use of criteria is a fruitful technique because it explicitly focuses data collection and analysis efforts around stated beliefs about the nature of good government management. Because the main impetus for our research is to explain how public managers can improve government performance, we must define what constitutes good management. It is vital to recognize, however, that we advocate using criteria that describe the positive attributes of sound management activities, not simple prescriptions for behavior. That is, we seek criteria that characterize a state of high management capacity, recognizing that any of a wide array of managerial tactics may be successfully applied to achieve high capacity levels.

In addition to its explicit focus on standards that support management capacity (and thus government performance), criteria-based assessment offers the benefit that both the level of a government's management capacity and the contributions to its capacity can be assessed. That is, by developing and applying a scheme of criteria that represents the desired characteristics of an array of management areas and various functions and activities within these areas, analysts can identify the particular strengths and weaknesses of a government's management systems and the degree to which these each affect the government's overall ability to manage. Moreover, the more detailed and sophisticated the scheme of criteria, the more information it can yield. The scheme included in appendix B, for example, includes both primary criteria that define major levels of a government's management capacity and secondary criteria that support the primary criteria and provide a higher degree of specificity. Thus we believe rating governments against a well-developed set of criteria has the potential to generate more informative analytical results than either an absolute scale, which makes no comment about what is good or bad, or a scale that ranks governments against one another, which emphasizes who performs better rather than who performs well or poorly and why.

Despite its advantages, criteria-based assessment poses some dilemmas that must be addressed. Probably the most significant issue is that this approach fails to control for the influence of environmental contingencies on managerial outcomes. That is, all governments under study are rated against the same criteria based on their management capacity and despite the fact that some may face relatively benign managerial environments while others may face harsher conditions. In short, criteria-based assessment emphasizes the capacity levels that result from managerial activities; it does not give "credit" for effort expended by governments simply to overcome obstacles to performance. This may be viewed as a positive attribute in the sense that, ultimately, citizens probably do not care as much about how hard governments work as about what they actually achieve. To the extent that criteria-based ratings reveal managerial end-results, these ratings therefore succeed. On the other hand, under such a scheme, Government A, operating under difficult circumstances, may be taking actions that, under the more favorable conditions faced by Government B, would actually result in a higher capacity rating than Government B receives. Conversely, Government B may not be performing up to its potential because the relaxed environment does not exert pressure on it to perform as well as possible. Failure to account for environmental disparities thus risks misrepresentation of the degree to which a government achieves its full potential in terms of management capacity.

An additional important challenge to using criteria-based assessment is choosing a coherent structure for the system. Here the most important concern is how to weight the criteria. That is, a well-managed (high capacity) government depends unevenly on the outcomes of its management systems. It may, for example, be less important that the government produce timely financial reports than it balance its budget, although both factors contribute to government management capacity. Moreover, the appropriate criteria weights may vary across governments. For example, it may be very important for one government that owns a large number of buildings to have sound capital plans, but this may be relatively trivial for a government that owns only a few buildings. Ratings of a government's management capacity ought, therefore, to account for not only the government's managerial strengths and weaknesses, but also the relative impact or importance of these strengths and weaknesses for capacity. We have attempted to address this issue by constructing a two-tiered scheme of criteria for assessing local government management. The criteria in the top tier are considered fairly equal in importance according to a notion of threshold achievements: if a government fails to accomplish any of these primary criteria, it cannot be optimally managed.

A final challenge to using criteria-based assessment that warrants discussion is defining the criteria themselves. The interested parties who would make use of an assessment of government management are likely to differ in what they consider to be the most important capacity determinants; a policy analyst would probably derive a different set of criteria by which to judge government management capacity than would a citizen. We have addressed that problem in our work very pragmatically. We convened a broad group of practitioners and researchers considered to be subject-matter experts for each of the management subsystems, as well as representatives of the many governments included in our pilot study efforts, and asked them what they considered to be the most significant elements of management. We discovered a high degree of consensus about what mattered most to successful government management, and converted these findings into evaluation criteria. Whether this is the "right" set of criteria may still be debated, but we are confident that each criterion would receive a great deal of support, although any one reviewer may approve of some and disapprove of others. Moreover, it is consensus about the framework for analysis that is important, and to the extent that our propositions spark debate about the appropriate focus for or content of assessment criteria, we only view that as productive.[3]

Conclusion

In earlier work, we have quoted Goggin et al. (1990, p. 120), who state, "A sophisticated understanding of organizational capacity and its subtle influences on policy implementation would require descriptions of virtually the whole gamut of administration, from financial management to motivation, from information systems to affirmative action plans and their impact on the workplace." We quote them because we think this statement represents the spirit of much contemporary public management literature and of the many scholars who implicitly call for rigorous analysis of government management systems. The conceptual framework presented in this chapter answers this call by taking key theoretical and initial methodological steps in the study of public management.

Substantively, our framework can lend realistic detail to existing models of bureaucracy by disclosing the complexity of management and its influence on organizational effectiveness. It can demonstrate the contribution of management capacity to the ability of government to fulfill its policy promises through implementation. It can also further the field of public management by specifying the dimensionality of performance-based activity in government settings. It tackles head-on one of the most troublesome and enduring dilemmas of public management research—the issue of the character, role, and impact of government management. We seek finally to shed bright light on the answers to two very difficult questions: What goes on inside the black box in terms of administration, and how does this matter?

References

Abramson, Mark. 1989. The leadership factor. *Public Administration Review,* 49 (November/December): 562–65.

Behn, Robert. 1991. *Leadership counts.* Cambridge, Mass.: Harvard University Press.

Easton, David. 1965. *A framework for political analysis.* Englewood Cliffs, N.J.: Prentice-Hall.

Gage, Robert, and Myrna Mandell, eds. 1990. *Strategies for managing intergovernmental policies and networks.* New York: Praeger.

Gargan, John. 1968. Consideration of local government capacity. *Public Administration Review,* 41: 649–58.

Goodnow, Frank. 1900. *Politics and administration: A study in government.* New York: Macmillan.

Goggin, Malcolm, Ann Bowman, James Leste, and Laurence O'Toole, Jr. 1990. *Implementation theory and practice: Toward a third generation.* New York: HarperCollins.

Hatry, Harry, David Ammons, Charles Coe, Mary Kopczynski, and Michael Lombardo. 1999. Mini-symposium on intergovernmental comparative performance data. *Public Administration Review,* 59: 101–34.

Honadle, Beth Walter. 1981. A capacity-building framework: A search for concept and purpose. *Public Administration Review,* 41: 575–80.

ICMA and the Urban Institute. 1998. *Comparative performance measurement: FY 1996 data report.* Washington, D.C.: ICMA and the Urban Institute.

Ingraham, Patricia, Jaes Thompson, and Ronald Sanders. 1997. *Transforming government: Lessons from the reinvention laboratories.* San Francisco: Jossey-Bass.

Ingraham, Patricia, and Amy Kneedler. 2000. Dissecting the black box: Toward a model and measures of government management performance. In *Advancing public management: New developments in theory, methods, and practice,* edited by Jeffrey L. Brudney, Laurence J. O'Toole, and Hal G. Rainey. Washington, D.C.: Georgetown University Press.

Kettl, Donald F. 1995. *Inside the reinvention machine: Appraising governmental reform.* Washington, D.C.: Brookings Institution.

Linder, Stephen, and B. Guy Peters. 1987. A design perspective on policy implementation: The fallacies of misplaced prescription. *Policy Studies Review*, 6: 459–75.

Lowi, Theodore. 1979. *The end of liberalism: The second republic of the United States,* 2d ed. New York: W.W. Norton.

Lynn, Laurence E., Jr. 1987. *Managing public policy.* Boston: Little, Brown.

Malysa, Lani Lee. 1996. A comparative assessment of state planning and management capacity: Tidal wetlands protection in Virginia and Maryland. *State and Local Government Review,* 28: 205–18.

Mazmanian, Daniel, and Paul Sabatier. 1989. *Implementation and public policy.* Lanham, Md.: University Press of America.

Meier, Kenneth. 1988. *The political economy of regulation: The case of insurance.* Albany: State University of New York Press.

———. 1994. *The politics of sin: Drugs, alcohol and public policy.* Armonk, N.Y.: M.E. Sharpe.

Meyers, Roy. 1996. *Strategic budgeting.* Ann Arbor: University of Michigan Press.

O'Toole, Laurence, and Robert Montjoy. 1984. Interorganizational policy implementation: A theoretical perspective. *Public Administration Review,* 44: 491–503.

Pressman, Jeffrey, and Aaron Wildavsky. 1984. *Implementation: How great expectations in Washington are dashed in Oakland.* Berkeley: University of California Press.

Rainey, Hal, and P. Steinbauer. 1999. Galloping elephants: Developing elements of a theory of effective government organizations. *Journal of Public Administration Research and Theory,* 9: 1–32.

Ricucci, Norma. 1995. *Unsung heroes: Federal executives making a difference.* Washington, D.C.: Georgetown University Press.

Schick, Allen. 1995. *The federal budget: Politics, policy, process.* Washington, D.C.: Brookings Institution.

———. 1999. Opportunity, strategy, and tactics in reforming public management. Paper presented at "Government of the Future: Getting from Here to There," an OECD Symposium, September 14–15, Paris, France.

Waldo, Dwight. 1980. *The enterprise of public administration.* Novato, Calif.: Chandler & Sharp.

Wilson, Woodrow. 1887. The study of administration. *Political Science Quarterly,* 2 (June).

Wildavsky, Aaron, and Naomi Caiden. 1997. *The new politics of the budgetary process.* 3d ed. New York: Longman.

Endnotes

1. We first presented our theoretical framework for examining government management at the Fourth National Public Management Research Conference in November 1997. This early model is in *Advancing public management: New developments in theory, methods, and practice,* edited by Jeffrey L. Brudney, Laurence J. O'Toole, and Hal G. Rainey (Washington, D.C.: Georgetown University Press, 2000). We have since refined our conceptualization of government management, as presented in this chapter. Our theory development has benefited greatly from the thoughtful comments of Laurence J. O'Toole, several participants at the Governance Workshop (Tucson, Ariz., May 1999), and other reviewers. The model and analytical rationale presented here also serve as the nucleus for papers related to our research on government management effectiveness and capacity; the explanation in this chapter appears, in part, in those publications.

2. Arguably these assertions could be framed as hypotheses rather than as assumptions. At this stage, our work is not aimed directly at testing these particular claims, and thus we have chosen to characterize them as assumptions, not hypotheses. They are not, however, considered invulnerable to adjustment; the research may reveal that these assumptions are incorrect.

3. The model presented in the previous section in combination with the criteria discussed here are facilitating cross-system, cross-government, and cross-time comparative study to a level of detail and breadth never before undertaken. The results of our first year of work were published in *Governing* and *Government Executive* magazines in February 1999. A more complete discussion of our empirical work, including explanation of our methods and preliminary findings, is forthcoming.

Appendix A:
The Management Subsystems

Financial Management. Government financial management systems distribute and manage money for public purposes through processes such as procurement, accounting, cash management, and reporting. Financial management includes both budget allocation and budget execution systems. A financial management system that supports performance must determine the appropriate level of resources, allocate those resources according to strategic priorities, and spend money effectively and accountably. Key components of the effectiveness of the financial management subsystem include the ability to engage in accurate revenue and expenditure forecasting, a long-term focus, the practice of planning for contingencies, awareness of the link between cost and performance, and appropriate flexibility (Meyers 1996).

Human Resources Management. Government activities are typically highly personnel intensive, and thus personnel systems are a key element of public institutions. Fundamentally, human resources systems are concerned with recruiting, retaining, motivating, training, and terminating public employees. Key components of the effectiveness of the human resources management subsystem include the use of coherent rules and procedures, efforts at workforce planning, timely hiring, sufficient professional development programs, and meaningful reward structures and disciplinary actions. An additional consideration when evaluating public human resources systems is the relationship between political appointees and career civil servants within governments—that is, political leadership of the career service. Because increased flexibility in the human resources management process has been a consistent focus of administrative reform, it is also important to consider where in the system and for whom such flexibility occurs.

Information Technology Management. The quality and availability of information is crucial to the ability of managers and policymakers to make decisions and carry out the key functions of acquiring resources and implementing policy. Managing information technology includes developing, maintaining, and using technological systems to collect, analyze, and communicate data. Especially in public institutions responsible for executing complicated programs and interfacing with large, diverse constituencies, information technology performs both primary and integrative functions. It not only responds to information demands particular to specific programs, but also supports the information needs of the other management subsystems. Key components of the effectiveness of the information technology management subsystem include the timeliness, accuracy, reliability, usefulness, and cost-effectiveness of data, and the ability of all personnel to use the information systems.

Capital Management. Capital management involves planning for, maintaining, and disposing of long-lived resources. This area is particularly salient for state and local governments, where capital spending and stock management demands are typically more frequent than in federal agencies (although many federal agencies have large capital responsibilities). Key components of the effectiveness of the capital management subsystem include actively engaging in long-range planning and prioritization of projects, adequate budgetary resources for infrastructure maintenance and repair, and attending to the relationship between the capital and the operating budget.

Appendix B:
City Government Assessment Criteria

Financial Management Criteria

Government has a multiyear perspective on budgeting.

Government produces meaningful current revenue and expenditure estimates.

Government produces meaningful future revenue and expenditure forecasts.

Government can gauge the future fiscal effect of financial decisions.

Government has mechanisms that preserve stability and fiscal health.

The budget reflects a structural balance between ongoing revenues and expenditures.

Government uses countercyclical or contingency planning devices effectively.

Appropriate management of long-term liabilities, including pension funds.

Appropriate use of debt and effective management.

Investment and cash management practices appropriately balance return and solvency.

Sufficient financial information is available to policymakers, managers, and citizens.

Government produces accurate, reliable, and thorough financial reports.

Useful financial data are available to managers.

Budgetary and financial data are communicated to citizens.

Government produces timely financial reports.

Government is able to gauge the cost of delivering programs or services.

Government budget adopted on time.

Government has appropriate control over financial operations.

Government exercises sufficient control over expenditures.

Government permits sufficient managerial flexibility.

Government effectively manages procurement, including contracts for delivery of goods and services.

Human Resources Management Criteria

Government conducts strategic analysis of present and future human resource needs.

> Government has sufficient data about its workforce to support
> analysis.
> Government plans ahead to meet its future workforce needs.

Government is able to obtain the employees it needs.

> Employees are hired in a timely manner.
> Managers have appropriate discretion in the hiring process.
> Government conducts effective recruiting efforts.
> Government hires appropriately skilled and qualified employees.

Government is able to maintain an appropriately skilled workforce.

> Government conducts appropriate training to develop and main-
> tain employee skills.
> Government is able to retain skilled and experienced employees.
> Government is able to discipline employees.
> Government is able to terminate employees.

Government is able to motivate employees to perform effectively in
support of the government's goals.

> Government is able to reward superior performance through pay
> and other cash and noncash incentives.
> Government is able to evaluate the performance of its employees
> effectively.
> Sufficient opportunity for employee feedback exists.
> Government is able to maintain productive labor-management re-
> lations.

Government has a civil service structure that supports its ability to
achieve its workforce goals.

> Classifications system is coherent and of the appropriate size.
> Personnel policies permit appropriate flexibility, including pay
> structure.

Government's human resources goals and policies are communicated to employees.

Information Technology Management Criteria

Government-wide and agency-level information technology systems provide information that adequately supports managers' needs and strategic goals.

Information technology systems form a coherent architecture.
  Strategies are in place to support present and future coherence in architecture.

Government conducts meaningful, multiyear information technology planning.

  Planning process is centralized.
  Managers have appropriate input into the planning process.
  Presence of formal government-wide and agency information technology plans.

Information technology training is adequate.

  Information technology end-users are adequately trained to use available systems.
  Information technology specialists are adequately trained to operate available systems.

Government can evaluate and validate the extent to which information technology system benefits justify investment.

Governments can procure the information technology systems they need in a timely manner.

Information technology systems support the government's ability to communicate with and provide services to its citizens.

Capital Management Criteria

Government conducts thorough analysis of future needs.

  Government has a formal capital plan that coordinates and prioritizes capital activities.
  Multiyear links between operating and capital budgeting.

Multiyear links between strategic planning and capital budgeting.

Government has sufficient data to support analysis.

Government monitors and evaluates projects throughout their implementation.

Government conducts appropriate maintenance of capital assets.

Government has sufficient data to plan maintenance adequately.

Maintenance is appropriately funded.

Managing for Results Criteria

Government engages in results-oriented, strategic planning.

Government leadership effectively communicates the strategic vision to all employees.

Government plans are responsive to input from citizens and other stakeholders.

Agency plans are coordinated with central government plans.

Government develops indicators and evaluative data that can measure progress toward results and accomplishments.

Government can ensure that data are valid and accurate.

Leaders and managers use results data for policymaking, management, and evaluation of progress.

Government clearly communicates the results of its activities to stakeholders.

Prospects for the Study of the Governance of Public Organizations and Policies

John W. Ellwood

The chapters in this volume are part of an attempt to foster and build a theoretical and empirically based literature on the governance of public policies and the institutions that lead to their creation, implementation, and administration. This chapter summarizes where we are today and suggests directions for future research. The bottom line is a mix of good news and bad news. The good news is that new theories and better data give promise to a much better understanding of how and why some governance mechanisms are effective while others are not. The bad news is that the inherent nature of public governance continues to place severe limits not only on the ability of practitioners to achieve better public policies but, and more important for this volume, also on our ability to model the causes of effective versus less effective governance practices and institutions.

Comments on the Nature of Public Governance

In the framing paper of this volume, Lynn, Heinrich, and Hill indicate that "in the empirical analysis of public policies and their implementation, the term 'governance' may be defined as *regimes of laws, administrative rules, judicial rulings, and practices that constrain, prescribe, and enable governmental activity*, where such activity is broadly defined as the production and delivery of publicly

supported goods and services." The chapters in this volume, therefore, are focused on governance of public policies.

It should also be noted that there is an older and extensive governance literature that focuses on issues of accountability. It is also
the case that the contributions to this volume focus on the achievement of positive governmental activity.[1] Some traditional American
governance literature focuses on limiting governmental activity in
order to achieve liberty. Finally, my reading of the Lynn, Heinrich,
and Hill definition leaves out the effects of markets, be they economic or political, as significant factors on the ability of governance
structures to remain stable over time.

In recent years, it has become fashionable to argue that public and
private organizations and policies are converging (Bozeman 1987).[2]
Those who hold this view point to the greater regulation of private-sector activity and the increase in the goals that private organizations seek or must achieve. Stakeholder models in which private
firms are seen as organizations with a variety of customers (clients),
ranging from shareholders to employees to lenders to purchasers of
products, seek to capture this "new" reality.[3] But these models have
very real limitations, as can be seen in the following comparison of
the market for corporate control versus the market for public control.

Public organizations (and governance regimes) differ from their
private-sector counterparts in two important respects: they exercise
monopoly power and, more important, they lack the balance sheet
(be it an accounting balance or stock price) that exposes them to single-issue accountability. Both factors insulate the public governance
regime from accountability. Of particular importance is the imper-
fection (if not absence) of the market for political and public policy
control. Students of public management are wont to point out that,
in practice, private firms manage day to day through a series of internal goals and guidelines and that there is no reason that public
organizations cannot do the same (Behn 1987). Although this observation is formally correct, it misses the fact that the balance sheet offers to the private-sector firm signals as to the appropriate weights
to be placed on each goal. Its presence allows the owners of the firm
(the holders of the firm's residual) to create strong incentives for the
firm's management.

This market for corporate control is at the heart of successfully applying principal-agent theory to the study of firm behavior (see
Alchian and Demsetz 1972; Jensen and Meckling 1976; Fama 1980;

and Fama and Jensen 1983). It is the bridge between the two intellectual traditions of modern business school scholarship—finance theory within economics and the findings of the behavioral sciences. It allows students of the private-sector firm to relate hierarchies to markets and markets to hierarchies. Signals are often very imprecise, if not crude; but the market for corporate control, with its threat of organizational death, provides the ultimate strong signal. In all cases where there is a separation of management and ownership, the ultimate threat of a hostile takeover constrains managerial behavior (including the behavior of boards of directors—the private-sector equivalent of the legislature).[4] Moreover, as Eugene Fama has argued (1980; Fama and Jensen 1983), private-sector firms also face a much stronger labor market for control in which inappropriate managerial action causes the best employees to seek employment in competing firms. This further drives down the performance of the mismanaged firm to the point at which either better management is applied or death results. The public-sector labor market, with tenure for civil service employees and short-term ticket-punching for political appointees, provides a much weaker, if not invisible, signal for public organizations. In short, the exit option is available to the owners and other stakeholders of the private sector firm in ways that are rarely available to voters and those who create, implement, administer, and are affected by public policies (Hirschman 1970).

The existence of monopoly status and the lack of clear signals allow public organizations to spiral down to a stable state of poor performance. In fact, James Morone (1998) has posited an American pattern in which citizen hostility to government (supported and induced by candidate attacks on government performance) causes a decline in resources devoted to government programs, which then perform poorly, thus confirming citizen opinion.

The modern public-choice literature is rarely about the increase in social welfare.[5] Rather, it centers around behaviors (rent-seeking on the part of legislators, bureaucrats, interest groups) that create situations in which individuals and groups profit at the expense of the society as a whole.[6] Because of Arrow's General Possibility Theorem, public choice students of decision making believe that there is no "right" or stable method of decision making (Riker 1982 and 1986; Levine and Plott 1977; and Plott and Levine 1978). Instead, stable results (creating a stable equilibrium) are induced (Shepsle and Weingast 1981) through organizational, procedural, or policy arrangements. The question then reverts to who has the power to create the decision-making institutions and processes that will cause their side of the policy debate to win. Everyone has his or her favorite. Currently, because of the power of the purse, those betting on the legislator are in ascendancy, but there are other candidates. Traditionally, some have pointed to the information asymmetry advantage of the bureaucracy as a source of its power (Bendor 1988). The legislator's need for resources to achieve reelection points to the power of interest groups as a key to understanding the development of policy. One recent rational expectations model posits that an all-dominant interest group will include due process provisions in a new policy so as to protect its interests when it is no longer dominant, but finds itself in the minority in a given policy area (Moe 1989). Another recent line of thought points to policy designs that create barriers to change in order to protect the policy. Sometimes this is labeled as "deck-stacking" (as in Lynn, Heinrich, and Hill, in this volume); others refer to it as the prevention of legislative or bureaucratic drift.

The differences between the signals and incentives faced by private-sector and public-sector organizations have implications for the practice and the research of creating, implementing, and administering public policies. As for practice, who should determine what the goals of a given policy should be? The simple answer is the legislature. However, the public-choice literature then forces us to ask: What governance mechanism or process should the legislature use to make the determination?[7] The Knott and Hammond chapter in this volume is clearly in this tradition.

Similar questions can be posed for each policy actor and administrator. What right does she or he have to determine what is correct policy? This is among the oldest questions of public administration (Wilson 1887). Although we have largely rejected the Wilsonian dichotomy between politics and policy on the one hand, and administration on the other, we have no real substitute. At the department level, at the bureau level, at the street level, should the policy analyst determine which policy alternative will increase social welfare? Should the administrator? Should the customer (client)? And where is the role for the taxpayer and the voter? It is discouraging that we have come such a small distance since Woodrow Wilson and the Progressives wrote about this at the end of the nineteenth century.

The lack of a stable equilibrium in the development, implementation, and administration of public policy also poses problems for the researcher. The lack of a stable equilibrium (prior to one being structurally induced) reflects the fact that principals and agents have different values and goals. In private firms, these goals are at least partially sorted out through the exit mechanism. With the high cost of exit, the goals are rarely sorted out when it comes to the design, creation, implementation, and administration of public policies. In a series of papers, Paul Milgrom and John Roberts (1988, 1990) have shown that, in a situation with multiple goals, principals lose control over agents as the agents reallocate effort among the goals. David Kreps (1990) and Gary Miller (1992) have shown that repeated games have multiple equilibria. Although they see this as a positive result, given that it opens the door for leadership into the economics of organization, it does not help much with governance because leadership through coordination occurs by leaders choosing among equilibria. Thus we are back with another version of structurally induced equilibrium.

To the extent that this remains the case, the researcher must impose the dependent variable for her or his study of the governance of public policies. For example, Ingraham and Donahue (in this volume) posit several sets of managerial capacities to distinguish good from not-so-good management of public policies (see appendixes A and B of their chapter). These were developed by elites and are highly normative. But are they what the public (a major set of principals) wants? For example, they call for multiyear budgeting and a structural balance across economic cycles. Not all economists, accountants, or budgeters—much less citizens—agree with these principles. For example, throughout the federal budget wars of the last two decades (1975–1995), it is impossible to find a single member of the U.S. Congress who was defeated because of the size of the U.S. budget deficit. It is possible to find many members who were defeated because they supported the increases in taxes or the reductions in spending that were required to shrink and then eliminate the deficit. Even presidents were not immune, as George Bush discovered when the budget agreement of 1990 contributed to his defeat. Bill Clinton lost Democratic control over the House of Representatives for the first time since 1954, at least in part because of the tax increases contained in the 1993 budget agreement.[8]

Different Types of Policies Lead to Different Governance Problems

All the chapters in this volume are focused on governance structures in which positive governmental action is used to achieve changes in individual or group behavior. However, the most successful governance structure in American history—the Madisonian model of the U.S. Constitution—used governance structures to retard positive policy action. As is set out in *The Federalist Papers*, the major goals of the Madisonian model were to preserve (negative) liberty and to create a stable, large republic (Wilson 1990). This was achieved through intentional fragmentation of governmental power and was brought about by separation of powers between the national government and the states as well as checks and balances among the branches of the national government. As James Madison pointed out in two of the *Federalist* papers (Numbers 10 and 51), although a faction might be able to dominate a state or several states, it is very unlikely that it could dominate all the states and the national government. Even within the national government, the multiple checks and balances created by a bicameral legislature, a chief executive with veto power, an ability for both chambers to override that veto only with a super majority in each chamber, and then judicial review all make it very difficult for any narrow interest to dominate the entire governance system. The result has been the most successful, longest-lasting, largest republic in history. There are significant costs, however. The Madisonian governance system is willing to sacrifice efficiency in the creation, adoption, implementation, and administration of public policy in order to maintain liberty. Thus the governance problems encountered in the chapters on job training (Heinrich and Lynn) and welfare reform (Jennings and Ewalt; Sandfort; and Riccio, Bloom, and Hill) occur, in part, because of the biases of the Madisonian governance system.

The policy papers in this volume analyze governance systems that seek to use government outputs to affect the behavior of individuals or groups. That is, welfare reform seeks to lower welfare caseloads by creating incentives for recipients to find jobs. Finding and holding a job is seen as a goal in and of itself. The reform also seeks to change the behavior of the welfare recipient in a variety of other ways, be it lowered rates of out-of-wedlock teenage pregnancy or less substance abuse among recipients.[9] The chapter by Roderick, Jacob, and Bryk analyzes the effectiveness of governance mechanisms that were put in place in Chicago to end social promotion in public schools. Among the goals of this program were to end social promotion, lower course failure rates, and raise student test scores. To achieve these goals, the policy governance structure had to change not only the behavior of students but also the behavior of teachers and school administrators.

Between the complex positive (action) policy goals of the governance structures analyzed in this volume and the relatively simple negative governance structure of the Madisonian model lies a series of governance structures that were the norm for public policy until the time of the Great Society. As Samuel Beer (1978) has pointed out, until the Great Society, domestic public policy involved two types of activities: providing resources (transfer payments as in veterans' payments or Social Security, and discrete public goods as with roads, canals, and dams) or a reallocation of political and economic power (as with the Wagner Act, which granted labor rights, and in creating the various independent commissions to regulate economic behavior). These activities are much easier to study and evaluate, and they require much simpler governance regimes.[10]

Thus governance structures exist on a continuum. The easiest to analyze are those that seek to prevent government action, what one might call negative governance regimes. The next easiest to study are those that are concentrated on government outputs, be they reallocation of power or the provision of direct public goods. The policies addressed in this volume involve the most difficult policies to study—those that seek to use government outputs to change individual and group behaviors. As Carol Weiss (1972) has pointed out, this is a much more difficult task because it involves at least two sets of models: why and how government is willing to provide a governmental output; and how that output will affect individual and group behavior.

Progress in the Study of Governance

Weimer and Vining (1996, p. 92) have pointed out four related bodies of knowledge that inform the study and practice of the management (and governance) of public policies:

- "Broadest in scope is knowledge about the political processes that place demands, provide opportunities, and impose constraints on public managers."
- "Next broadest in scope is policy analysis, which provides the conceptual foundations and craft skills for determining what government should do and how it should be done."
- "Organizational design, a subset of policy analysis, gives insight into how the public sector can be organized to facilitate the effective delivery of goods and services."
- "Narrowest in scope, but most directly relevant to the practice of management, is knowledge about how to carry out executive functions skillfully within existing organizational designs."

Although touching on all four categories, the chapters in this volume are mostly directed at the third point—organizational design.[11]

It is also the case that, although they rely on the most modern statistical techniques, the organizational design chapters fall nicely into the three traditions of research that flowed from the pioneering work of Chester Barnard (1938). As pointed out by Charles Perrow (1986, p. 77), three traditions flowed from Barnard's work: the institutional approach, the decision-making approach, and the human relations approach.

All three approaches are attempts to "scientifically" study organizational design. Each is a reaction to the classical management theory view that there was one "best" way to design and manage an organization.[12] The institutional approach reflects the structural-functional analysis that dominated sociology in the 1950s and 1960s. The decision-making approach centers around the work of Herbert Simon and what has come to be called the "Carnegie school" of organizational analysis. It starts from the notion that organizations are composed of individuals, and therefore, the best way to study organizations scientifically is to study how those individuals achieve their goals. Finally, the human relations approach has centered on the scientific studies of industrial psychologists. From the Hawthorne experiments on, it has focused on how to manage actual and potential conflict (among goals, individuals, groups, and so forth) so as to achieve organizational goals generally and increase worker productivity specifically.

Although other approaches to organizational design have sprung up over the last two decades (the contingency approach, the ecological approach, the economic institutions approach, for example), the original three approaches all sought to move beyond what Simon (1946) labeled the "proverbs of administration" to test hypotheses. Simon stressed (1996) the degree to which moving from a study of the outputs of public organizations to a study of organizational decision making allowed him (and his followers) to move from one of the least prestigious fields (public administration) to the practice of science. This occurred, at least in part, because decisions provided a database that could be used to test hypotheses. In fact, a focus on decisions even allows for a systematic study of cases by switching from an analysis across a few cases to an analysis of many decisions within a single case.[13]

The weakness of the three approaches for students of the creation, implementation, and administration of public policy is that scholars face a trade-off between policy relevance and scientific rigor. With better data and improved statistical techniques, the authors in this volume are able to escape this trade-off. Thus the chapters on implementing job training, welfare reform, and school reform have data and statistical models that enable their authors to assess the effects of the organizational structure, managerial roles and actions, the effects of various treatments, the effects of variations across clients, and the effects of the environment in which the policy is made, implemented, and administered. They represent a return to what Simon and his colleagues were attempting, but abandoned, in the late 1930s—to assess the effects of a wide variety of independent variables on policy outcomes.

Another rationale for moving away from the study of policy administration to a scientific endeavor is reflected in Charles Lindblom's critique of policy analysis (Lindblom and Woodhouse, 1993, pp. 13–32). Lindblom argues that the reliance on analysis for policymaking is limited owing to inadequate data and statistical techniques, imprecise models, and the inability of analysts to separate fact from value.[14] The papers in this volume offer hope that scholars have come some way toward overcoming all but the last of Lindblom's critiques.

Improvements in Data and Statistical Models

Over the past two decades, Eric Hanushek (1981, 1997) has become the bane of school reformers by consistently pointing out that almost nothing works when it comes to reforms to improve the academic performance of elementary and secondary school students. Smaller classes have had almost no effect. Better teacher pay has had almost no effect. Longer school years have had almost no effect. The studies that Hanushek summarized relied on data that, at best, were collected for individual schools (but often were collected for school districts, counties, or states). In recent years, however, Hanushek and his coauthors have begun analyzing a data set (the Harvard/UTD Texas Schools Project) in which the unit of analysis is individual classrooms in a series of schools in Dallas, Texas. With better data, teachers matter, class size begins to matter, special education programs begin to have positive effects, and so forth (Hanushek, Kain, and Rifkin 1999; 1998a; 1998b). What is true for Hanushek and his colleagues is also true for the authors of the chapters on job training, welfare reform, and Chicago school reform in this volume. Better data and statistical techniques cause relationships that were statistically unidentifiable to become significant and identifiable.

The Informal Organization

Two of the chapters—Milward and Provan, and O'Toole and Meier—are modern attempts to address the classic finding that an informal organization almost always exists within the formal hierarchical structure of an organization. From Barnard on, students of organizational design have sought to overcome internal organizational conflict. What is known is that as information requirements increase, either through an increase in complexity or an increase in the number of players or goals, formal hierarchical arrangements and decision making are likely to break down. One result is that conflict will increase between individuals or groups. Informal organizations exist (and are often created) to manage this stress and conflict. Milward and Provan and O'Toole and Meier set out conceptual and formal models of these networks. As indicated below, as is true in all scientific endeavors, determining the quality of these efforts awaits tests of the predictions of the models.

Next Steps in the Study of Governance

Although the authors are not specific on this point, one assumes that the chapters in this volume have two goals: to establish true statements about the governance of public policies; and to help practitioners design, adopt, implement, and administer public policies. Whether the first goal has been achieved depends on the quality of the science used by the authors. The purist position for the scientific method has been stated by many. But one clear view was set forth by Richard Feynman in the 1964 Messenger Lectures at Cornell University (quoted in Gribben and Gribben, 1997):

> In general we look for a new law by the following process. First we guess it. Then we compute the consequences of the guess to see what would be implied if this law that we guessed is right. Then we compare the result of the computation to nature, with experiment or experience, compare it directly with observation, to see if it works. If it disagrees with experiment it is wrong. In that simple statement is the key to science. It does not make any difference how smart you are, who made the guess, or what his name is—if it disagrees with experiment it is wrong (pp. 178–79).

This position requires a theory, a prediction (hypothesis) resulting from that theory, and a test of that prediction. On this ground, some of the chapters in this volume are quite strong. Several chapters (on job training, welfare reform, and school reform) develop and test models with data. What is evident is that, particularly in the case of those efforts that test models with data, the research agendas reported on in the volume are serious attempts to build a scientific literature of the governance of public policy.

Potential Problems

This is not to say, of course, that the authors have found the Holy Grail. Many standard problems remain. First, the reduced form equation set out by Lynn, Heinrich, and Hill, which motivates the work of the volume, comes close to the economist's criticism of political science: by including everything, one runs the danger of explaining nothing. One should, therefore, ask: Are all factors important? Which are the most important? Does the import of a variable—or a set of variables—vary across policy domains? Across political jurisdictions?

Second, can the results of these analyses be used by practitioners managing the same programs in other jurisdictions or those managing similar, but not quite the same, programs? On a scholarly level, this is the question of the power of the analysis (model, statistical techniques, and so forth). For practitioners, this relates to whether the results can be used to replicate the governance model in other jurisdictions or for other policies in the same jurisdiction.

Some students of governance believe that it is possible to build a structural model of the governance of a public policy that can be used to tell managers in other jurisdictions how to implement that policy. Others believe that successful design, implementation, and administration is so highly idiosyncratic to the nature of the jurisdiction that successful replication based on analysis is nearly impossible. An example of the first view is Lee Friedman (1997), who believes that his model of the governance of bail reform undertaken by the Manhattan Bail Project of the Vera Institute of Justice can be used to design reforms in other jurisdictions. On the other hand, Paul Berman takes the view that reforms in elementary and secondary education are idiosyncratic and cannot be replicated through the application of governance models (Berman and Nelson 1997). One possible next step for the authors in this volume is to take their models of governance and test them in other jurisdictions and for other policy programs.

Finally, one has to say that the fundamental problem of public policy—that its design, adoption, implementation, and administration are inherently political and therefore involve multiple actors holding multiple goals—while acknowledged, remains unsolved. So far, at least, neither principal-agent theory, nor transaction-cost economics, nor game theoretic models of institutions has provided a stable equilibrium that would lead the way to an analytic solution to the appropriate governance system. This remains the hardest problem to model. But that is why future conferences on the study of the governance of public policy will be held.

References

Alchian, Armen, and Harold Demsetz. 1972. Production, information cost, and economic organization. *American Economic Review:* 777–95.

Allison, Graham. 1980. Public and private management: Are they fundamentally alike in all unimportant aspects? In *Setting the public management agenda.* U.S. Office of Personnel Management, Document 127-53-1. Washington, D.C.: Government Printing Office.

Barnard, Chester. 1938. *The Functions of the Executive.* Cambridge, Mass.: Harvard University Press.

Beer, Samuel. 1978. In search of a new public philosophy. In *The new American political system,* edited by Anthony King. Washington, D.C.: The American Enterprise Institute, pp. 5–44.

Behn, Robert. 1987. (Teaching) notes on "The Registry of Motor Vehicles: Watertown Branch." Duke University, unpublished data.

Bendor, Jonathan. 1988. Formal models of bureaucracy. *British Journal of Political Science,* 18: 353–95.

Berman, Paul, and Beryl Nelson. 1997. Replication: Adapt or fail. In *Innovation in American government: Challenges, opportunities, and dilemmas,* edited by Alan Altshuler and Robert D. Behn. Washington, D.C.: Brookings Institution Press, pp. 319–31.

Bozeman, Barry. 1987. *All organizations are public: Bridging public and private organizational theories.* San Francisco: Jossey-Bass.

Cyert, Richard, and James March. 1963. *A behavioral theory of the firm.* Englewood Cliffs, N.J.: Prentice-Hall.

Fama, Eugene. 1980. Agency problems and the theory of the firm. *Journal of Political Economy,* 88: 288–305.

Fama, Eugene, and Michael Jensen. 1983. Separation of ownership and control. *Journal of Law and Economics* (June): 301–25.

Ferejohn, John. 1974. *Pork barrel politics: Rivers and harbors legislation, 1947–1968.* Stanford, Calif.: Stanford University Press.

Friedman, Lee. 1997. Public sector innovations and their diffusion: economic tools and managerial tasks. In *Innovation in American government: Challenges, opportunities, and dilemmas,* edited by Alan Altshuler and Robert D. Behn. Washington, D.C.: Brookings Institution Press, pp. 332–59.

Gribben, John, and Mary Gribben. 1997. *Richard Feynman: A life in science.* New York: Dutton.

Gulick, Luther, and Lyndall Urwick. 1937. *Papers on the science of administration.* New York: Institute of Public Administration, Columbia University.

Hanushek, Eric. 1981. Throwing money at schools. *Journal of Policy Analysis and Management,* 1: 19–41.

———. 1997. Assessing the effects of school resources on student performance: An update. *Education Evaluation and Policy Analysis,* 19 (2): 141–64.

Hanushek, Eric, John Kain, and Steven Rifkin. August 1998a. Teachers, schools, and academic achievement. Cambridge, Mass.: NBER working paper no. W6691.

————. August 1998b. Does special education raise academic achievement for students with disabilities? Cambridge, Mass.: NBER working paper no. W6690.

————. April 1999. Do higher salaries buy better teachers? Cambridge, Mass.: NBER working paper no. W7082.

Hirschman, Albert. 1970. *Exit, voice, and loyalty: Responses to decline in firms, organizations, and states.* Cambridge, Mass.: Harvard University Press.

Jensen, Michael, and William Meckling. 1976. Theory of the firm: Managerial behavior, agency costs, and ownership structure. *Journal of Financial Economics*, 3: 305–60.

King, Gary. 1993. The methodology of presidential research, In *Researching the presidency: Vital questions, new approaches,* edited by George C. Edwards, John H. Kessel, and Bert A. Rockman. Pittsburgh: University of Pittsburgh Press.

Kreps, David. 1990. Corporate culture and economic theory. In *Perspectives on positive political economy,* edited by James E. Alt and Kenneth A. Shepsle. New York: Cambridge University Press, pp. 90–143.

Levine, Michael, and Charles Plott. 1977. Agenda influence and its implications. *Virginia Law Review,* 63(4): 561–604.

Lindblom, Charles, and Edward Woodhouse. 1993. *The policy-making process,* 3d ed. Upper Saddle River, N.J.: Prentice-Hall.

March, James. 1962. The business firm as a political coalition. *Journal of Politics,* 24: 662–78.

March, James, and Herbert Simon. 1958. *Organizations.* New York: John Wiley & Sons.

Milgrom, Paul, and John Roberts. 1988. Employment contracts, influence activities and efficient organization design. *Journal of Political Economy,* 96(1): 42–60.

————. 1990. Bargaining costs, influence costs and the organization of economic activity. In *Perspectives on positive political economy,* edited by James E. Alt and Kenneth A. Shepsle. Cambridge: Cambridge University Press, pp. 57–89. Reprinted in Oliver Williamson, and Scott Masten (eds). *Transaction cost economics.* London: Edward Elgar Publishing Co.

Miller, Gary. 1992. *Managerial dilemmas: The political economy of hierarchy.* New York: Cambridge University Press.

Moe, Terry M. 1989. The politics of bureaucratic structure. In *Can the government govern?* edited by John Chubb and Paul Peterson. Washington, D.C.: The Brookings Institution, pp. 267–329.

Morone, James. 1998. *The democratic wish: Popular participation and the limits of American government.* New Haven, Conn.: Yale University Press.

Perrow, Charles. 1986. *Complex organizations: A critical essay*, 3d ed. New York: Random House.

Plott, Charles, and Michael Levine. 1978. A model of agenda influence in committee decisions. *American Economic Review*, 68: 146–60.

Riker, William. 1982. *Liberalism against populism: A confrontation between the theory of democracy and the theory of social choice*. San Francisco: W.H. Freeman.

———. 1986. *The art of political manipulation*. New Haven, Conn.: Yale University Press.

Shepsle, Kenneth, and Barry Weingast. 1981. Structure-induced equilibrium and legislative choice. *Public Choice*, 37 (3): 503–19.

Simon, Herbert. 1946. The proverbs of administration. *Public Administration Review*, 6: 53–67.

Simon, Herbert. 1996. *Models of my life*. Cambridge, Mass.: The MIT Press.

Weimer, David, and Aidan Vining. 1996. Economics. In *The state of public management*, edited by Donald F. Kettl and H. Brinton Milward. Baltimore: The Johns Hopkins University Press, pp. 92–117.

Weiss, Carol. 1972. *Evaluation research: Methods for assessing program effectiveness*. Englewood Cliffs, N.J.: Prentice-Hall.

Wilson, James Q. 1990. Interests and deliberation in the American republic, or why James Madison would never have received the James Madison award. *PS* (December): 558–62.

Wilson, Woodrow. 1887. The study of administration. *Political Science Quarterly*, 2: 197–222.

Endnotes

1. I use the word "positive" to indicate actions that require affirmative judgments and steps. I am contrasting positive actions with negative actions, which seek to preserve a goal, such as liberty, by preventing government from acting. Positive can also be used as a label for theories that seek to describe and explain phenomena. In this sense, they are to be contrasted with normative theories that seek to identify better, versus worse, results or phenomena.

2. On the other hand, see Allison (1980).

3. The classic exposition of the business firm where something other than the profit maximizing organization exists can be found in March and Simon (1958). See also March (1962) and Cyert and March (1963).

4. In *A Behavioral Theory of the Firm*, Richard Cyert and James March (1963) build a model of for-profit firms that seek to maximize or satisfy multiple goals—often sequentially. One question

is whether this view was more appropriate in the closed economy of the 1950s and 1960s, when firms could maintain significant amounts of slack, than is the case today. It is certainly true that when U.S. private firms are threatened in the marketplace, their first instinct is to cut costs to improve the bottom line (or improve the stock price if the firm is publicly traded).

5. In this discussion, I use the term "public choice" as a surrogate for the terms "public choice," "formal theory," and "political economy." Among political scientists and economists, these terms have slightly different meanings. Here they are used to indicate a formal application of microeconomics to political and public decision making.

6. A very clear exposition of economic models of the policymaking process is found in Weimer and Vining (1996), where they set out five economic approaches to the study of the governance—neoclassical welfare economics, agency (principal-agent) theory, transaction cost economics, social choice theory, and the economic theory of institutions. The final four approaches result either in multiple or induced equilibria. Welfare economics, while justifying government activity and providing normative answers to overcoming market failures, does not answer the question of how to adopt, implement, and administer these policies.

7. As part of the Watergate-era reforms in the U.S. House of Representatives (the Subcommittee Bill of Rights), members were allowed to run for their assignments on committees and subcommittees. The result was a self-selection in which members sat on those committees and subcommittees where they could better help their districts. The result was a significant increase in appropriations (Ferejohn 1974). The success of a given policy proposal often is determined by whether it requires an annual appropriation (and thus is under the jurisdiction of the fairly conservative appropriations committees) or whether the advocates of the program are successful in achieving entitlement status where funding is automatic and the funding formula is under the jurisdiction of an authorizing committee.

8. It is also the case that, until the Clinton administration's campaign finance scandals broke two weeks before the 1996 election, the Democrats were poised to regain the House of Representatives, at least in part because of the Republican-sponsored cuts in domestic spending.

9. There were many other goals of welfare reform. One was clearly to reduce the national government's expenditures on the Aid to Families with Dependent Children (AFDC) program. Some be-

lieved that the reform would lead to higher incomes for those who had been receiving welfare. The traditional "welfare triangle" points out that it is (almost) impossible to achieve all these goals at once.

10. Of course, the questions of whether the policy will be enacted and to what extent it will be funded are still applicable. However, these pre–Great Society policies are much easier to implement and administer than those policies that seek to change behavior in a particular way.

11. The obvious exception is the chapter by Knott and Hammond, which focuses almost entirely on the effects of institutions on political power and support.

12. The classical view is set out in Gulick and Urwick (1937).

13. This technique is recommended by Gary King (1993) as a way to foster the scientific study of the U.S. presidency.

14. Lindblom also stresses the inability of analysts to complete their work in time for it to be useful to decision makers and the fact that often the output of the analyst is not relevant enough to the specific options before the decision makers.

Subject Index

Author Index